Explicit Direct Instruction

for English Learners

John Hollingsworth • Silvia Ybarra

A Joint Publication

CORWIN
A SAGE Company

DataWORKS
Educational Research

CORWIN
A SAGE Company

FOR INFORMATION:

Corwin
A SAGE Company
2455 Teller Road
Thousand Oaks, California 91320
(800) 233-9936
www.corwin.com

SAGE Publications Ltd.
1 Oliver's Yard
55 City Road
London EC1Y 1SP
United Kingdom

SAGE Publications India Pvt. Ltd.
B 1/I 1 Mohan Cooperative Industrial Area
Mathura Road, New Delhi 110 044
India

SAGE Publications Asia-Pacific Pte. Ltd.
3 Church Street
#10-04 Samsung Hub
Singapore 049483

Acquisitions Editor: Robin Najar
Associate Editor: Julie Nemer
Editorial Assistant: Mayan White
Permissions Editor: Adele Hutchinson
Project Editor: Veronica Stapleton
Copy Editor: Diana Breti
Typesetter: C&M Digitals (P) Ltd.
Proofreader: Dennis W. Webb
Indexer: Kathleen Paparchontis
Cover Designer: Anthony Paular

Printed in the United States of America

Library of Congress Cataloging-in-Publication Data

Hollingsworth, John R.

Explicit Direct Instruction for English Learners /
John Hollingsworth, Silvia Ybarra.

pages cm
Includes bibliographical references and index.

ISBN 978-1-4129-8841-4 (pbk. : alk. paper)

1. English language—Study and teaching—Foreign speakers. 2. Education, Bilingual. I. Ybarra, Silvia, author. II. Title.

PE1128.A2H575 2013
428.0071—dc23   2012039612

This book is printed on acid-free paper.

SUSTAINABLE FORESTRY INITIATIVE
Certified Chain of Custody
Promoting Sustainable Forestry
www.sfiprogram.org
SFI-01268

SFI label applies to text stock

13 14 15 16 10 9 8 7 6 5 4 3 2

Contents

Additional sample lessons are available on our website at http://www
.dataworks-ed.com/resources

Preface

In our last book, *Explicit Direct Instruction® (EDI®): The Power of the Well-Crafted, Well-Taught Lesson,* we described how to design and deliver lessons that would help all students learn more and learn faster. This book takes the same approach but focuses even more specifically on strategies for using Explicit Direct Instruction to teach English Learners. Of course, the goal for this book is to ensure that *all* students, including English Learners, are successfully taught grade-level work, at school, every day. Students are successful as a direct result of your teaching. We also call this GIFT: *Great Initial First Teaching,* when students learn more the first time they are taught, the best school reform. To help you make this happen, we'll describe lesson design, lesson delivery, vocabulary development, language objectives, and how to make lessons more understandable for English Learners.

The ideas we present are research based but have been refined by extensive field research conducted by our company, DataWORKS Educational Research, including our analysis of more than 2.5 million student assignments and visitations to more than 35,000 classrooms. In addition, we—and the other DataWORKS consultants—have taught hundreds of demonstration lessons, from kindergarten to 12th grade, in all content areas so teachers can see the practices working with their students.

IDEAL FOR COMMON CORE STATE STANDARDS

Educators across the country are anticipating the implementation of the new Common Core State Standards. They're analyzing important shifts in the new standards, such as focusing on text and text-based answers, developing students' conceptual knowledge along with fluidity in skills, and increasing student reading and use of Academic Vocabulary in both reading and speaking.

Explicit Direct Instruction for English Learners is the ideal model for teaching the Common Core standards because of its balanced approach in teaching both Concepts and Skills along with integrated listening, speaking, reading, writing, and vocabulary development in every lesson.

CONTENTS AND SPECIAL FEATURES

We start this book with classroom examples of English Learners learning. In Part I, Getting Ready, we describe English Learners and their needs—learning grade-level content while simultaneously learning English. We present the importance of well-crafted lessons for English Learners. A quick overview of Explicit Direct Instruction is followed by a chapter on Checking for Understanding and specific modifications for English Learners.

In Part II, Strategies for English Learners, three chapters present the core of the English Learner strategies: Vocabulary Development, Language Objectives, and Content Access Strategies. The *Vocabulary Development* chapter describes how to teach new vocabulary—including Academic Vocabulary—within the context of each lesson, every day. We next describe how to implement *Language Objectives*—in which students continually Listen, Speak, Read, and Write using new English words and language structures from the lesson itself. In the *Content Access Strategies* chapter, we describe how to make spoken and written English more understandable for English Learners.

In Part III, Integrating Strategies for English Learners Into EDI Lessons, six chapters describe in detail how to teach English Learners—how to integrate English Learner strategies into each part of a well-crafted lesson, starting with a standards-based Learning Objective and ending with Closure and Independent Practice. Chapter 13 wraps up this part of the book, with feedback on actual classroom lessons plus a list of all the instructional techniques used throughout the book.

You will also find several special features throughout the text. "From John" and "From Silvia" notes have been included when one of us has an extra insight to add, and shaded boxes highlight key strategies and quick-reference tips in each chapter. In addition, end-of-chapter summary sections provide a brief recap of each chapter's contents.

Sample lessons are also included within the text and are presented in three ways: first, as short examples throughout the text, identified with markers indicating which portion of a lesson they illustrate (e.g., Learning Objective, Activate Prior Knowledge, Concept Development, Skill Development, Guided Practice, Importance, Closure, Independent Practice, and Checking for Understanding), second, as complete lessons in Appendix A, Sample Explicit Direct Instruction Lessons for English Learners, and third, on our website (http://www.dataworks-ed.com/resources).

Seven additional Appendices also provide a wealth of resources, including instructions on how to manage pair-shares, address subskill gaps, teach English Learners on grade level, design standards-based pacing guides, and design an EDI learning objective for English Learners. Appendix D provides a quick refresher on English phonemes and associated spelling patterns, which can be helpful when teaching ELs how to read specific words incorporated in EDI lessons.

Additional resources, including sample lessons and videos showing the strategies being used in actual classrooms, are on the DataWORKS website, www.dataworks-ed.com.

We invite you to discover step by step how to create success in every lesson—transforming your teaching and revolutionizing learning for your English Learners.

A final note for administrators reading this book: It's not a focus on test scores that raises test scores. It's a relentless pursuit of optimizing the effectiveness of the way students are taught—before the tests are given—that raises test scores. And that's what this book is all about.

Acknowledgments

We wish to thank all those who gave us the insight, inspiration, and knowledge to write this book. Without them, we could not have completed it.

All of our consultants, including those located in California and those on the East Coast led by Bill Gassman, have provided insights into classroom instruction. They have helped implement our vision of effective classroom practices while training and supporting thousands of teachers across the United States.

Bruce Berryhill, our linguistic expert, provided insight on English Learners and Language Objectives, especially on English phonics and the mechanics of English pronunciation.

Rewrites and proofing were supported with careful reading and analysis by Mike Neer and Katie Burchfield at the DataWORKS office. In addition, several DataWORKS consultants read the entire manuscript and added their suggestions—Gordon Carlson, Larry Federico, Linda Hale, and Alice Rodriquez.

We would like to thank those working at DataWORKS. Our dynamic programming team led by Roman Kolmakov has processed literally millions of pieces of data from schools across the United States. Without their efforts, we would never have been able to analyze and present the results of the vast amounts of information we collect. Our tireless production team led by Maria Cuadra has provided printing and mailing of materials to and from thousands of schools. Our outstanding research department led by Katie Burchfield has analyzed millions of student assignments and worked indefatigably to design and write powerful Explicit Direct Instruction lessons. Our client relations group led by Tina Anderson supports contracting and scheduling our work at schools across the United States.

We would like to thank Robin Najar, Julie Nemer, Mayan White, Veronica Stapleton, and Diana Breti at Corwin Press for their hard work, support, and faith in the project.

We would like to extend special thanks to the thousands of teachers whose classrooms we visited, both for observations and to teach lessons. And thanks to those tireless administrators who supported our vision of classroom instruction.

John Hollingsworth and
Silvia Ybarra, EdD

About the Authors

The authors, husband-and-wife team of John Hollingsworth and Silvia Ybarra, are the cofounders of DataWORKS Educational Research. The information in this book is based on research, their experience in education, and their 14 years of fieldwork with DataWORKS, working with thousands of educators across the United States and other countries, too.

 **John Hollingsworth** is president of DataWORKS Educational Research, a company originally created to use real data to improve student achievement. Although DataWORKS started by analyzing learning *outcomes* (test scores), it soon refocused on analyzing learning *inputs* (classroom instructional practices). DataWORKS now focuses mainly on providing staff development to schools on classroom instruction. John is an active researcher and presenter and has published numerous articles in educational publications. He spends much of his time on the road training teachers.

 **Dr. Silvia Ybarra, EdD,** began her career in education as a physics and chemistry teacher at Roosevelt High School in Fresno, California. Next, Silvia became principal of Wilson Middle School in Exeter, California, which under her leadership became a prestigious Distinguished School. Silvia was then named assistant superintendent of Coalinga-Huron School District. Her focus progressed from helping one classroom to helping one school to helping an entire district. Silvia is the head researcher at DataWORKS.

John and Silvia are coauthors of *Explicit Direct Instruction: The Power of the Well-Crafted, Well-Taught Lesson* (Corwin, 2009). They are also coauthors, with Joan Ardovino, of *Multiple Measures: Accurate Ways to Assess Student Achievement* (Corwin, 2000).

John and Silvia live on their organic vineyard in Fowler, California, along with their adopted farm dogs Antonia, Apollo, Ulysses, Virgil, and the newcomer, Tandora.

John Hollingsworth may be reached at john@dataworks-ed.com. Silvia Ybarra may be reached at silvia@dataworks-ed.com.

This book is dedicated to all educators who are working hard to improve learning for students, especially English Learners.

Part I
Getting Ready

1 English Learners Learning Every Day

Who Are They? What Do They Need?

T his book shows how to successfully teach English Learners (ELs). Before delving into specific practices, we want to relate two examples in which a few changes in teaching strategies produced immediate success for English Learners. Silvia describes two classrooms.

Mr. Nelson pointed to his Learning Objective written on the board: "Identify the title of a book." He immediately called on some students to read the Objective. Most of them were not able to read the word *title*. I could hear students struggling trying to sound it out. Some students used the short *i* sound. Some pronounced the silent *e* at the end of *title*.

In desperation, Mr. Nelson turned to me and whispered, "I have too many English Learners, and this is too hard for them."

I whispered back, "Let me try some strategies. Watch what I'm going to do, and then you can use the same techniques later on your own."

I pointed to the word *title* on the board.

Students, I want all of you to look carefully at this word. Put your eyes right here where I am pointing and listen very carefully while I say this word.

I waited a few seconds to check that all students were looking.

This word is title. *Listen one more time as I say it,* title.

I repeated *title* one more time, extending the long *i* sound, *tiiii-tle*. I asked the students to say the word *title* as I cued them by pointing to the word each time I wanted them to say it.

I stepped away from the board and toward the students.

Now, I am going to call on some of you to read the word to me. But first, I want all of you to point to the word title *on your handout and read it to your pair-share partner.*

I waited a moment for the students to pair-share and then I called on some random non-volunteers. The first one said it correctly.

I asked a second student. He looked at the word *title* and misread it, pronouncing the silent *e*. It almost sounded like *tightly*. I corrected the mispronunciation.

Listen carefully. The correct way to read this word is title.

I wanted to reduce the focus on him, so I asked the entire class including him to say *title* one more time. I returned to him and asked him to read it. "Title," he now correctly stated. I called on a third student who pronounced it correctly.

I then slowly read the entire Objective while having the entire class look at each word as I pointed to it.

Students, look at these words while I read: Identify the title of a book. Now we are going to read the Objective together.

I cued the class, *Today we will . . .*

The students joined in chorally, *Identify the title of a book.*

I turned to Mr. Nelson and whispered, "Now, have your students pair-share by reading the Learning Objective to each other. Then call on two non-volunteers to read today's Learning Objective." The students were successful, and it only took a couple of minutes.

After the lesson was completed, we debriefed about what had happened during the lesson. Mr. Nelson stated that it was great that his ELs were able to read and pronounce new words and to participate in the lesson. He went on to confess that in the past he had been hesitant to call on ELs.

I reminded him that nothing magical had taken place. All I did was implement research-based strategies that have been proven to work for ELs, such as pre-pronouncing and pre-reading difficult words, choral readings, pair-shares, Checking for Understanding, and providing Effective Feedback in direct response to student errors.

Now let's look at Silvia's second example, a lesson that addressed a different challenge.

Mr. Cunningham was part of a group of teachers I was working with. At this school, I taught the lesson first, and then teachers took turns teaching the same lesson with different students. After each lesson we debriefed, analyzing the strategies and practices used.

The lesson was "Describe the sequence and function of the digestive system." Mr. Cunningham used PowerPoint slides with written text and visuals. During Concept Development, the students read the text with him, and he referred to a diagram that illustrated the digestive system (see below). He followed up with some Checking for Understanding questions.

For his first question, he called on non-volunteers to define the digestive system in their own words. All the students were successful. Then he asked his students to list the sequence of the digestive system on their whiteboards. All of a sudden, the students started to ask questions such as "What do you want us to do?" "What do you mean by that?" Pointing to the diagram, one girl asked, "Do you want us to draw that?"

Mr. Cunningham looked at me, very puzzled because the lesson had been going very well up to this point. I had some ideas.

Sometimes, it appears that English Learners don't understand content when, in reality, they don't understand a specific English word. It's important to recognize the difference between ELs not understanding content and not understanding English. In this case, the students were having trouble with the word *sequence*. They didn't know what Mr. Cunningham was asking them to do. Some students guessed that he wanted a drawing of the digestive system.

I thought about my options. With Explicit Direct Instruction for English Learners, there are various strategies for dealing with words that students don't know. I could substitute an easier-to-understand word by rephrasing "sequence of digestion" as "order of digestion." I could quickly tell the students the meaning of *sequence* and move on. However, *sequence* is an academic word that will come up often at school. I decided to invest a moment in teaching its meaning and to follow up with a Checking for Understanding question.

I told the students to place their fingers underneath *sequence* and to read it with me. I explained that *sequence* means the order in which something happens or the order in which something is done. I elaborated.

Think about the alphabet. The letters are in a sequence: a, b, c, d, all the way to z. They are in order. We use words like first, next, then, and last to describe things that happen in sequence, in order.

I told the students to tell their pair-share partner the meaning of *sequence*. I waited a few moments while the students exchanged their answers and then called on non-volunteers to give the definition.

I turned and pointed toward the PowerPoint screen.

Students, explain to your pair-share partner what the sequence of the digestive system means.

I motioned to Mr. Cunningham to take over and to re-ask his question about the sequence of the digestive system. The students were successful in answering his question.

During the debriefing session afterward with the teachers, Mr. Cunningham stated it was hard to believe that ELs came to class not knowing the meaning of *sequence*. I explained to everyone that we should act preemptively as much as possible, anticipating where ELs might need help and then using Checking for Understanding to make decisions during the lesson. In this case, the fact that the students did not understand what *sequence* meant became apparent when they were not sure what the teacher wanted of them when the word was used in a Checking for Understanding question.

We'll be sharing more scenarios like the ones above in which ELs are successful. But before we go any further, let's spend a moment defining English Learners and their needs. Actually, the number of English Learners in your classroom includes more students than you might think.

WHO ARE ENGLISH LEARNERS?

English Learners are students whose first language is not English and who are in the process of learning English. Many years ago, when non-English speakers came to the United States, they learned English on their own. Today, teaching English to school-age children has become the responsibility of the school system.

These English-learning students are not equally distributed in schools across the United States. Some schools have very few ELs and other schools have very high populations. In the past, ELs were concentrated in a few states, but now they are distributed across the country so that more and more schools are addressing the needs and challenges of ELs. Although ELs include immigrants, the majority of ELs were born in the United States.

All Students Are English Learners for *New* Content

After visiting thousands of classrooms and working with content standards from several states, we have rethought the traditional definition of English Learners. They are not just the students who speak a different language at home. *When you teach grade-level, standards-based lessons, all your students take on some of the characteristics of English Learners.*

Here's why. Students don't already know the concepts and key vocabulary terms in most standards-based lessons because the vocabulary has never been presented at school before. Suddenly, everyone has to learn—listening, speaking, reading, writing, and understanding—new vocabulary.

Let's listen to Silvia describe how all students can be English Learners for new content:

> A few years ago, I taught a lesson at a middle school so teachers could see Explicit Direct Instruction using English Learner strategies in the classroom with their students. I included abundant student opportunities for listening and speaking, using the new vocabulary, during the lesson. I pronounced difficult words and had students repeat them. I read key concepts to the students and had them read them chorally. I called on individual students to pronounce specific words.
>
> After I had taught the EL class in first period, I was ready to repeat the lesson for second period. This time the teacher told me that this was her gifted class and asked me not use the pronunciations, repetition, and choral reading. She thought it would be demeaning for her gifted students.
>
> I pointed to the objective on the board and then called on some students to read the objective to the class. The first student read up to

the third word and got stuck trying to read and pronounce it. I turned to the teacher and whispered, "May I show the class how to pronounce the word?" The teacher slowly nodded yes. At that very moment, I was thinking all students are English Learners for new content. I continued, "Class, look at this word and listen very carefully while I pronounce it, and then I want you to read it with me." I slowed my rate of speech and continued, "This word is *theological.* Listen again, *theological.* Let's all read it together. Ready? *Theological.*"

All your students—not just ELs—will benefit from the strategies presented in this book. Look at these words—taken directly from standards, including Common Core State Standards—that students need to read, to write, to pronounce, and to understand:

Kindergarten: *character, setting, author, greater than, less than.*

First grade: *illustration, equivalent, distinguish, trapezoid.*

Second grade: *alliteration, organism, sequential, bar graph.*

Third grade: *conveyed, literal, Constitution, fraction.*

Fourth grade: *figurative language, decomposers, differentiate.*

Fifth grade: *tone, respiration, exponent.*

Sixth grade: *textual evidence, proportional relationships.*

Seventh grade: *soliloquy, additive inverse, mitochondria, theological.*

Eighth grade: *passive voice, incidents, absolute value, bivariate data, velocity.*

Ninth and 10th grades: *cumulative impact, transversal, elastic collisions, passive voice, matrices, prokaryotic cells.*

Eleventh and 12th grades: *rhetorical features, amplitude, neoclassic, nebular cloud, categorical and quantitative variables.*

From John: At a school where I was training, a teacher told me that state test questions were unfair for ELs. She showed me a released question addressing an author's assertion. She said it was unfair for ELs because they might not know what *assertion* meant. I opened my briefcase and lifted out a dog-eared copy of the standards. I flipped through the pages and pointed to the following standard: "Assess the adequacy, accuracy, and appropriateness of the author's evidence to support claims and *assertions*, noting instances of bias and stereotyping."

She was surprised when she saw the same word in the standard that was on the state test. I reminded her that every noun—actually every word—in the standard needs to be explicitly taught to all students, including English Learners.

English Language Fluency

Our goal when working with ELs is for them to learn grade-level content plus expand their knowledge of English. They must be able to *listen* to spoken English and understand what is said. They need to be able to *speak* English correctly using proper pronunciation, grammar, and syntax. They need to *read* English text with comprehension and *write* fluently in English.

From Silvia: I am a native Spanish speaker myself. I came to the U.S. from El Salvador when I was a teenager, not knowing a word of English. I can tell you that ELs can and do communicate in English that can be understood even when it is grammatically and syntactically incorrect, but this is not good enough. It is critical for English Learners to be taught correct English so they develop language fluency that matches a native speaker's. Language acquisition must be a focus of every classroom lesson.

The strategies in this book increase fluency by incorporating vocabulary development plus listening, speaking, reading, and writing in English into every lesson.

SUMMARY: ENGLISH LEARNER NEEDS

English Learners have a double duty in school. They must learn content while simultaneously learning English.

When you *teach* English Learners, you have a triple duty. You must provide well-crafted lessons so your ELs learn the content you are teaching them, plus you must consciously modify the English you use during the lesson so your ELs understand it, plus you need to support your ELs in learning more English every day.

English Learner Needs

Learn content

Learn English

Teachers meet English Learner needs by

Providing well-crafted lessons

Modifying English so ELs understand the lesson

Supporting English language acquisition every day

Whew! This sounds like a big job: providing well-crafted lessons in understandable English while supporting ELs in acquiring more English.

Over the course of this book, we'll describe how to do all three: well-crafted lessons, modifying English, and supporting English language acquisition. Chapter 2 provides an overview of Explicit Direct Instruction followed by a whole chapter on Checking for Understanding (Chapter 3).

Chapter 4, Vocabulary Development, and Chapter 5, Language Objectives, describe how to support English language acquisition within the context of every lesson.

Chapter 6, Content Access Strategies, describes how to make the English that teachers use easier to understand for ELs.

Chapters 7 to 12 show how to apply EL strategies within each component of an Explicit Direct Instruction lesson.

In Chapter 13, we discuss feedback and reflections from a school that saw Explicit Direct Instruction for English Learners in action. This chapter also includes a list of all the strategies described throughout the book, which can serve as a resource.

We're ready to go to the next chapter. You may be surprised to find out how important it is to have well-crafted lessons for English Learners.

2 English Learners Need Explicit Direct Instruction

The Well-Crafted, Powerfully Taught Lesson

In the previous chapter, we discussed meeting English Learner needs by using well-crafted lessons, modifying English to make it more understandable, and supporting English language acquisition daily. Let's start with the well-crafted lesson. It's important. It's the foundation.

ENGLISH LEARNERS NEED WELL-CRAFTED LESSONS

In our last book, *Explicit Direct Instruction (EDI): The Power of the Well-Crafted, Well-Taught Lesson* (Corwin, 2009), we described how to design and deliver lessons that would help all students, including English Learners, learn more and learn faster.

Soon, teachers and administrators were telling us how effective Explicit Direct Instruction is for English Learners. This confirmed what we saw when we visited schools, coaching teachers and teaching demonstration lessons ourselves.

> Good instruction for English Learners is similar to good instruction for English-speaking students.

While conducting research for this book, we came across an article by Dr. Claude Goldenberg, Professor of Education at Stanford University. His article described two major government-funded reviews of the research on English Learners which found that good instruction for English Learners is similar to good instruction for English-speaking students.

English Learners benefit from

- clear goals and objectives
- well-designed instructional routines
- active engagement and participation
- informative feedback
- opportunities to practice and apply new learning and transfer it to new situations
- periodic review and practice
- opportunities to interact with other students
- frequent assessments, with re-teaching as needed

From John: Recently, Silvia and I drove up to Stanford University Campus in Palo Alto, California, to meet with Dr. Goldenberg in person. He described his findings for English Learners, and then we explained how our Explicit Direct Instruction model implements the research. He went on to describe accommodations for ELs, but again emphasized the importance of having a well-crafted lesson for ELs.

As we drove home, Silvia and I reviewed the morning's meeting. It made sense. Adding accommodations, such as speaking slowly and clearly, doesn't turn a poorly designed lesson into a better one. Using clear enunciation or adding a visual to a below grade-level lesson doesn't suddenly raise it to grade level. Silvia and I looked at each other and nodded. The foundation of effective instruction for English Learners begins with a well-crafted lesson.

The Well-Crafted Lesson, Powerfully Taught

The research-based practices Dr. Goldenberg referred to are incorporated into the Explicit Direct Instruction model of the well-crafted and powerfully taught lesson.

To make a lesson well-crafted, Explicit Direct Instruction includes a well-tested, research-based sequence of lesson components, starting with a standards-based Learning Objective and ending with matching Independent Practice.

To make a lesson powerfully taught, Explicit Direct Instruction implements research-based delivery strategies, including non-volunteer Checking for Understanding, embedded Language Objectives and Vocabulary Development, student engagement every one to two minutes, teacher think-alouds, and much more.

Let's start with an overview of Explicit Direct Instruction. Then, as the book progresses, we'll describe in detail more than 40 strategies that make a lesson even more powerful for English Learners.

What Is Explicit Direct Instruction?

Explicit Direct Instruction, usually shortened to EDI, is a collection of effective, research-based instructional practices for designing and delivering powerful lessons that explicitly teach content, especially grade-level content, to all students. Lesson design and lesson delivery plus continuous Checking for Understanding create the powerful lesson.

> Lesson design plus lesson delivery plus continuous Checking for Understanding create the powerful lesson.

Explicit Direct Instruction lessons are not scripted lessons. Rather, this instructional model is a blueprint for designing and then delivering powerful lessons.

The focus of EDI is students learning more during *whole-class* instruction. The goal in EDI lessons is 80% of students achieving 80% correct answers during Independent Practice.

Even if you've read our first EDI book, be sure to read everything in this book, too. We've added some great new ideas and insights for using EDI in the classroom.

EXPLICIT DIRECT INSTRUCTION LESSON DESIGN COMPONENTS

Student Preparation

EDI lessons start with Student Preparation, during which you present a Learning Objective and then Activate Prior Knowledge. During these two lesson design components, you aren't presenting any new content yet. You're preparing your students for new content that will come shortly. The Learning Objective focuses the students, and you teach them how to pronounce and read the new Academic and Content vocabulary contained in the Objective. During Activate Prior Knowledge, you explicitly connect information that the students already know to what they are about to learn.

- **Learning Objective:** A statement describing what students will be able to do by the end of the lesson. It must match the Independent Practice and be clearly stated to the students at the start of the lesson. For grade-level, standards-based lessons, the Learning Objective is derived directly from state or Common Core standards.
- **Activate Prior Knowledge:** Purposefully revealing to students a connection between what they already know and what they are going to learn. This retrieves ideas or information from students' long-term memories and transfers it to their working memories so they can make connections to their existing knowledge.

Content Presentation

Well-crafted EDI lessons begin by preparing students to learn using a Learning Objective and Activating Prior Knowledge. Then the lesson shifts into the Content Presentation phase; you deliver new information to your students during Concept Development, Skill Development, Guided Practice, Lesson Importance, and Closure.

- **Concept Development:** Explicitly defining and teaching students the concepts (usually the nouns) contained in the Learning Objective. Concepts are the "big ideas" in a lesson.
- **Skill Development**: Explicitly teaching students the steps or processes necessary to execute the skill (the verb) in the Learning Objective. Teaching students how to do it.
- **Guided Practice:** Working problems with students using the steps from Skill Development while checking that they execute each step correctly.

New in This Edition

EDI Rule of Two. In EDI, Skill Development and Guided Practice are now combined using matched problems. For Skill Development, the teacher works the first problem, modeling the thinking processes used. Then for Guided Practice, the teacher guides the students through a matched problem (usually with whiteboards) while checking that students work each step correctly. Then repeat. Teacher works a problem. Students work a problem. Teacher works a problem. Students work a problem. I do one. You do one.

- **Lesson Importance:** Explicitly teaching students why the lesson is important for them to learn, how it is relevant to them.
- **Lesson Closure:** Having students work problems or answer questions to prove that they have learned the concepts and skills in the Learning Objective *before* they are given Independent Practice to do on their own.

Independent Practice

After an EDI lesson is completed, students continue practicing by themselves to develop automaticity and to remember what they were taught.

- **Classroom Independent Practice** and **Homework:** Having students successfully practice in class or at home exactly what they were just taught.
- **Periodic Review:** Providing additional practice spread out over time to facilitate long-term retention.

Below are some approximate times for each lesson component. Although not all lessons or all grade levels will use 52-minute lessons, the table can be used to pace the relative times spent during each EDI lesson component. About two-thirds of any lesson should be allocated to Concept Development, Skill Development, and Guided Practice.

Minutes	Lesson Component
2	Learning Objective
5	Activate Prior Knowledge
15	Concept Development
20	Skill Development and Guided Practice
5	Lesson Importance
5	Closure
52	**Total lesson time**

EXPLICIT DIRECT INSTRUCTION LESSON DELIVERY STRATEGIES

EDI lessons incorporate lesson delivery strategies, which are used continuously throughout the lesson. Delivery strategies are not usually in the textbook; you need to add them yourself. Lesson delivery strategies are what make a good lesson great!

- **Checking for Understanding:** Continually verifying that students are learning while they are being taught.
- **Explaining:** Teaching by telling.
- **Modeling:** Teaching using think-alouds to reveal to students the strategic thinking you use to solve a problem.
- **Demonstrating:** Teaching using physical objects to clarify the content and to support kinesthetic learning.
- **English Learner Language Acquisition Strategies** *(NEW):* Purposefully supporting ELs in learning more English within the context of every lesson. Includes *Language Objectives* (Listening, Speaking, Reading, Writing) and *Vocabulary Development* (Academic, Content, Support).
- **English Learner Content Access Strategies** *(NEW):* Purposefully making English easier to understand during a lesson. Includes *Comprehensible Delivery*, *Context Clues*, *Supplementary Materials*, and *Adaptations of Existing Materials*.
- **Cognitive Strategies:** Practices added to a lesson to help students remember information.

Figure 2.1 is a graphical representation of Explicit Direct Instruction. It shows the lesson design components of a well-crafted EDI lesson, starting with a Learning Objective and ending with lesson Closure. After Closure, teaching has ended, and students are ready for Independent Practice and later Periodic Review. On the outside, surrounding the design components—like layers of an onion—are the lesson delivery strategies. They are not specific to any design component and are used throughout the lesson.

From John: At DataWORKS, we have interacted with several State Departments of Education. At one session, the speaker presented a study covering 100 years of educational research (Chall, 2000). The study found that the traditional teacher-centered (direct instruction) approach produced higher achievement than the progressive approach. This was true for all students, and its effect was even stronger for students who were less prepared. Explicit Direct Instruction is our version of teacher-centered, direct instruction in which you directly teach content to your students.

How Often Do You Use Explicit Direct Instruction?

Well-crafted, powerfully taught EDI lessons should be used for initial instruction of the Learning Objectives contained in state content standards for your grade. The rule of thumb is that about two-thirds of classroom instructional time should be allocated to teaching grade-level, standards-based lessons.

Figure 2.1 Explicit Direct Instruction for English Learners

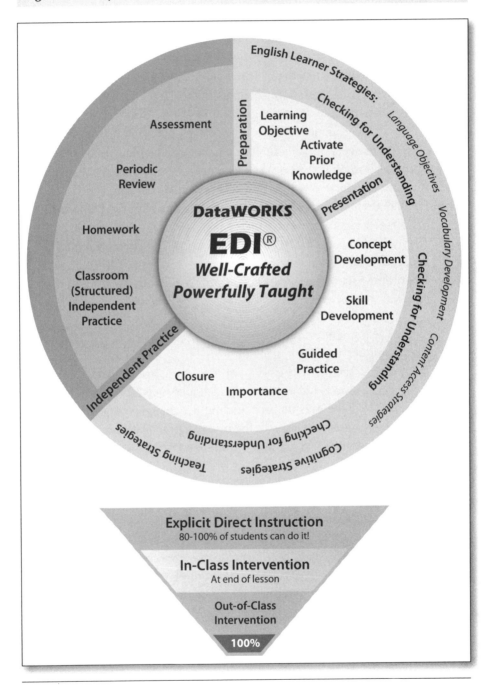

Source: © 2009 DataWORKS Educational Research.

(The two-thirds rule is over time, not for every day or every hour). The remaining time is used for Independent Practice, Periodic Review, tests, quizzes, and so forth.

Although fully developed EDI lessons are used two-thirds of the time, the various strategies, including English Learner Strategies, should be used *all the time*—slow and clear speech, non-volunteer Checking for Understanding, pair-shares, tracked reading, Listening and Speaking, Vocabulary Development, Content Access Strategies, and so forth. These strategies should be part of your every day repertoire of teaching tools.

Student Engagement

An important part of any lesson is student engagement. This is even more critical for English Learners. ELs need to be engaged in learning both new content and new language in every lesson. In EDI, teachers create engagement by having students do something every 1 to 2 minutes—whiteboards, pair-shares, tracked and choral reading, answering Checking for Understanding questions, and so forth.

From John: Recently, I taught an EDI math demo lesson on exponents as part of an instructional leadership training. I had 10 principals in the back of the room observing. During the debriefing session afterward, one principal reported that he had counted the number of student interactions. He reported that I had 107 student interactions in 50 minutes. This led to an insightful discussion about how engaged and on-task the students were throughout my EDI lesson. I replied that I created this engagement by directing students to do a lot during the lesson. ***Student engagement is created when the teacher asks the students to do something.***

From Silvia: I have a saying that applies to EDI: ***The brain that is not processing is not learning.*** This is why EDI has so much student engagement—so students will learn. When lessons are primarily lectures, learning is compromised because of the absence of student interaction.

SUMMARY: ENGLISH LEARNERS NEED WELL-CRAFTED LESSONS

- English Learners need well-crafted lessons.
- Explicit Direct Instruction combines research-based lesson design components and research-based lesson delivery strategies to produce well-crafted, powerfully taught lessons.

- Explicit Direct Instruction includes English Learner strategies to support English language acquisition and to make the English in the lesson understandable.
- Explicit Direct Instruction practices create student engagement to optimize learning and retention of content.

In the next chapter, we describe Checking for Understanding, which is the key to measuring student learning. Turn the page and read how to Check for Understanding for English Learners and why it's so important.

3 Checking for Understanding

How to Verify That English Learners Are Learning

EDI lessons are put together with design components, starting with a Learning Objective and ending with Closure, followed by Independent Practice. The design components are related to the content you are teaching. For example, Concept Development defines the concepts in the lesson.

What separates EDI from some other direct instruction models is the consistent use of a broad range of delivery strategies. The term *delivery strategies* refers to practices you use to teach the content, to deliver the lesson to your students. The *number one* delivery strategy in EDI is continuous Checking for Understanding. *Checking for Understanding* is a long phrase, so we often shorten it to CFU.

Checking for Understanding is the teacher continually verifying that students, including English Learners, are learning *what* is being taught *while* it is being taught. It's easy to do. You stop every few minutes and ask questions about what you just taught.

Students, how did I identify the simile in paragraph number one?

Notice we said "every few minutes." Don't wait until the end of the lesson to find out whether some students are confused. Intersperse your questions during the lesson while you are teaching. This makes the lesson more engaging and provides more student interaction. It also allows you to check that your students are with you throughout the lesson.

From John: In our last EDI book, we suggested that Checking for Understanding questions should be asked about every two minutes. This doesn't mean you use an egg timer and ask a question every two minutes. Instead, you follow the flow of the lesson, interspersing questions as you present meaningful chunks of information. I have had principals time my lessons and tally the number of questions. I might use 28 questions during a 50-minute lesson, in a combination of calling on individual students and having all students hold up whiteboards to show answers.

Checking for Understanding is the teacher continually verifying that students are learning *what* is being taught *while* it is being taught.

WHY IS CONTINUAL CHECKING FOR UNDERSTANDING SO BENEFICIAL FOR ENGLISH LEARNERS AND TEACHERS?

First, Checking for Understanding is your primary formative assessment, informing you in real time whether ELs are learning.

Second, Checking for Understanding allows you to make instructional decisions during the lesson. If you wait and look at Independent Practice, homework, quizzes, or state tests to find out whether ELs have learned, it's too late to modify your instruction. The lesson is already done.

Third, Checking for Understanding generates a high success rate for ELs because you speed up, slow down, and re-teach in direct response to their ability to answer your CFU questions. The fact that you check every few minutes means that you teach—and re-teach, when necessary—in small chunks, bringing the students with you through the entire lesson.

Fourth, Checking for Understanding allows you to confirm that ELs know how to do the homework before being asked to do it. You don't want your students to reinforce any misconceptions or to internalize the wrong way of doing it. There is an old saying: "Practice makes perfect." Actually, this is not correct. Have you ever seen students do every problem wrong? Do these students need to be assigned more problems? Not until they know how to do them—because practice doesn't make perfect; *practice makes permanent.* Always Check for Understanding so students are not practicing their mistakes into permanence.

Fifth, Checking for Understanding improves classroom dynamics. Your questions break up lectures, making the classroom more interactive for students. When you present questions every few minutes, students are more engaged and pay more attention. As an added bonus, when students are engaged, discipline problems are reduced. In fact, the best discipline program of all is using practices that prevent problems from occurring!

CHECK FOR UNDERSTANDING USING TAPPLE

Source: © 2009 DataWORKS Educational Research.

Several years ago we created TAPPLE as an easy-to-remember acronym for the steps of Checking for Understanding. The TAPPLE poster shown above is taped to thousands of classroom walls across the United States. You can download a color version from our website (www.dataworks-ed.com).

Put it on a wall where you can see it. You don't need to be able to read it, but every time you see it out of the corner of your eye, it will remind you to Check for Understanding.

We're going to go over each of the TAPPLE steps in this chapter. In a broad sense, Checking for Understanding starts with teaching, questioning, and picking students. Checking for Understanding ends with diagnosing errors and providing corrective feedback.

TAPPLE: Teach First So All Students Are Prepared to Respond

The *T* in TAPPLE stands for *Teach First* so all students, including English Learners, are prepared to respond. *Teach First* means you explicitly present the content before asking any questions about it. Remember the Checking for Understanding definition: You are verifying that your students are learning *what* you are teaching *while* you are teaching. You're monitoring whether they are following you. When you don't Teach First, it's not possible to measure learning; you're assessing background knowledge instead. (We'll talk more about activating and *providing* background knowledge during the Activate Prior Knowledge component of an EDI lesson.)

> *From Silvia:* Teach First. DataWORKS has found that students are often asked question after question about something that has not been taught yet. For example, a lesson on persuasive essays starts by questioning students on what a persuasive essay is. Invariably, the students cannot answer because they don't know what a persuasive essay is before they have been taught. This is more detrimental for ELs as they might know the concept of convincing someone, but they don't know the meaning of the word *persuasive*.

> *Remember:* Always Teach First so all students, including English Learners, can answer successfully.

Teach First includes more than content. You also teach ELs the language required for the new lesson during the lesson itself. You teach them how to pronounce and read new words and their definitions. In addition, you also teach how to answer in complete sentences that incorporate the new vocabulary from the lesson. We'll describe in detail how to do this in Chapter 4, Vocabulary Development, and Chapter 5, Language Objectives.

Teaching First greatly increases learning opportunities for English Learners because you provide both the content and language they need to be successful in class.

TAPPLE: Ask a Specific Question About What You Just Taught

After you have taught something, you are ready to ask specific questions about what you just taught.

Here are some examples of specific questions to measure whether English Learners are following what you are teaching. They're also higher order questions.

- *Students, in your own words, what is alliteration?*
- *Why is sentence number two an example of hyperbole?*
- *What was the difference between the Virginia Plan and the New Jersey plan at the Constitutional Convention in 1787?*
- *Students, what is one difference between plant cells and animal cells?*
- *Students, I just solved this one-step linear equation. How did I solve it?*
- *Students, you just added two fractions on your whiteboards. How did you calculate the sum?*
- *Students, I just identified the setting in the first paragraph. Now, you read the second paragraph and be ready to tell me the setting and how you know it's the setting.*

Avoid opinion questions such as *Does everyone understand how to do this? Ready to go on? Do I need to work another problem?* Ask specific questions.

Ask English Learners High-Level Questions

Sometimes, teachers drop the level of their questions for ELs, thinking ELs can't answer more sophisticated questions or don't have the language skills to answer. On the contrary, it's important for English Learners at all levels to be presented with questions that promote high levels of thinking, including questions they may not be able to answer orally. This means that ELs should be presented with higher-order questions (such as the ones above) so they have the opportunity to think and process information at a high level. ELs have the same capability to think and process information at high levels as native English speakers, even if they can't completely express their thoughts orally in English.

Generally, EDI lessons have only one low-level question: "What is our Learning Objective?" All other CFU questions are higher-order questions.

Support Language Acquisition During Questioning

Now we are going to add some powerful refinements to "Ask a Specific Question" that specifically support language acquisition for ELs.

Cue ELs to answer in complete sentences using the new Academic and Content Vocabulary words from the lesson.

ELs (and other students) typically respond to questions with a word or a short phrase. When told to answer in a complete sentence, they often use short sentences with pronouns. With EDI, you prompt and support ELs in answering in complete sentences, incorporating the new Academic and Content Vocabulary from the lesson.

Look at the responses in Table 2.1, ranging from phrases, to complete sentences, to complete sentences with vocabulary.

Table 2.1 Academic and Content Vocabulary

CFU Question	Word or phrase response	Complete sentence	Complete sentence with new vocabulary
Which sentence, A or B, uses alliteration?	B.	It's B. The answer is B. I wrote B on my whiteboard.	Sentence B uses *alliteration*.
What is the setting in the first paragraph?	The forest.	It is the forest.	The *setting* in the first paragraph is the forest.
What was the first step in solving the linear equation?	Subtracted two.	I subtracted two.	I used the *inverse operation* and subtracted two from each side of the *linear equation*.
What was the author's assertion in the passage?	Wear uniforms.	Students should wear uniforms to school.	The *author's assertion* in the passage is that students should wear uniforms to school.
What is one check and balance in the Constitution?	Veto.	An example is the veto.	One *check and balance* in the Constitution is the President's veto.

From John: Complete sentences can make any lesson better. However, I have found that teachers need to develop what I call "teacher discipline" to remember to require complete sentences every time. When students are consistently prompted to use complete sentences, they will do it automatically without prompting. Complete sentences should be a schoolwide norm. I saw a poster in a school the other day: "We always answer in complete sentences."

Sentence Frames

There is an easy way to support ELs to answer in complete sentences using academic English: you provide a sentence frame or a sentence stem showing them how to respond. Include it as part of your question and then have the students practice their complete sentences during a pair-share before you call on anyone to respond.

Students, get out your whiteboards. I want you to calculate the perimeter of the parallelogram in Example 4. In a moment, I'm going to call on some of you to read your answer. I want you to answer like this: The perimeter of the parallelogram is . . . I also want you to include the units. The units in Example 4 are meters. Your answer should include the word meters.

Students, turn to Figure 2 on page 349. Why is Figure 2 an example of the second Postulate of the Kinetic Molecular Theory? I want you to answer: Figure 2 is an example of the second Postulate of the Kinetic Molecular Theory because . . .

Let's read this sentence together. Ready? "After the rain stopped, Jennifer went outside to play." Students, why is this sentence a complex sentence? I want you to answer: It is a complex sentence because . . .

Besides using oral sentence frames, you can provide written sentence frames for students to use. This can be effective because students won't spend time trying to remember the sentence frame while they are composing their answer, and they will be practicing reading and recognizing new words contained in the sentence frame.

Cue English Learners to answer using language that is higher than their current English Language Development (ELD) level.

To advance ELs' language level, cue and support them in using new language that is higher than their current level. ELs need to learn and practice *new* words, not just the ones they know.

Students, I have a question. What are the two components, the two parts, of Lewis Dot Structures? I don't want you to say, "The two parts are . . ." I want you to say, "The two components of Lewis Dot Structures are . . ."

Students, I want you to tell me something that is the same about the two characters.

I want you to say, "One similarity is . . ."
(later during the lesson)
I want you to say, "Something they have in common is . . ."

Cue students to use a public voice.

Train students, especially ELs, to speak up when they respond so all students can hear. At DataWORKS we are using "Stand and Deliver." We direct elementary and middle school students to stand up and respond in a loud public voice. One of the advantages to the public voice and Stand and Deliver is that all the other students turn to listen to the response.

> **From John:** Experiment with your students using Stand and Deliver and complete sentences to answer questions. It is very effective. Most schools who try it adopt it right away.

TAPPLE: Pause, Pair-Share, Point

The TAPPLE Pause means you provide some time between asking the question and selecting someone to respond. This is called wait time or think time.

When you ask a question, students need time to prepare an answer. Generally, it takes about 3 to 5 seconds to recall information and mentally put together an answer. English Learners may require additional time, as much as 8 to 10 seconds. Beginning English learners often translate the question from English to their native language, compose an answer, and then construct an approximation of the answer in English. This translation process takes time.

The wait time you provide after asking a question allows all students time to process an answer. You don't need to wait again when you select the second or third student to respond. The wait time is provided once for the entire class. However, be ready to wait for individual students to orally state their answer after you call on them.

Pair-Share

The first *P* in TAPPLE now includes *pair-share,* one of the most powerful strategies for you to take from this book, especially for ELs.

Pair-share means to direct your students to explain something to the person sitting next to them. For example, every time you ask a CFU question, you tell your students to discuss their answers with each other before you select someone to respond. It is easy to do. Pair off your students and have them explain their answers to their pair-share partner.

Students, we just went over the Learning Objective together. I am going to ask one of you what we are going to do today. Before I select someone, I want you to read the Learning Objective to your partner so you are ready in case I call on you.

Students, identify and underline a supporting detail in the first paragraph. In a minute I am going to call on someone to tell me a supporting detail. Use a complete sentence like this: "One supporting detail is . . ." Tell your partner your supporting detail and why it is a supporting detail. Be ready to tell me if I call on you.

On your whiteboards, do Step 1: Simplify the expressions on both sides of the linear equation. Then explain to your partner how you did it. If you don't have the same answer, check each other for errors.

During pair-shares, students often teach each other the content you just taught. You turn the students into teachers.

Students, I just solved this problem. Explain to your partner how I solved it.

From Silvia: Pair-shares, during which ELs discuss academic content, should not be confused with ELs talking to each other using language they already know. During pair-shares, ELs should be practicing new language from the lesson.

Point and Explain: Students point to information on the page and explain it to their pair-share partner.

Pair-shares can be enhanced by asking students to point to specific textual information on the page and explain it to their partners. Point and Explain is an effective language strategy for ELs because they are connecting ideas to text, explaining ideas in text, and describing and explaining visuals to their partners.

The most engaging method of doing this is directing students to reach out and point to the information on their *partner's* paper. The kinesthetic aspect of this practice is amazing to watch: arms crossing throughout the classroom, fingers pointing to specific information directly related to the content you are teaching, animated discussions.

Students, where does the author use personification in the second paragraph? Partner A, point to a sentence in the second paragraph in your partner's textbook where the author uses personification. Explain to your partner why it is personification.

Pair-shares without questions.

Sometimes, if you have a series of items to cover, you can direct students to pair-share and explain individual items without asking CFU questions until you have covered several or all of the items. In other words, you can have students pair-share and explain information to each other even if you don't ask an immediate CFU question.

Pair-shares are especially important for ELs.

Pair-shares are the primary method of implementing Language Objectives for English Learners.

Pair-shares are so beneficial for English Learners that they should be used for almost every question. In fact, pair-shares are the primary method of implementing Language Objectives for ELs because they are listening and speaking using the new language from your lesson. Pair-shares create engagement as ELs exchange information with each other. Pair-shares also allow ELs time to compose and practice their answers before being called upon to respond.

Appendices B and C provide additional information on how to manage the classroom for pair-shares and why pair-shares are so beneficial for ELs.

From John: I find that students have focused attention spans of less than five minutes. However, every time I direct students to pair-share, they become engaged. The interaction of the pair-share resets their "attention clock." Then they can concentrate for another few minutes. Constant use of strategies like pair-shares keeps students engaged for the entire lesson.

TAPPLE: Pick a Non-Volunteer

We've talked about pair-shares. Let's get to the next step of TAPPLE. You Taught First. You Asked a specific question about what you just taught. You then Paused and Pair-shared using a sentence frame. You had students Point and Explain relevant information, if applicable. Now you're ready to Pick a Non-Volunteer to answer your question to verify that everyone— including ELs—is learning.

In EDI, a randomizing system is used to select non-volunteer students during the lesson. The most widely used method is to write the student names on Popsicle sticks and place them in a cup. Each time you ask a question, you pull a stick from the cup to select a student to answer. In fact, the general phrase "pull a stick" now means to select a non-volunteer no matter what system is actually used.

Any method can be used, but keep in mind, Checking for Understanding is valid only when you call on random non-volunteers. Also, randomizing ensures that ELs are always included among the selected students.

From Silvia: Many teachers express serious concerns about having to ask ELs to respond to questions during a lesson. They state that ELs should not be forced to talk in class. However, students need a moderate level of concern to stimulate their efforts to learn. One way of raising student level of concern is by calling on non-volunteers. Everyone needs to be ready to respond. In addition, ELs need ample opportunities to express their ideas in English (oral language development). ELs answering questions also gives opportunities for teachers to monitor students' English Language Development proficiency.

Unfortunately, with multiple opportunities for students to use English in the classroom, we often see the same volunteers answering questions. Under the volunteer system, ELs are not given equal opportunity to participate in class.

DataWORKS has found that ELs are very successful in answering questions during EDI lessons. Of course, that's because they are well-prepared to answer. Using TAPPLE, the teacher Teaches First, and the students Pair-share to practice their answers before being asked to respond.

The responses shown below are from a survey of ELs who participated in a DataWORKS StepUP Academy summer school program designed to accelerate English Learners by pre-teaching the next year's standards during the summer. The Academy teachers taught EDI lessons every day and consistently called on non-volunteers to answer CFU questions. You can see from the responses that calling on non-volunteers also motivates students to pay attention.

Fifth-grade survey: *Write a sentence telling how you felt when the teacher asked questions.*

- I was hoping to get picked.
- I felt okay because I pay attention.
- I felt prepared.
- I was hoping my teacher would pick me.
- I was thinking I was going to get picked.
- I felt like I needed to pay attention to get it right.

How Many Students Should Be Called on for Each CFU Question?

We used to have a rule of thumb: Call on three non-volunteers students for each question. Our latest action research during the past year working with hundreds of teachers—and teaching kindergarten to 12th-grade lessons ourselves—has caused us to fine tune our thinking: Depending on the question asked, adjust the number of students you call on to respond.

1. Call on fewer students for questions that have a single answer.

2. Call on more students for higher order and divergent questions that do not have one answer.

3. Call on more students when answers have linguistic demands.

4. Call on more students when students need to remember the answer.

We're halfway through Checking for Understanding. We focused on asking questions and preparing ELs to respond. Now we'll continue, describing how to provide effective feedback for correct and incorrect student answers. Then we'll complete this chapter by discussing how to use whiteboards to Check for Understanding of the entire class at once.

HOW TO PROVIDE EFFECTIVE FEEDBACK FOR ENGLISH LEARNERS

You've Taught first, Asked a specific CFU question, had students Pair-share using a sentence frame, and Picked a non-volunteer. Now you're ready to shift gears from asking questions to *listening* to the responses to decide what to do next. Do you need to re-teach the content to the whole class? Do some individual students need support? Are ELs having trouble with the language of the lesson?

TAPPLE: Listen to the Response

The *L* in TAPPLE stands for *Listen to the Response.* When delivering an EDI lesson, you listen carefully to each student's response because what you do next depends on your analysis of the student's answer. Your initial diagnosis is to determine (1) Is the student's answer correct? (2) Is it partially correct? or (3) Is it wrong?

Note: With whiteboards, Listen to the Response also means look at the student answers, and then listen to non-volunteers read and explain their whiteboard answers.

TAPPLE: Effective Feedback (Echo, Elaborate, or Explain)

The *E* in TAPPLE stands for Effective Feedback: Echo, Elaborate, or Explain. After you listen and analyze the student's response, you provide Effective Feedback: (1) echo correct answers, (2) elaborate on partially correct answers, and (3) explain incorrect answers.

Let's look at providing effective feedback for both content and ELs' use of language.

Echo Correct Answers

When students have the correct answer to a CFU question, echo the answer to the entire class for everyone to hear. The echoing is beneficial for the student who answered and for everyone else, too.

First, you acknowledge and affirm that the student had the correct answer. *That's correct, Adriana. We can determine character traits from the character's words, the character's thoughts, and the character's actions.*

Second, the echo allows all students to hear important information more often, especially if the original student had a soft voice, and the other students did not hear the answer. The echoing is especially beneficial for something students need to remember. When Adriana's response is echoed in a clear adult voice, all the students are hearing it again. These repetitions are important to help transfer the information into permanent, long-term memory.

Finally, the echoing allows ELs additional repetitions of correctly worded English sentences so they develop an ear for English syntax.

Elaborate on Partially Correct Answers

When a student's answer is mostly correct, you don't need to re-teach. You paraphrase and elaborate on the student's answer so all students hear a more effectively worded answer with proper English syntax. ELs sometimes have a hard time verbalizing their thoughts even when they know the answer. So, you clean up their answers using understandable vocabulary. You can have the student or whole class repeat the corrected answer.

Student: I picked sentence two. It's a simile because . . . there . . . there are two things . . . and as.

Teacher: That's correct. Sentence two is a simile because it compares two unlike things using the word as. Class, let's say that together: Sentence two is a simile because it compares two unlike things using the word as.

Again, you want students to hear the correct answer and for ELs to hear (and practice) correctly worded sentences.

Explain the Answer

Here's the rule: If two non-volunteers in a row have the wrong answers, stop and *re-teach* the entire class. Avoid the temptation of calling on additional students, searching for someone who can provide a correct answer. Remember, the purpose of Checking for Understanding questions is to determine whether students are confused. It's not a search to uncover a student who can respond correctly.

> If two non-volunteers in a row have the wrong answers, stop and re-teach the whole class.

What If Students Can't Answer a Question?

There are several strategies you can use to ensure high student success, as shown in the box below.

Creating Student Success

Students are never allowed not to know the answer.

Teach the whole class to the 80% success level.

Provide corrective feedback to individual students.

1. Provide the student with prompts or hints.

2. Tell student, "Listen carefully to the next student. *I will come back to you.*"

3. If two students in a row cannot answer correctly, re-teach the entire class.

(The next two strategies can be useful for beginning ELs.)

4. De-escalate by rephrasing to a multiple-choice question.

5. Have students read the answer with you.

CHECKING FOR UNDERSTANDING TO MAKE INSTRUCTIONAL DECISIONS

Teacher as Decision Maker

You've probably heard the expression "use assessments to modify instruction." This is usually interpreted to mean modify your instruction the next time you teach the same content, probably next year. Well, the most timely assessments you can use are the Checking for Understanding questions during the lesson itself. Then you can modify instruction—while you teach—in direct response to student learning.

Now, we're going to combine the TAPPLE *L* (Listen to student responses) and the TAPPLE *E* (Effective Feedback: Echo, Elaborate, or Explain) to make instructional decisions.

What Corrective Action Should You Take?

The corrective action you take during a lesson also depends on correctly assessing the *cause* of student errors. There are four broad types of errors: (1) errors in learning the *new* content; (2) subskill errors; and, for ELs, (3) errors in understanding the English used during the lesson; and (4) student English language errors—incorrect use of English when responding. Let's start with content and subskill errors.

Content Errors

You use continual Checking for Understanding to determine whether students are learning the new content you are teaching. When many students are making errors in answering your content-related CFU questions, you stop and re-teach with a slightly different approach. When individual students make errors, you provide corrective feedback.

Subskill Errors

Subskills are skills from prior grades that are used in a new lesson. For example, multiplication facts from third grade are a subskill used to calculate the circumference of a circle in a sixth-grade lesson. Often students understand the new concept but make an error in a subskill operation, which then leads to an incorrect answer. The errors we see most often are math fact errors and low reading fluency.

Addressing Subskill Gaps

At DataWORKS we have used EDI to successfully teach grade-level content to all levels of students, from kindergarten to 12th grade. In fact, the DataWORKS company motto is *All Students Successfully Taught Grade-Level Work Every Day.* The expanded motto is *All Students, Including English Learners, Successfully Taught, at School, Grade-Level Work Every Day.*

All students, including English Learners,

successfully taught, at school,

grade-level work

every day!

Content standards are not beyond the cognitive ability of ELs. ELs can learn and understand grade-level concepts and skills before they are completely English proficient.

Also, you need to completely separate student reading level from student grade level. The content standards to teach are determined by the grade the students are in, not the grade level at which they are reading. For example, all high school students can be taught the concepts and skills contained in high school content standards even if they are reading below grade level.

At DataWORKS, we use a three-pronged approach to subskill gaps so we can teach grade-level lessons to all students, including ELs: (a) improve subskills within the context of an EDI lesson, (b) differentiate to work around subskills, and (c) improve subskills directly. Appendix C provides additional information on these three approaches.

Now let's return to our previous discussion of the types of student errors encountered in a lesson. We have discussed (1) errors in learning new content and (2) subskill errors. Now we will discuss the EL-specific third and fourth types of errors.

Errors in Understanding the English Used During the Lesson

Part of TAPPLE's "Listen carefully to each student's response" includes explicitly distinguishing between misunderstanding of the content being taught and misunderstanding of words or phrases used to teach the content. Misunderstanding of specific words is most often revealed when you ask ELs to justify and explain their incorrect answers. Below are three examples in which the teacher uncovers language errors and provides immediate feedback. You will see the importance of having ELs explain their incorrect answers. Notice in the examples that the ELs understood the concepts.

Example 1. The lesson was *using context clues to determine the meaning of unknown words.* One English Learner misunderstood the word *meager* as *major* and then had the wrong answer. When the teacher asked the student to explain his incorrect answer, the student described how he tried to use the context clues that matched *major* or large. He said that the context clues did not make sense. The teacher corrected the error and the student explained the correct answer.

Example 2. The lesson was *finding the greatest common factor of two numbers.* When the teacher called on a student, the student stated that the common factors were calling each other to "come on" next to each other. The teacher corrected "come on factors" as "common factors" and re-explained the concept.

Example 3. The lesson addressed *explaining shades of meaning of related words*. During the lesson the students were to select *slender* or *scrawny* when referring to a starving, stray cat. A student who had the wrong answer explained that the sentence referred to a starving *straight* cat. (If you say the words *stray* and *straight* a few times, you can hear that there is only a slight difference at the end of the word, especially if you say *stray cat* and *straight cat* quickly.) The student felt that a *straight* cat, standing straight would best be described as slender, not scrawny. The teacher corrected the meaning of *stray* and the student described the correct answer.

EDI preemptively reduces these errors through clear enunciation, pre-pronunciation of words, pre-reading of text, contextual definitions, and defining new vocabulary words in context. We'll cover these strategies in Chapter 4, Vocabulary Development; Chapter 5, Language Objectives; and Chapter 6, Content Access Strategies.

Student English Language Errors

Providing feedback on errors is an integral part of Checking for Understanding and TAPPLE. You always provide feedback on content errors. However, since ELs are in the process of learning English, they also need to be given corrective feedback on their use of English.

Correcting language errors is important. Beginning English speakers receive extensive language support and corrections from friends and acquaintances. However, once ELs reach a certain level of being understood—even when using incorrect English—the corrective feedback ceases and they continue practicing at their existing level for a lifetime without ever being shown how to improve their language.

In addition, many English Learners are not receiving *any* feedback for language errors from their peers or family. You, the classroom teacher, are the only one providing a role model, correcting English usage. You must correct ELs' language errors. In many cases, no one else is. In fact, many schools are adopting a policy of correcting all language errors anywhere, anytime—from the playground to the classroom.

We have three strategies you can use to correct English language errors during EDI lessons.

Language Correction

I. **Explicit Language Correction Strategy.** You explicitly note the type of language error to the whole class and explicitly correct it.

(Continued)

(Continued)

2. **Implicit Language Correction Strategy.** When you hear a language error, you don't actually state that an error was made. Instead, you echo a corrected answer to the entire class.

3. **Elicit a Language Correction Strategy.** With this method, you cue the English Learner to self-correct the error without actually giving the correction yourself.

The three methods each have their advantages and disadvantages.

The EDI-EL Explicit Correction Strategy identifies the specific error and takes more time, but it has the advantage of your emphasizing a rule of English grammar or pronunciation that all ELs can apply to other situations.

Using the EDI-EL Implicit Correction Strategy, you echo the correct language, but English Learners might not be aware of the correction.

With the EDI-EL Elicit a Correction Strategy, you cue and prompt English Learners to self-correct their language errors. Caution—eliciting corrections can *only* be used for language errors that have been previously discussed. ELs cannot self-correct unless they know the correct linguistic form.

Corrective Feedback on Student English Language Errors

Let's look at some examples of addressing different types of student English language errors.

Grammar errors. These are errors ELs make because of misunderstanding or lack of mastery of English grammar and syntax rules. When you hear these errors, you don't stop and teach a grammar lesson, but you can include a brief explanation so ELs can generalize beyond the specific sentence just used.

In the example below, the teacher uses the EDI-EL Explicit Correction Strategy, explicitly correcting a grammatical error, and includes the reason. Then the teacher has the whole class state the corrected answer and returns to the specific student to restate the grammatically correct answer. Having the whole class repeat the corrected response reduces the focus on the individual student.

Teacher:	What is something similar about trapezoids and rectangles?
Nicola:	Trapezoids and rectangles is quadrilaterals. They both have four sides.
Teacher corrects:	Yes, that is correct. They are quadrilaterals with four sides, but we say, "Trapezoids and rectangles *are* quadrilaterals." We say *are* because we are talking about more than one. Trapezoids and rectangles *are* quadrilaterals.

| Teacher turns to the class: | Class, let's say it together. Ready? Trapezoids and rectangles are quadrilaterals. |

Teacher
turns to
the class: Class, let's say it together. Ready? Trapezoids and rectangles
                are quadrilaterals.

Teacher
turns back
to Nicola: Nicola, can you tell me one more time?

Nicola: Trapezoids and rectangles are quadrilaterals.

> **From John:** I was in a classroom coaching a teacher when I heard three students in a row respond, "Me and my partner decided ..." I cued the teacher to correct the error. The students weren't embarrassed and answered, "My partner and I ..." from then on.

Oral reading pronunciation errors. Pronunciation errors made while students read orally are often due to misunderstanding of phonics rules or lack of decoding skills. Quite often, pronunciation errors occur *because* students use phonics rules to pronounce a word that does not follow the rules.

Students may be able to self-correct when they sound out enough of a difficult-to-read word such as *marshmallow* to recognize that it's a word they already know orally. However, pronunciation errors are compounded when ELs try to read or sound out words they don't already know, such as *omniscient point of view* or *multiplicative inverse.*

In EDI, you preempt reading errors by pre-pronouncing individual difficult words for your students while they are looking at the word. To support word recognition, it's important that they actually are looking at the word. If they are not looking at the word, they are practicing listening and speaking but not reading. In addition, you pre-read all difficult academic text.

Pronunciation errors. An additional pronunciation difficulty for ELs is the English sounds themselves, especially sounds that are not in the home language. For example, ELs who do not have the *th* sound in their home language might say *dis* and *dat* for *this* and *that.* For some sounds, you may need to teach mouth and tongue placement as if you were teaching first-time phonics.

We will cover language errors in greater detail while discussing Language Objectives in Chapter 5.

HOW TO USE WHITEBOARDS FOR CHECKING FOR UNDERSTANDING AND EFFECTIVE FEEDBACK

Whiteboards are small boards that students write answers on to show the teacher. (At DataWORKS we make our own whiteboards using plastic sheet protectors with stiff paper inside. The students write directly on the plastic using erasable marking pens. We use pieces of black felt cloth for erasers. In a pinch, we use paper towels for erasers.)

Whiteboards are extremely effective for Checking for Understanding. Every student solves every problem, and you see everyone's answer. All students participate. Also, when students raise whiteboards, you can often see specific errors that you can address immediately.

In mathematics, students solve problems step by step on whiteboards for you to see. However, whiteboards are not just for math. Whiteboards can be used any time you have a short answer. However, you still have students explain their answers orally in complete sentences, even if they only wrote one or two words on their whiteboards.

When possible, design your whiteboard questions so students answer using Academic and Content Vocabulary. This promotes the use of new vocabulary, whereas having students write "a" or "b" for their answers bypasses the use of vocabulary.

Whiteboard answers don't always need to be words; they can be examples or illustrations of concepts being taught. In these cases, students still must explain their whiteboards using complete sentences.

Draw an obtuse angle, an acute angle, and a right angle. Label them.

Write an integer that is greater than 6 and less than 14.

Draw the Lewis dot structure for oxygen on your whiteboard.

Draw a cell in mitosis during metaphase.

Explain your whiteboard drawing to your partner (pair-share).

Use Whiteboard Responses to Make Decisions

With whiteboards, you don't always need to pull sticks to select non-volunteers. You are seeing all the answers at once. Often, depending on what you see, your focus will be on corrective feedback and making instructional decisions. You scan the room and then call on specific students—depending on their answer—to reinforce an idea or to uncover student misunderstanding. Let's look at the general process for using whiteboards.

Whiteboards

1. Teacher asks a question.

2. Students write answer.

3. Pair-share. Direct students to *explain* their whiteboard answer to their partners, to *describe* how they got their answer, or to *interpret* its meaning.

4. Signal students to raise whiteboards in unison.

5. Call on students to read their answers and then to justify or interpret their answers to the class using complete sentences.

Error Correction for Whiteboards

Go for 80% and Then 100% Correct Answers

The EDI goal is teach the entire class to 80% correct answers and then to provide corrective feedback until you have 100% correct answers. Measuring student success is easy to do with whiteboards because you see all the answers at once.

When you look at whiteboard responses, you are making two broad determinations. First, you are trying to distinguish between systemic conceptual errors and individual student random errors. When you see many conceptual errors, do a quick error analysis and then re-teach the class.

Going for 100% Correct Answers

You've re-taught to the 80% level and corrected some errors. Now let's go over how to address any remaining students who have errors.

1. **Identify who has wrong answers.** Look around at the raised boards and mentally note which students have the wrong answer. Also, mentally note any students who you think are just copying answers onto their white-boards. In a few minutes, you are going to ask them to explain how they determined their answer.

2. **Call on correct answers first.** Call on non-volunteer *correct* answers. Ask these students to explain and justify their answers. Echo the correct answers clearly in the direction of the incorrect answers. Note: You call on correct answers first so the few incorrect students can hear a correct explanation. In most cases, as the correct-answer students describe how they got their answers, the incorrect-answer students have an "aha" moment of enlightenment and erase their boards quietly and write in the correct answer.

From John: If you call on an incorrect whiteboard answer first, every student in the class—including the 80% who have the correct answer—is listening to an incorrect answer. This is a slight change from calling on random non-volunteer students to answer oral questions. With oral questions, you don't yet know how many students are correct. You are going to find out by calling on a few random students to represent the entire class.

> With whiteboards, you already know how many students are correct. Now you are in corrective feedback mode to support the few students who are incorrect.

3. **Call on students who changed their answers.** After calling on correct answers, you look around and call on the students who changed and corrected their answer. You matter-of-factly ask them to explain and justify their answer. They can usually verbalize the correct process now.

4. **Call on incorrect answers.** By now almost all students have the correct answer. If there are any holdouts still holding up the incorrect answer, call on them to explain. Avoid blurting out, "You are wrong." Instead, ask them to describe how they determined their answer. Many students will self-correct when asked to describe their thinking. For the remaining students, correct any subskill errors directly. Then provide hints and prompts, de-escalate, or just tell them the answer. Have incorrect-answer students correct their whiteboard answers. In the end, 100% of the students will be holding up correct answers.

SUMMARY: HOW TO VERIFY THAT ENGLISH LEARNERS ARE LEARNING

We covered a lot of important ideas on Checking for Understanding. We focused not just on what to do, but how to do it—TAPPLE. Because Checking for Understanding is the backbone of effective instruction, you need to practice the CFU strategies until you develop fluency and automaticity. Then you won't need to think about them; you will just use them as a natural part of your teaching practices.

Some Big Ideas

- Teach first before asking a question—not only content but language.
- Ask higher-order questions to the entire class. Adjust responses for student language levels.
- Provide sentence frames and have students pair-share in complete sentences using new vocabulary from the lesson.
- Call on non-volunteers to explain or justify their answers.
- Use whiteboards whenever possible. Re-teach to 80% correct answers. Provide corrective feedback until everyone (100%) has the correct answer.
- Give feedback on both content errors and language errors.

Now we are ready to discuss strategies for Vocabulary Development in the next chapter. English Learners need to learn new vocabulary every day in every lesson.

Part II

Strategies for English Learners

4 Vocabulary Development

How to Teach English Learners New Words in Every Lesson

Let's recap English Learner needs. They have a double duty in school: ELs need to learn content while simultaneously learning English. We've discussed how ELs need well-crafted lessons. In this chapter, we'll describe how to provide vocabulary development for ELs within the context of EDI lessons.

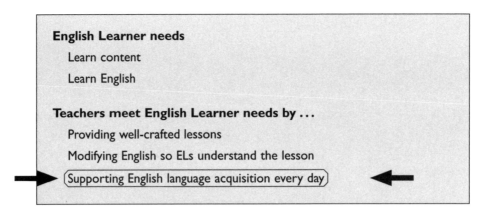

English Learner needs
   Learn content
   Learn English

Teachers meet English Learner needs by ...
   Providing well-crafted lessons
   Modifying English so ELs understand the lesson
   (Supporting English language acquisition every day)

We'll start by classifying vocabulary words into three categories to clarify our thinking on the relative importance of learning specific words. Then, we'll describe eight field-tested strategies that can be used to convey the meaning of new words and how to select which strategy to use.

VOCABULARY DEVELOPMENT

What is vocabulary development? *Vocabulary* refers to all the words that make up a language. *Development* is the process of enlarging or advancing something. So, "vocabulary development" means "learning more and more words."

There are two schools of thought on vocabulary development. One states that vocabulary should be taught *implicitly.* The other states that it should be taught *explicitly.* Both methods are used in school.

The *implicit vocabulary development* approach assumes that students learn vocabulary by exposure, mainly through independent reading. The logic behind this idea is that the number of words an average adult recognizes is too large to have been taught, so it must have been picked up through reading or conversing with others.

Implicit vocabulary development is promoted by programs or content standards that require students to read independently. Here's a Common Core Content Standard for independent reading for seventh graders:

> By the end of the year, read and comprehend literary nonfiction at the high end of the Grades 6-8 text complexity band independently and proficiently, with scaffolding as needed at the high end of the range.

The *explicit vocabulary development* approach calls for teachers to overtly teach vocabulary to their students. The intent is improved reading comprehension when the pre-taught words show up in written text.

Sample Vocabulary Words for Sixth Grade

accurate, acquire, adapt, additional, adequate, affect, analyze, approach, appropriate, assertion, calculate, clarify, coherent, collaborate, command, compare, complex, component, comprehend, computation

---

Vocabulary Strategies Instruction

Besides teaching individual words, effective vocabulary development for English Learners includes teaching vocabulary *strategies* they can apply to new words they encounter; for example, the meaning of *audi* (to hear, to listen) can be used to determine the meaning of many English words such as *audio, audible, auditorium, audiologist, audition,* and *audiotape.*

Most language arts standards call for teaching vocabulary strategies. The Common Core State Standards, for example, call for teachers to teach lessons explicitly showing students how to determine or clarify the meaning of unknown words by analyzing meaningful word parts. Vocabulary standards such as these are taught with fully developed EDI lessons. However, you can use word parts as a vocabulary strategy in any lesson.

EDI VOCABULARY DEVELOPMENT

Teach Vocabulary Within the Context of the Lesson

In *EDI for English Learners,* we adopted a unique approach to vocabulary development. English Learners need to learn more English words every day. English Learners also need to understand the specific words and language structures contained in each lesson in order to fully participate successfully in the lesson and to learn the new content. So, what we do is strategically identify and teach two to seven new vocabulary words that are already contained in each lesson. And we do this for every lesson, every day, for the entire year.

The EDI approach, therefore, is not to pre-teach vocabulary words in isolation before the lesson. Instead, we define and teach vocabulary words as they show up during the lesson.

With this method, ELs are continually learning new vocabulary, plus their understanding of the lesson is increased because they are being taught the meanings of the specific words needed to understand the lesson itself.

It's important not to overwhelm ELs with too many new words at once. Table 4.1 shows the approximate number of new words to teach in each lesson for different grade levels.

Table 4.1 Number of New Words by Grade Level

Grade	Number of new words per lesson
K–2nd	2–3
3rd–5th	3–4
6th–8th	3–6
9th-12th	4–7

In *EDI for English Learners,* you identify vocabulary words already contained in the lesson and then teach them within the context of the lesson—two to seven new words in every lesson, every day, for the entire year.

Classification of Vocabulary

Before selecting specific vocabulary words to teach, you need to have criteria for identifying them. Some words are more important than others in advancing English Learners' understanding of academic content.

For EDI, we divide words into three vocabulary categories: Content, Academic, and Support. The amount of effort and the approach taken for teaching the meaning of words often depend on the category of the word. Let's examine each category.

Content Vocabulary

Content Vocabulary includes words that are specific to a given subject area. These words are rarely used outside of their content areas. Content Vocabulary for language arts includes words such as *character, plot, theme, soliloquy,* and *future perfect progressive verb tense.* Mathematics Content Vocabulary includes words such as *place value, fraction, linear inequality, x-intercept,* and *quadratic equation.* Science Content Vocabulary includes *herbivore, solar system, meiosis,* and *photosynthesis.* Social Science Content Vocabulary includes words or phrases such as *Manifest Destiny, checks and balances (of the three branches of government),* and *Great Depression.*

The Common Core State Standards has its own term for Content Vocabulary: They label these "domain-specific words" *Tier Three Words.*

The key Content Vocabulary words in every lesson come directly from the content standards themselves and are included in the lesson's Learning Objective. During Concept Development, you teach the definitions of the lesson's Content Vocabulary. Here are some Learning Objectives with the Content Vocabulary shown in bold.

Recognize simple **affixes**.

Identify and describe the function of **dialogue**.

Write numbers in **scientific notation**.

Describe the process of **respiration** in plant and animal cells.

Analyze the effects of the **Industrial Revolution**.

Many lessons contain additional Content Vocabulary words besides those contained in the Learning Objective. For example, a lesson on the Pythagorean Theorem would include mathematics Content Vocabulary words such as *right angle, right triangle, hypotenuse,* and *legs* (of a triangle). ELs need to be taught, to understand, and to be able to use all the Content Vocabulary contained in each lesson.

For the most part, Content Vocabulary words are nouns. Be careful, however, because they can occasionally be verbs, especially the first time the standards introduce a new skill. For example, in the kindergarten objective "Add numbers using objects," *addition* is the new concept. You need to teach your ELs that "addition means finding out how much you have altogether."

Below are some additional examples of Learning Objectives in which you need to explicitly define the Skill (the verb) in the Learning Objective, and teach it as a Concept during Concept Development. Note: Sometimes a phrase or the entire Learning Objective is a concept.

Compare and **contrast** characters from two different stories.

Compare and **contrast** means to describe how two or more things are the same and how they are different.

Solve linear equations.

Solving linear equations means finding the value of the unknown that makes the equation true. For example, $x + 3 = 5$ is true only if $x = 2$.

Teach Content Vocabulary During Concept Development

Content-specific vocabulary words in standards-based lessons are usually new words for all students in the class, not just for ELs. In EDI, a significant part of every lesson is spent explicitly teaching Content Vocabulary. You do this during Concept Development using formal, written Concept Definitions; examples that show what the concept means; and Checking for Understanding questions. You use pair-shares before each question and provide sentence frames, cueing your ELs to answer in complete sentences so they start using the new Content Vocabulary words right away. With these strategies, ELs have ample opportunity to learn the Content Vocabulary necessary to be successful in the lesson.

We'll cover some strategies for introducing the meaning of Content Vocabulary later in this chapter. Then, in Chapter 9, we'll describe the formal teaching of Content Vocabulary during the Concept Development component of an EDI lesson.

Teaching Content Vocabulary Is Important

Although ELs need to be taught new Content Vocabulary in every lesson, the words are actually low-frequency words not used often in general conversation or text. However, teaching these words is essential to enable ELs to learn new concepts, to successfully complete grade-level work, to prepare them for college and careers, and to prepare them to answer state test questions.

Test questions often directly assess knowledge of Content Vocabulary words. *Which phrase from the passage is a simile? Which of the following statements correctly describes meiosis? What was the purpose of the Manhattan Project in World War II?*

Even state questions that look like computational questions are concept-based questions. *A Ferris wheel at the local fair has a diameter of 52 meters. Which expression can be used to find its circumference, C, in meters?* This is actually a conceptual question. If ELs don't know the definition of *circumference* and its formula, they can't answer the question. And the state test writers will definitely include one answer (a distractor) that is actually the area of the circle. This will cause some students who can't explicitly connect the Content Vocabulary word *circumference* to its formula to select the wrong answer.

From John: Students who mix up a circle's circumference with its area on a state test did not receive enough Concept Development during the initial teaching. Their circumference lesson probably focused on decimal arithmetic; they multiplied 3.14 by various diameters over and over. The students didn't connect their answers to the concept—the distance around the circle, the circumference.

Academic Vocabulary

Our second category of vocabulary words for EDI is Academic Vocabulary. Academic Vocabulary includes words that appear regularly in academic texts and tests. Academic Vocabulary words are not content specific and are used across content areas.

consist, constitute, distribute, establish, evident, indicate, occur, significant, recognize, respond

The Common Core State Standards use the term *Tier Two Words* to refer to "general academic words." Here are examples they provide:

relative, vary, formulate, specificity, accumulate, calibrate, itemize, periphery

Academic Vocabulary words often show up as the skills (verbs) in content standards and Learning Objectives.

analyze, critique, determine, evaluate, interpret, synthesize

Academic Vocabulary can appear anywhere in a lesson, including the Learning Objective, Concept Development definitions, Skill Development steps, or lesson Importance. Academic Vocabulary also occurs in the passages ELs read, especially in expository text. Let's look at how Academic Vocabulary words (shown in bold) are interspersed throughout a lesson.

Learning Objectives

Today, we will **trace** the historic influence of manufactured products in China.

Determine how a central idea of a text is **conveyed** through **particular** details.

Analyze how **particular** lines of dialogue in a story **propel** the action and **reveal aspects** of a character.

Measure temperature with **appropriate** tools.

Concept Development

Mitosis is the **process** in which cells divide to **increase** their numbers. The result is two daughter cells with **identical** sets of chromosomes.

Hyperbole is a way of describing something using **exaggeration**.

Importance

It is important to **recognize** idioms because idioms have **specific** meanings in **different** languages. You need to know what idioms mean so you understand what people say.

Skill Development and Guided Practice

Interpret the connotative meaning of words.

Step 1: Read the **passage** carefully.

Step 2: **Analyze** the underlined word. **Describe** what the word **suggests** or how it makes you feel.

Step 3: **Interpret** the connotative meaning in the **passage**.

Academic words occur in passages students read.

Chinese printers **developed** movable type. Each piece of type had one Chinese **character** carved on it. The pieces could be **assembled** as needed to print a page of text. This **eliminated** the need to carve a new block of text for every page of a book.

Teach Academic Words as They Show up During an EDI Lesson

English Learners need to be taught Academic Vocabulary in order to be successful at school during lessons and on assessments. However, because it's not unique to specific content, Academic Vocabulary is not always sufficiently addressed by teachers or textbook writers.

> *From Silvia:* The other day in a classroom with a high percentage of ELs, the teacher kept asking the students to interpret their answer after solving a linear equation. The students kept responding "4," which was the answer. The teacher kept saying that "4" was the answer but that she wanted them to interpret the answer. The students kept saying that the answer was "4."
>
> At the end of the lesson, the teacher concluded that the students were not successful in the lesson. In reality, the students were successful in mechanically solving the equation, but since they were not taught the meaning of *interpret*, they did not know that the teacher wanted them to explain the meaning of their answer.
>
> The teacher should have defined *interpret* during the lesson and then modeled interpreting an answer herself first.

In EDI, you support ELs by teaching Academic Vocabulary during every lesson. You teach academic words when they show up during the lesson. You don't need to pre-teach the words. Just teach them in context as they occur naturally during the lesson.

We'll go over strategies to do this in a moment, but first let's look at another type of Academic Vocabulary: Relationship Vocabulary.

Academic Vocabulary Includes Relationship Vocabulary

The term "mortar words" has been used to describe a set of Academic Vocabulary words that connect or show relationships between ideas. Table 4.2 shows these words organized by relationship and student English language development level. As you look across the table, you can see how the vocabulary becomes more sophisticated.

To support ELs in advancing their use of English, don't just use words from their *current* language level. Teach words from higher levels. In general, teach ELs at a level higher than their current language development level in order to advance their use of English.

Table 4.2 Relationship Vocabulary (Mortar Words)

Relationship	English Learner Differentiation		
	Beginning	*Intermediate*	*Advanced*
Compare	like, are the same, both, __er, __est	just like, are similar, have in common, compared to	just as, share/common attributes, by comparison
Contrast	but, however, unlike, _____er than	in contrast, on the other hand, differences between	whereas, as opposed to, a distinction between
Cause and Effect	because, because of, so	as a result of, therefore, if then, the cause was	consequently, thus, due to, this led to (caused)
Sequence	first, second, then, next, later, before, after	while, now, finally, earlier, for the past	prior to, previously, since, eventually, subsequently
Summarize	The author (story) tells/says	in summary, explains, discusses	illustrates, mentions, concludes, explores, focuses on

Teach ELs at a level higher than their current language development level in order to advance their use of English.

Incorporating Relationship Academic Vocabulary Into Lessons

There are many opportunities in lessons when you can promote the use of Relationship Vocabulary. Many Learning Objectives directly address the relationship structures shown in Table 4.2, and you can incorporate Relationship Vocabulary in the lesson and in sentence frames to promote ELs' use of new relationship Academic Vocabulary words. Imagine how impressive your ELs will sound using your sentence frames to respond.

Relationship-Based Learning Objectives With Sample Sentence Frames Using Relationship Vocabulary

Compare and Contrast Lessons

Compare and contrast two versions of the same story.

Compare a summary to an original.

Compare attributes of quadrilaterals.

Distinguish plant cells from animal cells.

Compare the processes of lawmaking at each of the three branches of government.

Sentence Frames Using Compare and Contrast Relationship Vocabulary

____ and ____ are the **same** because ____.

____ and ____ are **similar** because ____.

Something both passages **have in common** is ____.

Both ____ and ____ **share** these **common attributes** ____.

One of the **differences between** ____ and ____ is ____.

A **distinction** between ____ and ____ was ____.

Cause and Effect Lessons

Recognize cause and effect relationships in a text.

Identify the causes and effects of different types of severe weather.

Analyze the causes and effects of the vast expansion and ultimate disintegration of the Roman Empire.

Sentence Frames Using Cause and Effect Relationship Vocabulary

____happened **because** ____.

As a result of _____, _____.

Due to ____, **this led to** ____.

Sequential Order Lessons

Identify text that uses sequence.

Identify changes in natural phenomena over time.

Trace the development of Buddhism in Medieval Japan.

(Continued)

(Continued)

Sentence Frames Using Sequential Order Relationship Vocabulary

> **Before** ___, ___.
>
> **After**___, **then** ___.
>
> **Earlier** ___.
>
> **Prior to** ___, ___.
>
> **Subsequently,** ___.

Summarize Lessons

Summarize the key supporting details and ideas.

Summarize the text distinct from personal opinions or judgments.

Summarize the points a speaker makes.

(Students can also summarize any lesson for note taking or for Checking for Understanding questions.)

Sentence Frames Using Summarizing Relationship Vocabulary

> The story **tells** ___.
>
> The author **says** ___.
>
> The article **discusses** ___.
>
> The passage **illustrates** ___.
>
> The author **explores** the idea that ___.

Support Vocabulary

Support Vocabulary is the third category of vocabulary words used in EDI. Support Vocabulary refers to additional words that English Learners need to know so they can understand the meaning of a specific sentence or phrase used in the lesson. Support words are unrelated to grade-level Concepts and Skills and occur most often in text or passages that ELs read. For example, *The ship turned to starboard.* ELs might need to know that "port" means "left" and "starboard" means "right" to understand which direction the ship turned in a story, but EDI does not focus on teaching Support Vocabulary.

Distinguishing Support Vocabulary from Academic and Content Vocabulary is very important so you can effectively allocate your class time to advancing ELs' knowledge of the proper words.

From John: Silvia and I have seen many examples of lessons focusing on students being taught Support Vocabulary instead of Content and Academic Vocabulary. I was in a class where the teacher was working hard teaching students the meaning of these words flagged in the passage: hammock, halibut, port, and starboard. The definition of a tall tale was written on the top of the worksheet. "A tall tale is an exaggerated story." A more important word to teach English Learners in this lesson would have been *exaggerated*, yet it was not defined.

Support Vocabulary can show up anywhere in a lesson. It can be in the sentences ELs are reading to locate a noun or pronoun. It can be in a poem ELs are reading to recognize alliteration. Support Vocabulary can show up in the word problems used in math or in history or science passages.

Let's look at some examples of Support Vocabulary (shown in bold).

In the language arts lesson below, ELs need to recognize the items they are to separate with commas. They don't need to learn the Support Vocabulary words *attic* or *marbled cane* to be successful in the lesson.

Add commas to separate three or more items.

1. Our **attic** is filled with boxes bags and books.

2. The **marbled cane** was carved with tigers lions and elephants.

Solve simple interest problems.

3. David **invested** $1,000 in **stocks**. The value of the **stock** increased 15%. What is the current value of the **stock**?

In the math word problem above, *invested* and *stocks* are Support Vocabulary. ELs need to be given enough information about these words to understand the problem, but they don't need to learn these terms to be successful in *this* lesson. Note: In a high school economics lesson, however, *invested* and *stocks* would be Content Vocabulary, and these words should be explicitly taught.

We've spent a lot of time classifying vocabulary words. This is mainly so you can identify which words ELs need to learn and where to focus your efforts. It doesn't matter if you spend extra time on a Support word here and there, but you must stay focused on continually expanding your ELs' knowledge of Content and Academic Vocabulary. Now, let's look at the strategies for teaching vocabulary.

From John: State tests assess student knowledge of Content and Academic Vocabulary, not conversational English or Support words. Teach Content and Academic Vocabulary every day.

EDI-EL VOCABULARY STRATEGIES

We adapted, developed, and field-tested eight strategies to teach vocabulary embedded in EDI lessons. Although the strategies are not limited to one vocabulary type, we have grouped the strategies by the type of vocabulary they are most often used for—Support, Content, or Academic. And remember, in EDI, the general approach is to define new words as they show up in a lesson.

EDI-EL Vocabulary Development Strategies

Support Vocabulary

　1. Contextualized Definitions Strategy

Content Vocabulary

　2. Develop Concept Strategy

　3. Attach a Label Strategy

　4. Multiple-Meaning Words Strategy

　5. Homophone Strategy

Academic Vocabulary

　6. Synonyms Strategy

　7. Definitions Strategy

　8. Word Morphology Strategy

　9. Relationship Vocabulary Strategy

Support Vocabulary Strategies

In EDI lessons, we don't spend extensive instructional time on Support Vocabulary because our goal is different. We want ELs to understand, learn, and use more and more Content and Academic Vocabulary every day. On the other hand, ELs need to understand Support Vocabulary in order to understand a specific piece of text or passage used in a lesson. We are not trying to teach ELs the Support Vocabulary words. We provide meaning for Support Vocabulary in order to teach content, which leads us to our Support Vocabulary strategy.

EDI-EL Vocabulary Development

1. Contextualized Definitions Strategy
　A. Insert a definition near an unknown word.

When you provide a contextualized definition for Support Vocabulary, you purposefully insert a definition (or a few words of explanation) near an unknown word. There is little or no student interaction. You don't stop and have the students copy down the word or add Checking for Understanding questions. Just insert the definition and move on with the lesson. Contextualized definitions are generally added orally during a lesson.

In front of the old inn sat the ostler. **An ostler is a person who takes care of the travelers' horses.**

The captain saw the galleon, **the large sailing ship,** *far off on the horizon.*

Blue whales look blue underwater, but their skin is actually a mottled blue-gray. **Mottled skin means the skin has spots of blue and gray.**

Using contextualized definitions is the primary strategy for providing meaning of Support Vocabulary. ELs only need to know these words to follow the lesson.

Use Contextualized Definitions to Reinforce Content and Academic Vocabulary Definitions

We have talked about using contextualized definitions for Support words you are not going to formally teach. However, contextualized definitions can be very effective in reinforcing definitions of Content and Academic Vocabulary you have already taught. Just include contextualized definitions as you use new words. The repetition helps ELs remember and provides a transition as they learn the new words.

I am going to look for the **setting,** *where the story takes place.*

I need to **determine,** *to figure out, the meaning of the unknown word.*

Content Vocabulary Strategies

Content Vocabulary is lesson specific, and the words have only one meaning in the lesson. You teach Content Vocabulary using strategies that include extensive student interaction—including Checking for Understanding with sentence frames and pair-shares—so ELs learn, remember, and start using the new vocabulary right away.

Now we will look at strategies that address Content Vocabulary.

EDI-EL Vocabulary Development

2. Develop Concept Strategy

   A. Develop concept and label (new vocabulary word).
      ○ Provide formal, written Concept Definition.
      ○ Explain definition using examples and non-examples.
      ○ Include extensive student interaction.

In EDI, key Content Vocabulary is explicitly taught during Concept Development, a major part of every EDI lesson. You present formal, written definitions along with examples and non-examples (if applicable) of the concept. You provide extensive student interaction including Checking for Understanding with sentence frames and pair-shares. It is important that the Concept Definitions are written for ELs to read and refer to throughout the entire lesson.

Content Vocabulary is the most important vocabulary in every lesson. English Learners need to learn, remember, and use Content Vocabulary. Teaching Content Vocabulary is described in detail in Chapter 9 under Concept Development.

EDI-EL Vocabulary Development

3. Attach a Label Strategy

A. Attach a label to a concept students already know.

- ○ Teacher activates—asks students to do something they already know that connects to the new vocabulary word.
- ○ Students interact.
- ○ Teacher labels—provides the new vocabulary word that labels what students already know.

This approach is used when ELs already understand the concept, but they don't know the new vocabulary word that defines it. In other words, they know the idea, but they don't know the label. In EDI lessons, this approach is often used during Activate Prior Knowledge to connect existing knowledge to new vocabulary prior to the introduction of a formal, written definition during Concept Development.

Attach a Label Strategy Example 1

Mrs. Jackson is preparing a language arts lesson: "Draw inferences from text." The most important Content Vocabulary word in this lesson is *inference*. Students already know how to infer in daily life, but they don't know the specific word *inference*. Because students already know how to infer, she decides to use the EDI-EL Attach a Label Strategy. She will use it during Activate Prior Knowledge.

(Teacher activates by asking students to do something they already know that connects to the new vocabulary word.)

Mrs. Jackson points to a sentence on the board and says, *Students, let's read this sentence together . . .*

> **Activate Prior Knowledge**
>
> The principal would like to see Roberto in the office.

She continues, *Why do you think the principal wants to see Roberto in the office?*

(Student interaction)

Get out your whiteboards. Write your answer on your whiteboards. Then turn to your partner and explain what you wrote and why you think the principal wants to see Roberto. Partner B explains first.

She waits a moment while the students write on their whiteboards and pair-share. Then she continues, *Students, chin-it! Hold up your whiteboards for me to see.* She looks around the room from left to right. Most students have written *in trouble*.

Mrs. Johnson calls a non-volunteer Angelica. "I think Roberto is in trouble." Mrs. Jackson follows up, *Why do you think Roberto is in trouble at school?* Angelica responds, "I know that when you are in trouble, you get sent to the principal's office."

(Teacher labels by providing the new vocabulary word that labels what students already know.)

Mrs. Jackson turns away from Angelica to address the entire class, *Students, most of you wrote* in trouble *on your whiteboards. You read the sentence about Roberto and then you thought about what you already know about being sent to the office.*

She continues, *Today, we have a new word for what you just did. It's* inference. *You just made an inference. You wrote what you think is happening based on the information that you had, including what you already know.*

Look up here on the board where I have the definition of inference. I am going to read the definition first and then we will read together . . .

Attach a Label Strategy—Example 2

Students, look at these sentences. Which one is probably not true? Write the answer on your whiteboard and then tell your partner why you picked your answer. You can say, Sentence _____ is probably not true because _____. Partner B go first and then A.

> **Activate Prior Knowledge**
>
> 1. Jesse, I told you a million times to clean your room.
>
> 2. Jesse, I told you three times to clean you room.

Chin-it. Good, I see that you all selected sentence number 1. I am going to select some of you to tell me why. After calling on non-volunteers to answer in complete sentences, the teacher says, *You're correct, Jesse was not actually told to clean his room one million times, yet we talk like this all the time.*

There is a name for this type of sentence. It is called hyperbole. Students, look up here at the definition of hyperbole on the board. I'm going to read it first and then we'll read it together . . .

EDI-EL Vocabulary Development

4. Multiple-Meaning Words Strategy

   A. Provide new meanings for known words.

      o Present the new multiple-meaning word.
      o Acknowledge the known meaning.
      o Provide the new meaning.
      o Note the similarities between the meanings (if any).
      o Provide student interaction (CFU of definition of word).

Multiple-meaning words are words that have more than one meaning, such as plane (airplane), plane (flat surface), and plane (tool for smoothing wood). Often, ELs already know one of the meanings but not the specific new meaning used in the lesson.

Multiple-meaning words can show up anywhere in a lesson and can be Academic, Content, or Support Vocabulary. It's important for you to recognize and teach multiple-meaning words because ELs often apply their existing definitions to the words instead of the new content-specific definitions. For example, some students might think a right triangle points to the right instead of knowing that *right* in this case refers to a 90-degree angle.

Sometimes, the multiple meanings are an extension of the same idea. When they are, you use this as a strategy and acknowledge the similarity when teaching new meanings to known words. For example, the *drop-down menu* in a computer program is similar to the *menu* in a restaurant. They both provide choices.

Use the EDI-EL Multiple Meaning Word Strategy when ELs already know a common meaning and the lesson is using a new meaning.

Multiple-Meaning Words Strategy Example 1

From Silvia: I wrote and taught an EDI science lesson recently and was surprised at the number of multiple-meaning words it contained. Here's how I addressed the multiple-meaning words in this lesson

---

Learning Objective

Describe the parts of a tree.

Content Vocabulary for this lesson included *crown, trunk, bark, cambium,* and *roots.* Except for cambium, these are all multiple-meaning words. ELs are more than likely already familiar with some of the common meanings, but not necessarily with the meanings used in science. I wrote my definitions for Concept Development.

Concept Development

A **tree** is a woody plant that usually is more than 10 feet tall and has one main stem. Trees come in different shapes and sizes but have the same basic parts.

The **crown** of a tree is the upper leaves and branches. *(Point to illustration.)*

The **trunk** of a tree supports the crown and serves as a highway for food. *(Point to illustration.)*

The **bark** layer is on the outside of the trunk and branches and protects the tree from insects and disease. *(Point to illustration.)*

The **cambium** is a layer of cells inside the bark. *(Point to illustration.)*

The **roots** are underground and hold the tree in the soil. *(Point to illustration.)*

Here is how I addressed *crown* using the EDI-EL Multiple-Meaning Words Strategy.

- Present the word. *Students, look at this word while I say it: crown.*
- Acknowledge the known meaning. *Students, you already know that a crown is the round ring that kings and queens wear on their heads.*
- Give the new meaning. *In today's science lesson, the word* crown *is the name for the top of a tree.*
- Note the similarities between the meanings, if any. *Students, the new meaning of crown is similar to the old meaning. A king wears a crown on top of his head. The top of a tree is also called a crown. The meanings are close and that will help you remember the new meaning.* Point to the king's crown and the crown of a tree.
- Student interaction. *Students, I have a question for you. I want you to tell me the meaning of crown as we will use it today. And how does the meaning compare with the meaning of crown that you already know? Partner A, point to the crown of the tree in the picture and explain to your partner.* Call on non-volunteers.

My approach was slightly different for *bark* and *trunk*. For *bark*, ELs probably already know that dogs *bark.* I told them that they already know this meaning, but we have a new meaning for *bark* today, and I defined it. I didn't provide any connection between the *bark* of a dog and the *bark* of a tree.

Some ELs may already know *trunk* (large suitcase), *trunk* of an elephant, *trunk* of a car, swimming *trunks,* or *trunk* (upper body). I stated these meanings and acknowledged that they already know some of these meanings. I continued saying that we would learn a new meaning today. I didn't try to connect the meanings.

(Actually, *trunk* in the sense of upper body is similar to the *trunk* of a tree. Both words refer to a main part that has limbs attached. I could have used this relationship when teaching *trunk* in a different class, but I didn't use it here. When building on multiple-meaning words, I always connect from a more common meaning to a new meaning.)

I did not teach *root* as a multiple-meaning word because ELs most likely already know the meaning of *root* in relation to a tree, which is the meaning used in this lesson. *Root,* however, could be taught as a multiple-meaning word if the lesson were addressing the "roots of capitalism" or "square root" because these would be new meanings.

EDI-EL Vocabulary Development

5. Homophone Strategy

    A. Provide meanings for new words that sound like known words.

        ○ Present the new word.

        ○ Acknowledge the known homophone.

        ○ Provide the new meaning.

        ○ Provide student interaction (CFU of definition of word).

We just talked about multiple-meaning words and how ELs tend to use their existing definitions if they aren't explicitly provided new definitions. A similar effect occurs with homophones. Homophones are words that sound the same but have different spellings and meanings, for example, *mode, mowed*; *coarse, course*; *cell, sell*; *pie, pi* (3.14); and *sum, some*. It's important to recognize and define homophones whenever they occur during EDI lessons because ELs will often "hear" the meaning they are most familiar with.

The approach to use for these homophones is similar to the EDI-EL Multiple-Meaning Strategy.

Homophone Strategy Example 1

Students, an important word in our science lesson is cell. *This new word sounds like a word you already know—sell, as in they sell food at the grocery store. Cell is a completely different word. It's even spelled differently:* c-e-1-1. *I am going to read the definition and then we will read it together.* (Teacher continues teaching the definition of cell and asks CFU questions about its meaning.)

Use this strategy anytime homophones might lead to misunderstandings. Be on the lookout for homophones. They can show up as Content, Academic, or Support Vocabulary in a lesson: *jeans, genes; martial, marshal; medal, meddle; tide, tied; attendance, attendants; and cymbal, symbol.*

Academic Vocabulary Strategies

We have just discussed strategies to teach Content Vocabulary. These words have very specific meanings in standards-based lessons, and explicitly teaching their definitions is included in every EDI lesson during Concept Development.

Now, we are going to shift to strategies for Academic Vocabulary. These words are not discipline specific. Academic words are used in multiple situations across multiple subject areas. Because of this, *when teaching Academic Vocabulary, you generalize the definitions so your ELs can recognize and understand the words when they show up in another subject area, too.*

There are several strategies for teaching Academic Vocabulary. You can teach definitions orally, or you can refer to footnotes or definitions. When you write your own lessons, you can add footnoted definitions.

EDI-EL Vocabulary Development

6. Synonyms Strategy

Define new words using synonyms.

○ Present the new word.
○ Provide synonyms that are easy to understand.
○ Generalize the new word to other situations and to other word forms.
○ Provide student interaction (CFU of word definition).

Use the EDI-EL Synonyms Strategy when a new word can be defined using common synonyms that ELs already know. For example, *enormous* means *large, big.* Also, this strategy is used for words that can be explained with synonyms. It is not for words that need a definition or more elaborate explanation.

Synonyms Strategy Example 1

Learning Objective

Describe the Kinetic Molecular Theory of Gases.

The Kinetic Molecular Theory of Gases is composed of several postulates that explain the behavior of gases. One of the postulates states that "gas particles are in constant, rapid, random motion, continually colliding." *Colliding* is an important word in this lesson because it explains some of the gas behaviors.

- Present the new word. *Students, look up here. There's an important word in the third postulate:* colliding. *Let's read it together. Colliding. One more time. Colliding.*
- Provide easy-to-understand synonyms. *If you look at the footnote, you can see that "colliding" means "crashing and bumping."*
- Generalize to other situations and to other word forms. *For example, sometimes we see students colliding in the hallways. They are crashing or bumping into each other. We sometimes see cars colliding*

on the freeway. Television news sometimes shows car collisions, cars crashing into each other.

- Student interaction. *Students, what does it mean when we say that the gas particles are continually colliding? Tell your partner.* Call on non-volunteers.
- Cross-reference the brain to help students remember definitions.

Use the Cross-Reference the Brain technique to help students remember synonym definitions. You say the word, and the students call out the synonym. You say the synonym, and students call out the word.

Students, if I say "colliding," you say "crashing and bumping." If I say "crashing and bumping," you say "colliding." Ready?
Colliding.
Crashing and bumping.
Colliding.
Crashing and bumping.
Crashing and bumping.
Colliding.
Students, repeat after me. Colliding means crashing and bumping. Crashing and bumping means colliding.

Not all Academic words are suitable to be taught using synonyms. Some will require a short definition, which is our next strategy.

EDI Vocabulary Development

7. Definitions Strategy

  A. Define complicated words.
    ○ Present the word.
    ○ Provide a definition.
    ○ Generalize to other situations.
    ○ Provide student interaction (CFU of meaning of word).

When you provide your definition, check that the words in it are appropriate for your grade level. Often definitions are provided using vocabulary that is more difficult than the word being defined.

From John: I observed an elementary school science class in which the teacher asked a student to look up the dictionary definition of *vibration.* I remember the student reading, "Vibration: equilateral displacement across a neutral point." This was too complicated for the elementary school students.

The strategy of providing quick, short definitions is fine for Academic Vocabulary, but don't use it for Concepts. Concepts are formally taught during Concept Development using written definitions, examples and non-examples, and extensive Checking for Understanding. We'll cover Concept Development in Chapter 9.

> ***From John:*** The next example has both Academic and Content Vocabulary in the Learning Objective. Here is my thinking on how to address the vocabulary using EDI.

Definitions Strategy Example 1

> **Learning Objective** ▶
>
> Today, we will use prefixes and suffixes to determine the meanings of words.

There are three vocabulary words in this Objective: *prefixes, suffixes,* and *determine.* The words *prefixes* and *suffixes* are Content Vocabulary for this lesson. I teach them during Concept Development with formal, written definitions; tracked reading; examples; non-examples; and extensive Checking for Understanding.

The word *determine* is Academic Vocabulary. It can be used across content areas. I could use a synonym such as "figure out," but I use a more comprehensive definition: "use information to figure out." I teach the definition of *determine* while I present the Learning Objective because that is the first time the word occurs in the lesson. I refer to the definition again during Skill Development when I actually use the meaning of prefixes and suffixes to *determine* the meaning of words.

- Present the word. *Students, look at this word in our Objective. The word is* determine. *Let's say it together,* determine.
- Provide an easy-to-understand definition. *Look at the footnote. You can see that "determine" means "to use information to figure out or find out something."*
- Generalize to other situations. *For example, we might need to determine whether we have enough money to go to the movies. We would use information such as how much money we have and how much the tickets cost to figure out whether we have enough money to buy the tickets.*

  Teachers use information, including your test scores, to determine your grade in the class. Look at our Objective. Today, we will use information—in this case, prefixes and suffixes—to determine, or figure out, the meaning of words.

- Student interaction. I could ask the students to restate the definition of *determine* in a complete sentence. *Determine means . . .* However, I want to use a higher order application question, so I ask them to create their own sentence using the new word. Also, hearing the new word in different sentences helps ELs develop an ear for the use of the word. It's better than just hearing the definition. I provide an example first.

  Students, I want you to use determine *in your own sentence. For example, you could say, I want to determine when my favorite TV show starts. Talk with your partner and create your own sentence using* determine. *Be ready, in case I call on you.*

  If some students' sentences are not perfect, I will elaborate (reword) them when I echo their sentences. That's the Effective Feedback in TAPPLE: Echo, Elaborate or Explain.

EDI-EL Vocabulary Development

8. Word Morphology Strategy

   A. Use word parts to understand new words.

     ○ Present the word.
     ○ Point to and define the word parts.
     ○ Generalize to other words.
     ○ Student interaction (CFU of meaning of word).

Here's our next strategy for vocabulary development: Word Morphology. Words that contain recognizable roots, prefixes, or suffixes can be taught using the meanings of the word parts.

When using this approach, you generalize the word parts so your English Learners can apply this knowledge to other words they encounter. In this manner, you are building their capacity to understand additional words, not just the specific word you are teaching at the moment.

Word Morphology Strategy Example I

Learning Objective

Describe the theological, political, and economic ideas of the major figures during the Reformation.

> *From Silvia:* I have taught this lesson several times. I don't define *theological* during the Learning Objective. Instead, I define *theological, political,* and *economic* during Concept Development because the bulk of the lesson is spent classifying the ideas of Martin Luther, John Calvin, and Desiderius Erasmus into these three areas. I use the Word Morphology strategy for *theological.*

- Present the word. *Students, look closely at this word:* theological.
- Point and define word parts. *Look at the first part of* theological. *Point to* theo. Theo *is from an old word that meant God. Today,* theo *is used in words to refer to religion in general. So, "theological" means "related to religion."*
- Generalize to other words. Theo *is used with the same meaning in other words, too. For example, "theology" means "the study of religion." "Theocratic" means "government by a god or religious leaders."*
- Student interaction. *Students, I want you to tell me the meaning of theological and how you can remember it just by looking at the word. Make sure you answer in a complete sentence. Theological means_____. I can remember because _____. Tell your partner your answer. Partner B go first and then partner A.* Call on non-volunteers.

Word Morphology Strategy Example 2

Concept Development

Homophones are words that have the same sound but different meanings and spelling.

Examples: blue, blew; hair, hare; no, know; ate, eight

The word *homophone* is Content Vocabulary in this lesson. Its definition would be taught during Concept Development using a written definition and examples. The teacher can then follow up with the EDI-EL Word Morphology Strategy to provide additional meaning and to show how to remember the definition.

- Present the word. *Students, let's look closely at the word* homophone *one more time.*
- Point to the word parts. *This first part—homo—means "the same." The last part—phone—means "sound." So, the word "homophone" means "same sounds" or words that sound the same.*

- Generalize to other words. *These word parts—homo and phone—have the same meanings in many words. Here are some other words related to sound: telephone and microphone. The word* homograph *refers to words that have the same spelling.*
- Student interaction. *Students, I want you to tell me the meaning of homophones and how you can tell just by looking at the word. Make sure you answer in a complete sentence. Homophones are _____ . I know this from the word homophone because _____ . Tell your partner first. Be ready in case I call on you.*

EDI-EL Vocabulary Development

9. Relationship Vocabulary Strategy

   A. Support students in using new Relationship Vocabulary.
- Replace simple relationship words with more sophisticated relationship words.
- Provide a sentence frame with Relationship Vocabulary.
- Define the Relationship Word, if necessary.

We've already described Relationship Vocabulary. When you have lessons, or Checking for Understanding questions, based on relationships (compare and contrast, cause and effect, sequence, and summarize), you can support ELs' use of Relationship Words. The goal is for ELs to use more sophisticated vocabulary. Most often, Relationship Vocabulary is used in sentence frames to answer CFU questions. In the examples below, you can see how Relationship Vocabulary became more sophisticated.

___ and ___ are ~~the same~~ similar because ___ .

The passage ~~tells about~~ discusses ____ .

One ~~difference~~ distinction between the characters is ____ .

SUMMARY: VOCABULARY DEVELOPMENT

This chapter contained many strategies for vocabulary development. Let's recap what we covered.

- English Learners have dual needs in school: learning content while simultaneously learning English.
- Although vocabulary words can be taught from lists, EDI focuses on teaching English Learners two to seven new vocabulary words in every lesson, every hour, for the whole school year. The vocabulary words to teach are selected from the words contained in the lesson.

Types of Vocabulary

Content Vocabulary is the discipline-specific vocabulary unique to a given lesson. The most important Content Vocabulary is contained in the Learning Objective and is explicitly taught during Concept Development. Content Vocabulary includes words such as *personification, compound sentence, fraction, decimal, atmospheric pressure, cell wall, Bill of Rights,* and *Age of Enlightenment.*

Academic Vocabulary is the vocabulary used in academic text and tests. These words are used across disciplines. Examples include *appropriate, correspond, distinguish, interpret, organize, preliminary,* and *statement.* Because Academic Vocabulary words are not discipline specific, they are not always well covered in textbooks. EDI lessons teach the Academic Vocabulary contained in the lesson. Academic Vocabulary includes Relationship Vocabulary that describes relationships between ideas.

Support Vocabulary is the vocabulary that needs to be defined for ELs so they can follow the lesson, but the focus is not on learning these words. Support Vocabulary most often occurs in texts ELs read. Examples are words such as *whistled, humongous, smeared,* and *grinned.* Examples also include old-fashioned or archaic words found in literature: "They talked in the *parlor.*"

This chapter provided nine strategies to address lesson-embedded vocabulary:

EDI-EL Vocabulary Development Strategies

Support Vocabulary

1. Contextualized Definitions Strategy

Content Vocabulary

2. Develop Concept Strategy

3. Attach a Label Strategy

4. Multiple-Meaning Words Strategy

5. Homophone Strategy

Academic Vocabulary

6. Synonyms Strategy

7. Definitions Strategy

8. Word Morphology Strategy

9. Relationship Vocabulary Strategy

Now we're ready for the next chapter, in which we describe more strategies to support English Learners—Language Objectives: Listening, Speaking, Reading, and Writing.

5 Language Objectives

*How to Have English
Learners Listening,
Speaking, Reading,
and Writing English in
Every Lesson*

English Learners need to learn new grade-level content while simultaneously learning English. The previous chapter addressed vocabulary development. When you embed vocabulary development in an EDI lesson, you teach ELs the *meanings* of new words they need to know to be successful in the lesson. But you also need to teach ELs how to pronounce the new words, to read them, to distinguish them when stated orally, and how to write them. These are Language Objectives.

In the classroom, Vocabulary Development and Language Objectives are almost always done together. For example, when deoxyribonucleic acid is introduced in a science class, you need to teach ELs what it is plus how to pronounce it, read it, and write it.

In this chapter, we will describe how to incorporate Language Objectives—Listening, Speaking, Reading, and Writing—into every EDI lesson.

LANGUAGE OBJECTIVES

Language refers to human communication using spoken or written symbols. In EDI lessons, you use Language Objectives to advance ELs' use of the academic English—already contained in a lesson—that is necessary for them to be successful in the lesson. You do this by purposefully engaging ELs in structured Listening, Speaking, Reading, and Writing.

Language Objectives serve two purposes. First, they identify and support new language ELs must use to be successful in a *specific* lesson. Second, Language Objectives advance ELs' use of English in general so they are more successful in *all* lessons.

Language can be classified into receptive and expressive skills. The receptive skills are Listening and Reading. The expressive skills are Speaking and Writing. These four skills can also be classified as *sound-related:* aural (listening) and oral (speaking) and *text-related:* reading and writing (see Table 5.1).

At DataWORKS, we have had endless conversations, actually heated debates, about the types of classroom activities that count as Language Objectives. We initially considered any word that ELs uttered as a Language Objective. We have since refined our thoughts on what qualifies as a Language Objective.

Language Objectives Intentionally Advance ELs' Knowledge of English

First, Language Objectives must intentionally *advance* ELs' knowledge and use of English. Directed by the teacher, ELs practice using *new* words that are explicitly taught, not the words they already know.

Also, Language Objectives describe what you will teach your ELs to do to further their language development so they can fully participate successfully in the lesson and learn the new content. For example, you teach ELs

Table 5.1   Language Objectives

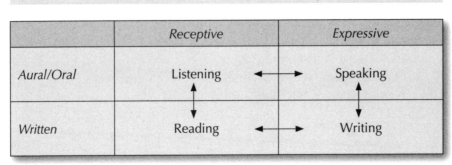

	Receptive	*Expressive*
Aural/Oral	Listening ←→	Speaking
Written	Reading ←→	Writing

how to pronounce new content-related words contained in a lesson. You explicitly pronounce new words and direct your students to pronounce the words themselves using choral responses, pair-shares, and Checking for Understanding questions.

EDI lessons explicitly support English Learners by intentionally embedding Language Objectives and Vocabulary Development into every lesson. You spend part of every EDI lesson teaching ELs new vocabulary and language.

From Silvia: *Language Objectives* is a term that has a very loose interpretation in the field. Here are some examples that are often thought to be Language Objectives that wouldn't be considered EDI Language Objectives because they don't focus on acquisition of new content-related language:

- English Learners will listen attentively to the story. A story is read to the ELs but there is no language in the story targeted for them.
- English Learners will talk to each other throughout the lesson. ELs are told to tell each other some adjectives they already know. ELs share what they know but aren't presented with any new words.
- English Learners will read about the Civil War and then answer questions using past tense. ELs are directed to use the past tense but there is no directed teaching or support to do so.

Implementing Language Objectives

Language Objectives are *intentionally* included in every EDI lesson. The Language Objectives are not the same as the Learning Objective of the lesson; instead, they are added to develop and support new language contained within the lesson.

Listening, Speaking, Reading, and Writing

Now let's look at each Language Objective in detail and then we'll go over strategies for incorporating them into lessons. Keep in mind that you rarely do only one Language Objective in isolation. You almost always do several Objectives at once and incorporate vocabulary development at the same time.

Listening. Listening as a Language Objective occurs when you focus your students to listen to specific words, sentences, phrases, or language structures that advance their knowledge of English. This occurs, for example, when you have them listen to you pronounce a new word such as *onomatopoeia* during a lesson. You are implementing Listening Objectives when you intentionally cue your students to listen to you read the Learning Objective, Concept Definitions, or steps to execute a skill. Pair-shares count as Listening Objectives whenever students listen to each other while discussing new academic content.

Speaking. After you pronounce new words, students are executing Speaking Objectives when they pronounce new words or read aloud phrases containing new Academic and Content Vocabulary. When students pair-share using Content and Academic Vocabulary, they are executing Speaking Objectives.

As the teacher, you usually cue students for Speaking Objectives.

Students, say "character." Ready? Character.

Students, say "multiplicative inverse." Multiplicative inverse.

Students, tell your neighbor what Ohm's Law is. Use a complete sentence. "In an electrical circuit, Ohm's Law describes the relationship between . . ."

> ***From Silvia:*** I must emphasize that English Learners must be working with new words and language structures when they execute EDI Language Objectives. For example, having ELs talk conversationally does not count as an EDI Speaking Objective when they are just using words and language structures they already know.

Reading. Language arts standards call for lessons in decoding and reading. In these cases, you are directly teaching students *how* to read. In EDI, when you *facilitate* your students in reading academic text in any content area lesson, you are executing Reading Language Objectives. We use the term "facilitate" because you are not directly teaching students how to read, yet you are supporting them in reading text, mainly the new academic text contained in the lesson.

Reading in EDI lessons is done mostly through Tracked Choral Reading. You pre-read important text first while your students are looking at the words, and then you have them read the same text chorally. Following your pre-read, every student, including poor readers, can participate in the choral read. And as a bonus, choral reading counts as both Reading and Speaking.

In the example below, a chemistry teacher pre-reads and then has her students read a definition that contains mostly Content Vocabulary: *Lewis dot structures, valence electrons,* and *element symbol.*

Students, eyes on the board while I read the definition of Lewis dot structures. Then we will read the definition together. Lewis dot structures show valence electrons represented as dots placed around the element symbol. Let's read together. Ready? Go. Lewis dot structures show valence electrons represented as dots placed around the element symbol. Now, look at Figure 1. That's the Lewis dot structure for oxygen . . .

Writing. Language Objectives for writing are directly addressed in EDI lessons that teach writing standards. This would include lessons in sentence, paragraph, or essay writing, plus lessons in editing and revising, parallel structure, active and passive voice, and so forth. In these cases, you would explicitly teach your students writing skills that they would execute during Skill Development, Guided Practice, Closure, and Independent Practice.

Writing can also be embedded into any EDI lesson. You are not teaching writing per se but are facilitating ELs to write using the new vocabulary and language contained in the lesson.

Language Objectives Are Not Presented to Students

Unlike Learning Objectives, which are explicitly stated to students at the beginning of a lesson, we don't state EDI Language Objectives to students. You just *execute* them with the whole class throughout the lesson.

We don't state Language Objectives because there are too many of them. Listing all of them and going over them sequentially would slow down the lesson. As students participate in EDI lessons, they practice Language Objectives when you direct them to pronounce words chorally with the class, read important text in a lesson, exchange ideas orally with their pair-share partners, and answer in complete sentences using new vocabulary.

Shown below are the Language Objectives for a math lesson. As you can see, there are many, many Language Objectives. (It's surprising to see just how many there can be in one lesson.) It just isn't practical to list all of the Language Objectives at the start of every lesson and present them to the students.

Learning Objective ▶

Calculate the circumference of a circle.

Language Objectives

Listening Objectives

- Listen to teacher (and pair-share partner) pronounce *calculate, circumference, radius, diameter,* and *π (pi)*.
- Listen to teacher (and pair-share partner) read Learning Objective and the definitions of *radius, diameter,* and *circumference*. Listen to teacher read the steps used to calculate circumference.
- Listen to teacher read circumference word problems.

(Continued)

(Continued)

Speaking Objectives

- Students pronounce *calculate, circumference, radius, diameter,* and π *(pi)*.
- Students speak while reading Learning Objective and the definitions of *radius, diameter,* and *circumference*.
- Students speak as they read steps used to calculate circumference.
- Students speak while reading circumference word problems.
- Note: the teacher always pre-pronounces difficult words.

Reading Objectives

- Students read vocabulary words including *calculate, circumference, radius, diameter,* and π *(pi)*.
- Students read the Learning Objective and the definitions of *radius, diameter,* and *circumference*. Students read the math formulas $C = \pi d$ and $C = 2\pi r$.
- Students read steps used to calculate circumference. Students read circumference word problems.
- Students read why it is important to learn how to calculate the circumference of a circle.
- Note: the teacher always pre-reads difficult text before students read.

Writing Objectives

- Students write *radius, diameter, circumference,* and π *(pi)* on their whiteboards as they label the parts of a circle and work problems.
- Students write units such as *meters, feet, inches,* and *yards* as they calculate circumferences.

ENGLISH LANGUAGE CONSTRUCTION

Before we look at Language Strategies, let's take a moment to examine some of the components of English and their connections to English Learners.

To be proficient in English, ELs must acquire knowledge of the mechanics of English including phonemes (sounds), letter-sound correspondence, subject-verb agreement, verb tenses, and sentence structures.

Native English speakers generally pick up much of the mechanics of English through listening and speaking with their native English-speaking parents and peers. ELs often don't have these experiences and need to learn English at school. If you teach English Language Development, you teach lessons in learning English. Many language arts lessons, such as phonics, reading, and grammar, teach English. If you are a content area teacher—even though you don't teach English directly—you support ELs' English language acquisition through Language Objectives of Listening, Speaking, Reading, and Writing using the vocabulary already embedded in your lessons. Plus, you provide corrective feedback for language errors such as subject-verb agreement that students might make during your lessons.

Now we are going to define some of the mechanics of English that ELs need to be taught in order to become English proficient.

English Phonemes and Letter-Sound Correspondence

Phonemes are the distinct sounds used in a language. English uses 44 phonemes. ELs must be able to correctly distinguish between the sounds when they hear spoken English, and they must be able to create the sounds when pronouncing words. ELs may have difficulties pronouncing sounds not present in their primary language. For example, Spanish does not contain many of the English short vowel sounds, such as those in "pit," "pet," "put." In addition, English uses between 46 and 53 consonant clusters at the beginning of words and more than 36 consonant clusters at the end of words (bo**ld**, ho**ld**, a**sk**, fla**sk**). Spanish, however, uses only 12 consonant clusters (Kramer, Schell, & Rubison, 1983).

"Letter-sound correspondence" refers to how letters are used to represent sounds. The 26 letters of the English alphabet are used to represent the 44 English sounds, which include 18 consonant sounds, seven digraph sounds, and 19 vowel sounds. Almost all of these 44 sounds have multiple spellings. In fact, there are over 300 spelling patterns to represent the 44 sounds. This makes it difficult for ELs (and native speakers) to read English and to spell English words correctly.

In addition, English has r-controlled sounds (*car, are*) and diphthongs, a vowel sound that gradually moves toward a second vowel so that both sounds form one syllable (*toy, foil*).

The box below shows 22 different ways of spelling just the English long *e* sound.

---

22 Spelling Patterns for the Long *E* Sound

e, y, ee, ea, e_e, i_e, ie, ei, ei_e, ey, ae, ay, oe, eo, is, eip, ie_e, i, ea_e, it, eigh, ois

b**e**, c**i**ty, b**ee**, b**ea**ch, c**e**de, mach**i**ne, f**ie**ld, dec**ei**t, dec**ei**ve, k**ey**, C**ae**sar, qu**ay**, am**oe**ba, p**eo**ple, debr**is**, rec**eip**t, bel**ie**ve, sk**i**, l**ea**ve, espr**it**, Ral**eigh**, cham**ois**

It's an eye opener to see just how many different spellings English uses for the same sound. And to be a proficient reader and writer in English requires knowing most of them.

You can look at additional examples of sounds and spelling variations in Appendix D.

English Subject-Verb Agreement and Verb Tense

As in all languages, English has its own methods for subject-verb agreement, including regular verbs, which follow rules, and irregular verbs that don't. ELs need to be taught subject-verb agreement and verb tenses. Here are some examples.

Verbs and Verb Tenses

Regular Verbs (follow rules)

I jump. He jumps. You jump. We jump.

I jumped. He jumped. You jumped. We jumped.

Irregular verbs (don't follow rules):

I am. He is. You are. We are.

I was. He was. You were. We were.

Verb Tenses

English has many verb tenses to convey different ideas.

He **eats**.

He **is eating**.

He **ate**.

He **has been eating**.

He **will have eaten** three hot dogs by 6:00 o'clock.

He **has been eating** hot dogs for 40 minutes.

He **would have eaten** three hot dogs if he had had more time.

The hot dog **was eaten** by him.

Subject-verb agreement is explicitly taught during English Language Development and language arts lessons. Subject-verb agreement is implicitly taught in all EDI lessons using sentence frames and language error feedback corrections during CFU responses.

English Sentence Structure

English has conventions for different types of sentences and sentence structures.

Sentence Structure

Statement

I have a pencil.

Negative Statement

I do not have a pencil.

Question

Do you have a pencil?

Direct and Indirect Object

I gave Philip the pencil.

I gave it to him.

ELs often use rules from their primary language, which can lead to language errors, such as *I no have a pencil.* (These are called language transfer errors.)

English sentence structure is directly taught during language arts lessons and then implicitly taught in EDI lessons through sentence frames and corrective feedback for language errors during CFU responses.

LANGUAGE STRATEGIES

Language Strategies are tools, techniques, or methods used to promote English language acquisition through Listening, Speaking, Reading, and Writing. Language Strategies are not considered to be effective unless the *students* are involved with them. Language Strategies must include student interaction. It's the students who need to practice and develop language, not the teacher.

The box below summarizes the Listening, Speaking, Reading, and Writing strategies that we will describe in the remainder of this chapter.

EDI-EL Language Objective Strategies

Listening and Speaking Strategies (With Reading)

1. Clear Enunciation Strategy

2. Physical Pronunciation Strategy

3. Connect to Known Sounds Strategy

4. Minimal Pairs Strategy

5. Word Chunking for Pronunciation Strategy

6. Backward Syllabication Strategy

7. Inflectional Endings Emphasis Strategy

8. Inflectional Endings Buildup Strategy

9. Pair-Share Strategy

Reading Strategies

Sentence Reading

1. Tracked Choral Reading Strategy

Word Reading

2. Read Whole Word Strategy

3. Use Phonics Rules Strategy

4. Syllabication Strategy

5. Initial Letter Sounds Word Reading Strategy

Writing Strategies

1. Write New Words on Whiteboards Strategy

2. Write Vocabulary-Based Answers on Whiteboards Strategy

3. Elaboration Writing Strategy

Now let's go over some specific Language Strategies.

LISTENING AND SPEAKING STRATEGIES (WITH READING)

Listening and Speaking Objectives address spoken words. English Learners need to be taught to differentiate between English sounds aurally (auditory discrimination) and to pronounce English sounds orally (create the sounds). Since listening, speaking, reading, and writing are interrelated, many strategies address multiple language skills. For example, you almost always teach listening, speaking, and reading at the same time and generally in concert with vocabulary development.

Over the years at DataWORKS, we refined and field-tested nine Listening and Speaking Strategies for ELs.

EDI-EL Listening and Speaking Strategies (With Reading)

1. Clear Enunciation Strategy

2. Physical Pronunciation Strategy

3. Connect to Known Sounds Strategy

4. Minimal Pairs Strategy

5. Word Chunking for Pronunciation Strategy

6. Backward Syllabication Strategy

7. Inflectional Endings Emphasis Strategy

8. Inflectional Endings Buildup Strategy

9. Pair-Share Strategy

Let's go over each strategy, one at a time.

EDI-EL Listening and Speaking

1. Clear Enunciation Strategy

   A. Enunciate clearly while students listen and look at the word.

   B. Students imitate, repeat, and pair-share.

   C. CFU of pronunciation.

The most basic method of Listening and Speaking is directing ELs to imitate you as they practice saying new words. One important consideration is that you clearly pronounce the new word enough times. You need to say it over and over. The students may have never heard it before. You even repeat the word again when Checking for Understanding for pronunciation. (In Chapter 6, we'll present specific strategies that promote clear enunciation, such as extending vowels, stressing consonants, and emphasizing each syllable.)

Note in the example below that students are directed to look at the new word while Listening and Speaking, to support reading of the new word.

1. Clear Enunciation Strategy

   A. Enunciate clearly while students listen and look at the word.

Students, look at this word on the board. It is the most important word for today's science lesson. The word is meiosis. Listen while I say it, mei-o-sis. Listen again, mei-o-sis.

> B. Students imitate, repeat, and pair-share.

Let's say it together: meiosis. One more time, meiosis. Point to meiosis on your partner's page and say meiosis three times. Partner "A" goes first. Then I am going to call on some of you to pronounce meiosis.

> C. Check for Understanding of pronunciation.

Call on random non-volunteers. Use the new word in your question so students hear it again. *Rubin, please say meiosis. Robert, how do you pronounce meiosis? Maria, say meiosis for me.* Be sure you Echo so students hear the new word again. *That's right, Rubin, meiosis.*

If individual students mispronounce a word, you repeat the word and show them how to pronounce it. To reduce the emphasis on a single student, have the entire class pronounce the word and then call on the individual student who mispronounced.

> **EDI-EL Listening and Speaking**
>
> 2. Physical Pronunciation Strategy
>   A. Model lip and tongue movements.
>   B. Students practice.
>   C. CFU of pronunciation.

Sometimes, just asking ELs to mimic your pronunciation will not work because they are not proficient in recognizing or producing the specific English phonemes (sounds) required.

The phonemes in every language require specific lip, tongue, and air movements to create them correctly. Many ELs need to be taught the mouth movements required for the correct pronunciation of English phonemes, especially those not in their home language. For example, some ELs say *dis* and *dat* instead of *this* and *that* because they are using the wrong tongue movements. They are using an explosive air sound made by quickly moving the tongue forward from the roof of the mouth giving *dis* and *dat. This* and *that* are pronounced with the mouth partly open and the tongue starting from between the teeth and then being pulled back to allow the air to be released more slowly to make the *th* sound.

With the Physical Pronunciation Strategy, you show and model the proper mouth, lip, and tongue movement and then have the students practice chorally and with partners. Then you call on individual non-volunteers to check on pronunciation.

In the scenario below, Mr. Reyes is teaching his students *b* and *v* sounds. He starts with Listening so students can hear the difference between the *b* and *v* sound. He states several words and uses finger signals to Check for Understanding. Students raise one finger for the *b* sound and raise two fingers like a V for the *v* sound. Then he moves to Speaking: His students practice saying the sounds using the proper lip and tongue movements.

A. Model lip and tongue movements.

Mr. Reyes points to his mouth and says, *Students, look at my mouth while I say* boat. *My lips are together and then the air blasts out when I make the* b *sound. Look closely at my lips. Boat. Boat. The air blasts out on the* b *sound. Boat.*

He continues, *Now look at my lips while I say* vote. *My teeth are over my bottom lip. Look at my mouth. Vote. Vote. The air slips out in a sort of buzzing sound. Listen one more time. Vote. Vote.*

Mr. Reyes is ready to Check for Understanding for Listening. *Now I am going to say* vote *or* boat. *I want you to put up one finger if I say* boat. *If I say* vote*, put up two fingers that look like a V. All I want you to do is to look at my mouth and tell me which sound I said. Just look.* He continues, emphasizing the mouth movements while scanning the student hands as he says boat and vote. Then he adds base, vase, very, berry, bat, vat.

Students, you have been watching my lips. Now I am going to cover my mouth, and I want you to listen to the difference between the explosive b *sound and the buzzing* v *sound. Use your fingers to show me which sound you hear.* He holds up a piece of paper to prevent his students from seeing his mouth and continues saying the *b* and *v* words. When a few students show the wrong fingers, he lowers the paper and lets them look at his mouth.

B. Students practice.

Mr. Reyes is ready to move from Listening to Speaking. *Now you're going to say the words. Look at me. My lips are together, and then I let the air blast out. Listen. Boat. Boat. Put your lips together and say boat. Boat. Put your hand in front of your mouth and feel the air blast out when you say boat.* The students raise their hands to feel the air as they speak. He continues having the students practice the *b* and *v* sounds with their partners.

C. CFU of pronunciation.

He calls on non-volunteers to say the words and provides feedback to a few students on proper tongue and lip movements.

EDI-EL Listening and Speaking

3. Connect to Known Sounds Strategy
   A. Present a similar-sounding known word.
   B. Students pronounce known word.
   C. Connect known sound to new word.
   D. Students pronounce known word and new word.
   E. CFU of pronunciation.

With our third strategy, you support listening and speaking by connecting sounds in new words to the same sound in familiar words that ELs can already pronounce.

3. Connect to Known Sounds Strategy

   A. Present a similar-sounding known word.

Students, look at this word you already know. The word is nation.

   B. Students pronounce known word.

Say nation with me. Nation.

   C. Connect known sound to new word.

Look at this new word and listen carefully. Connotation. The ending sounds like nation. Listen. Nation, connotation. Nation, connotation.

   D. Students pronounce known word and new word.

Let's say nation, connotation. One more time: nation, connotation. Tell your partner our new word twice, connotation, connotation.

   E. Check for Understanding of pronunciation.

I'm going to call on some of you to pronounce connotation. Call on random non-volunteers.

Minimal Pairs

Minimal pairs can be very difficult for ELs. The term *minimal pairs* refers to two words that are pronounced the same except for one sound, for example, *collect* and *correct, pen* and *pin, sat* and *hat, bad* and *bat,* and *John* and *Joan.*

Distinguishing between minimal pairs is important. In addition to caus-ing pronunciation difficulties, the lack of discrimination between minimal pairs can cause ELs to mix up words and word meanings.

The specific minimal pairs that cause student difficulty depend on the phonetics of their native language. For example, Spanish speakers have dif-ficulty hearing and pronouncing the difference in *very* and *berry* because Spanish does not distinguish between *b* and *v* sounds. (We practiced these sounds in the Physical Pronunciation Strategy above.) Japanese students might have problems with *fad* and *food* because their language lacks the sound for the English *f.* Another example would be *eel* and *heel* for a French learner of English since the letter *h* is silent in the French language. Again, the lack of discrimination of minimal pairs can cause ELs to mix up words and their meanings.

Classic tongue-twisters are difficult because of the number of minimal pairs and the rapid tongue movements required. Listen to the subtle minimal pair difference between *shall, shell, she'll.*

She sells seashells by the seashore.

If neither he sells seashells,

Nor she sells seashells,

Who shall sell seashells?

Shall seashells be sold?

EDI-EL Listening and Speaking

4. Minimal Pairs Strategy
   A. Present the new word.
   B. Pre-empt minimal pair errors.
   C. Students practice.
   D. CFU of pronunciation.

In the Minimal Pairs Strategy, you preempt minimal pair errors when students might think they are hearing a different word. You acknowledge the minimal pair words and emphasize the correct word and pronunciation.

4. Minimal Pairs Strategy
   A. Present the new word.

Students, a group of lines that form a unit in a poem or song is called a verse. Listen as I say "verse." Again, verse.

> **B. Pre-empt minimal pair errors.**

Don't confuse our new word "verse" with a word you already know, "worse." Listen as I say the two words. Verse. Worse.

> **C. Students practice.**

Let's pronounce the two words. Verse, worse. Again. Verse, worse. Now point to the word verse *on your page and say it twice.*

> **D. Check for Understanding of pronunciation.**

I'm going to call on some of you to pronounce verse. Call on random non-volunteers.

> **EDI-EL Listening and Speaking**
>
> 5. Word Chunking for Pronunciation Strategy
>   A. Break word into oral word parts.
>   B. Have students repeat parts.
>   C. Have students repeat entire word.
>   D. CFU of pronunciation.

Many words, when spoken, do not exactly match the written syllables. It's as if words have another set of syllables when pronounced. Often it's easier for ELs to say a new word when you break the word into word chunks (oral syllables) instead of referring to the actual syllables in text. For example, it's easier to teach ELs how to say the word *analyze* by having them repeat the word chunks *an-nal-lize* rather than repeating the actually syllables *a-nal-yze*.

Students, look at our new word, "disturbing." Listen to the parts of disturbing: dis-stur-bing. Disturbing. Repeat after me, dis-stur-bing. Disturbing. One more time, dis-stur-bing. Disturbing. Say disturbing *to your partner twice. Then I will call on some of you to read and pronounce* disturbing.

> **EDI-EL Listening and Speaking**
>
> 6. Backward Syllabication Strategy
>   A. Present the new word.
>   B. Use backward syllabication.
>   C. CFU of pronunciation.

Our strategies so far work well until you come across a long, difficult word. Imagine trying to do this:

Students, listen carefully: deoxyribonucleic. Let's say it together . . .

We need a new strategy. With the EDI Backward Syllabication strategy, you practice pronouncing the word starting from the end until ELs are saying the entire word. It works especially well for long words. Here's why: If you just keep saying a long word over and over, the ELs tend to hear the beginning over and over and don't quite get the ending part. With backward syllabication, by the time ELs say the beginning of the word they have already heard and said the ending several times.

To make this strategy work, you need to have a copy of the word to refer to. It's hard to use backward syllabication orally without looking at the word. And, of course, looking at the word supports students in being able to read the word.

You don't need to separately pronounce each and every syllable starting from the end of the word. Just use pronounceable chunks.

6. Backward Syllabication Strategy

    A. Present the new word.

Students, our new word is "deoxyribonucleic." Look at it here on the board.

    B. Use backward syllabication.

We are going to say this big word from the end and then say the entire phrase. Look up here at the board where I'm pointing and repeat after me:

(teacher)	(students)
*nu-**cle**-ic*	*nu-**cle**-ic*
Again.	
*nu-**cle**-ic*	*nu-**cle**-ic*
***ri**-bo-nucleic*	*ribo-nucleic*
***ri**-bo-nucleic*	*ribo-nucleic*
***oxy**-**ribo**-nucleic*	***oxy**-**ribo**-nucleic*
***oxy**-**ribo**-nucleic*	***oxy**-**ribo**-nucleic*
*de-**oxy**-**ribo**-nucleic*	*de-**oxy**-**ribo**-nucleic*
*de-**oxy**-**ribo**-nucleic*	*de-**oxy**-**ribo**-nucleic*
Now let's say the entire phrase twice. *deoxyribonucleic acid* *deoxyribonucleic acid*	

> C. Check for Understanding of pronunciation.

Point to "deoxyribonucleic acid" on your partner's handout, and say the words twice. Be ready to say deoxyribonucleic acid *if I call on you.*

Inflectional Endings

Inflectional endings are suffixes added to a base word to show tense, plurality, possession, or comparison. Inflectional endings for verb tenses include present tense (enjoy, enjoy*s*); past tense and past participle (enjoy*ed*); and present participle (enjoy*ing*). Inflectional endings are also used to show plural nouns (dog*s*, dress*es*); possession (John*'s* hat); and comparisons in adjective and adverbs (small*er*, small*est*).

Although English has relatively few inflectional endings, ELs frequently make errors using them. For example, they will omit the third person singular *s* or the past tense *ed*.

To make matters more complicated, some of the inflectional endings have multiple pronunciations depending on the ending sound of the base word they are attached to. Although there are complicated rules to do this, which could be explicitly taught, most teachers just teach ELs the correct pronunciation of inflectional endings as the words show up during the lesson or when they hear mispronunciations.

Below are two types of inflectional endings that are difficult for English Learners.

Pronunciation of Verbs and Nouns Ending in s *and* es

Possessives, verbs, and nouns ending in *s* and *es* are pronounced as /s/, /z/, or as an extra syllable /iz/ depending on the final sound of the verb or noun.

Pronunciation of Endings *s* and *es*

1. Pronounce *s* as /s/

hit	hits
Philip	Philip's
fifth	fifths

2. Pronounce *s* as /z/

go	goes
Bill	Bill's
name	names

3. Pronounce s and es as extra syllable /iz/

judge	judges
inch	inches

Pronunciation of Verbs Ending in ed

ELs often have a hard time hearing and pronouncing the *ed* on the end of verbs. In addition, since they are in the process of learning English, they may not be completely sure when verbs require an *ed* ending. *I could have helped you.* To make matters more difficult, the ending *ed* can be pronounced in three different ways: as /t/, /d/, or as an extra syllable /id/.

Pronunciation of Ending *ed*

1. Pronounce *ed* as /t/

help	helped
look	looked
watch	watched

2. Pronounce *ed* as /d/

order	ordered
judge	judged
wave	waved

3. Pronounce *ed* as an extra syllable /id/

start	started
need	needed
wait	waited

From Silvia: The *ed* pronounced as /t/ is especially hard for ELs to hear. Say these words out loud: help, helped. Now, say this out loud quickly: "He helped me at school." When spoken rapidly, the *ed* is almost dropped. As an English Learner myself, I need to pay attention to the *ed* endings.

From John: I believe the confusing variations of English pronunciations have occurred because of the difficulty of the mouth movements required to make some combinations of sounds. As humans, we have changed the pronunciations over time to make them easier to say but kept the spelling and grammatical rules. For example, the plural of *act* is *acts*. However, we often pronounce *acts* closer to *axe* because it is too difficult to pronounce the explosive ending *t* sound followed by the hissing sound of the *s*. Act-s. A similar example is *prompt* and *prompts*. We say the plural as *promps* because it is too hard to pronounce the ending letters *mpts*.

We have two inflectional endings strategies. Let's look at the first one.

EDI-EL Listening and Speaking

7. Inflectional Endings Emphasis Strategy
   A. Present new word while emphasizing the inflectional ending sound.
   B. Students imitate and practice.
   C. CFU of pronunciation.

7. Inflectional Endings Emphasis Strategy
   A. Present new word while emphasizing the inflectional ending sound.

Students, twelve percent expressed as a fraction is twelve one-hundredths. Listen carefully. There is an s on the end of hundredths that makes a hissing sound. Listen. Hundredths. Hundredths. Listen while I read the equation. Twelve percent equals twelve one-hundredths.

   B. Students imitate and practice.

Let's read the equation together. Make sure you say the s on the end of hundredths. Ready? Go. Twelve percent equals twelve one-hundredths.

   C. Check for Understanding of pronunciation.

Students, read this equation to your partner: 15% = 15/100. Then I will call on some of you to read it to me.

Our second inflection ending strategy focuses on *adding* an inflectional ending to a base word. In this case, you practice the base word first and then add the inflectional ending.

EDI-EL Listening and Speaking

8. Inflectional Endings Buildup Strategy
   A. Pronounce the base word.
   B. Add the inflectional ending.
   C. Practice the base word with inflectional ending added.
   D. CFU of pronunciation.

In this inflectional ending strategy, you focus on *adding* an inflectional ending to a word.

Inflectional Endings Buildup Strategy Example 1

> **Learning Objective**
>
> Today, we will analyze text that uses the compare-and-contrast organizational pattern.

8. Inflectional Endings Buildup Strategy

   A. Pronounce the base word.

Students, look at the word uses *in our Objective. It is based on the word* use. *Let's all say* use.

B. Add the inflectional ending.

With the s on the end, use [yooz] becomes uses [yooz-iz]. It almost sounds like the word "is" was added. Uses [yooz-iz].

C. Practice base word with inflectional ending added.

Let's say the word uses *together. Uses. One more time. Uses. Point to* uses *on your page and say it to your partner.*

D. Check for Understanding of pronunciation.

I am going to call on some of you to say uses.

Inflectional Endings Buildup Strategy Example 2

> **Learning Objective**
>
> Trace the historic influence of Chinese inventions.
>
> **Concept Development**
>
> The Chinese combined sulfur, saltpeter, and charcoal to create an explosive mixture that became gunpowder.

Students, the word combined *comes from* combine. *Let's say combine. Combine. Now listen while I say combined. There is a* duh *sound on the end. Combined. Combined. Say combined with me. Combined. Point to* combined *on your handout and read it to your partner. I am going to call on some of you to pronounce combined.*

From Silvia: The concept of selecting words to pre-pronounce for ELs is a simple one. Unfortunately, it is an instructional practice that is rarely observed in the classroom, even in schools with high populations of ELs.

For example, the other day we were conducting classroom observations. The Learning Objective for the lesson was to identify the author's purpose in a selection. The teacher asked the students to write the Learning Objective in their notes. When she called on students to read the *Objective* to her, it was obvious that the students did not know how to pronounce *author's*. She used cheerleading to get the students to say the word. "Come on, you know better than that. We have done this in the past. You are always reading in class." The outcome was that most of the students were not able to pronounce the word. The solution would have been so simple: teach the students how to pronounce *author's*. Instead, the result was a very frustrated teacher and students who did not advance in their language.

EDI-EL Listening and Speaking

9. Pair-Share Strategy

   A. Provide a sentence frame with Academic or Content Vocabulary.

   B. Direct students to explain to each other.

So far, we have discussed Listening and Speaking strategies that focus on showing ELs what specific words *sound* like (Listening) and how to *pronounce* them (Speaking). A pair-share is your most important Listening and Speaking strategy for ELs. It gives them an opportunity to practice using new language as they engage in academic discourse with their pair-share partners.

Pair-share every question.

Pair-shares are discussed extensively in Chapters 2 and 3, so we won't repeat the information here. But do remember the EDI-EL rule: pair-share every question. (The only exception to pair-sharing every question is a Skill-Based Closure question, when you want to measure individual accountability.)

READING STRATEGIES

We've been discussing Listening and Speaking strategies, which often include Reading. Now we are ready to move on to specific Reading Strategies. At DataWORKS, we refined and field-tested five English Learner Reading Strategies to support and improve student reading during all EDI lessons.

EDI-EL Reading Strategies

Sentence Reading

　1. Tracked Choral Reading Strategy

Word Reading

　2. Read Whole Word Strategy

　3. Use Phonics Rules Strategy

　4. Syllabication Strategy

　5. Initial Letter Sounds Word Reading Strategy

Tracked Choral Reading Strategy

As mentioned at the beginning of this chapter, the primary Reading strategy in EDI is Tracked Choral Reading. Although you are not teaching reading, you are using a strategy that improves reading fluency every time you use it.

With Tracked Choral Reading, you read a sentence (or a few sentences) while your students follow along silently looking at the words. Then they read chorally after you. The fact that you *read the words first* enables all students, including ELs, to participate successfully in the choral read.

Avoid cold reads of difficult text. Whenever students are asked to read difficult text chorally with no pre-read, they inevitably stumble on words they don't know. Similar reading errors occur during popcorn or round-robin reading, where each student is asked to read one sentence with no pre-reading or support.

There are a few nuances that need to be followed to maximize the effectiveness of tracked reading:

First, it is very important that your students actually look at the words while you pre-read so they see the printed word that represents the spoken word. It's best to have students track with their fingers, especially for difficult text. It cues all students to participate and keeps their eyes on the printed words as you read them.

Second, you must read at your students' decoding rate. If you read too fast, then students are moving their fingers on the page, but they are not connecting your spoken words to specific printed words on the page.

Table 5.2 shows typical reading rates for students in words per minute. Use the Oral rate. For high school, start with the 7th-grade rate.

Table 5.2 Silent and Oral Reading Rates (Words per Minute)

Silent and Oral Reading Rates (Words per Minute)						
	Grade 2	Grade 3	Grade 4	Grade 5	Grade 6	Grade 7
Silent	70–100	95–130	120–170	160–210	180–230	180–240
Oral	66–104	86–124	95–130	108–140	112–145	122–155
Weekly improvement = 1.5 to 2.0 words per minute						

Of course, you must read in a formal register with clear enunciation. This means you say *running,* not *runnin'*. You say *going to,* not *gonna.* You pause at commas and raise and lower your voice as you read.

Sometimes, it is not necessary to pre-read when students are reading easy text or reading words that have already been practiced during the lesson. Choral reading of easy text is also a good engagement strategy. *Students, let's all read question one together . . .*

From Silvia: Some schools use books on tape or recorded versions of textbooks. These recordings are often read too fast for students to track while looking at the text. Also, if students just listen (without looking at the text), the lesson is promoting oral comprehension as opposed to reading comprehension. Sometimes, in schools with low reading scores, we see that students are not reading enough. ELs are listening rather than reading, and they are using resources with excessive pictures that allow them to bypass reading.

Tracked Choral Reading Adds Reading to Every Lesson

Tracked Choral Reading is an excellent method of integrating reading into any lesson, in any content area. If ELs spent five minutes in each lesson reading the Learning Objective, concept definitions, and a few other parts of the lesson, they could add up to 90 hours of expository text reading to each school year.

Have Beginning Readers Read Every Word in the Lesson

Beginning readers include all students from kindergarten to third grade plus any ELs who are learning to read. For these students, pre-read (while students track with their fingers) and then have them chorally read every word in the lesson. This means you pre-read and have students read text from every lesson component, starting with the Learning Objective and including all the text-based questions and answers in the lesson. Read the text from the Independent Practice, too.

With tracked reading, every lesson improves students' reading fluency. Even though you are not teaching reading per se, you are supporting improved reading fluency. Students are learning to recognize new words and practicing reading words they already know.

Air Tracking

Emergent readers—especially kindergarteners—often don't have enough reading ability to look at a page and track individual words with their fingers while you read. In these cases, have students "air track" by pointing to words on the board, flip chart, or other large print text. You pre-read, pointing to each word while the students point in the air toward each word at the same time. Then have students read chorally while you point to each word, and they point in the air to each word.

EDI-EL Reading

Sentence Reading

I. Tracked Choral Reading Strategy

A. Cue students to look at the text.

B. Teacher reads while students track.

C. Students read.

D. Check for Understanding.

I. Tracked Choral Reading Strategy

A. Cue students to look at the text.

Students, look at the definition of the Manhattan Project on page 34. Put your finger on the word Manhattan *and track while I read the definition.*

B. Teacher reads while students track.

The Manhattan Project was the American effort during World War II to develop and deploy nuclear weapons.

> C. Students read.

Let's read this definition together. Go. The Manhattan Project was the American effort during World War II to develop and deploy nuclear weapons. Students, what this means is . . .

> D. Check for Understanding.

What comes next depends on the lesson. When you are focusing on reading, your CFU question addresses reading. Have students pair-share by reading the sentence to each other and then call on non-volunteers to read the sentence.

Most often, however, you are focusing on content, not reading. In the example above, you continue by explaining and elaborating on the Manhattan Project. Then, your follow-up CFU questions address something about the Manhattan Project. In this case, you are Checking for Understanding of the content, not the students' ability to read the content.

Word Reading Strategies

We just talked about using tracked reading to read entire sentences. Sometimes, we need to show ELs how to read an individual word. We have three single-word reading strategies. These strategies are rarely done in isolation. They are almost always done concurrently with Listening, Speaking, and Vocabulary Development. Let's look at each one in detail.

> **EDI-EL Reading**
>
> *Word Reading*
>
> 2. Read Whole Word Strategy
>   A. Teacher reads word while students look at word.
>   B. Students imitate, repeat, and pair-share.
>   C. CFU of reading, if applicable.

This reading strategy is almost the same as the EDI-EL Clear Enunciation Listening and Speaking Strategy, with the emphasis now on reading rather than pronunciation.

With the Read Whole Word Strategy, you read the word while having students look at the word. There is no attempt to sound out the word or apply any strategy. You just say it. To support reading, it is important that your students look at the word while you and they say it. If they don't look at the word, they are practicing Listening and Speaking Language Objectives, but not Reading.

The Read Whole Word strategy can be used with words that are easy to say but have difficult or confusing spelling. It can be used with words students know orally but haven't seen before in print, such as *marshmallow,* or *whistling.* If the word is a new word, then reading should be followed by a definition.

Students, look at the first word in the sentence. The word is magma. *Point to the word* magma *in your text and read it to your partner. Now, let's read the definition together. Magma is hot, melted rock below the earth's surface.*

Phonics

"Phonics" refers to associating letters or groups of letters with the sounds they represent. (We described letter-sound correspondence at the beginning of this chapter.) When students learn the sound of the letter *b* or that *tion* sounds like /shun/, they are learning phonics. Mastery of phonics is an important tool in helping ELs read, pronounce, and spell words.

Native English speakers and ELs both benefit from explicit, systematic phonics instruction. There is one difference, however. Native English speakers are often decoding words they already know, whereas non-native speakers may be trying to decode words they don't yet know. In this case, ELs also need vocabulary development while reading.

English is a complex language with many phonics rules, but you can use the more common ones to help ELs decode words during EDI lessons.

Useful Phonics Rules for English Learners

1. **Syllables**. Every syllable in every word must contain a vowel.

2. **The letter "c" has two sounds.** The hard "c" sounds like a "k" (cat, cape, constant). When "c" is followed by "e," "i," or "y," it usually has the soft sound of "s" (city, cycle, cylinder).

3. **The letter "g" has two sounds.** The hard "g" is used in gate, goat, and go. When "g" is followed by e, i, or y, it usually has the soft sound of "j" (gem, giant, gyroscope).

4. **Consonant digraphs make one sound.** A consonant digraph is two or more consonants grouped together that represent a *single* sound. Common consonant digraphs include wh (what), sh (shout), wr (write), kn (know), th (that), ch (children, watch), ph (pharmacy), tch (watch), gh (laugh), ng (ring). Note: Don't confuse consonant digraphs (single sound) with consonant blends. In consonant blends, each consonant can be heard: st (store); br (brake).

(Continued)

(Continued)

5. **Syllables with short vowels.** Syllables with one vowel and ending in a consonant are usually short (tap, bed, wish, lock, bug).

6. **Silent "e."** In English an "e" is often added to the end of a word to indicate the long vowel sound (take, gene, bite, hope, fuse). The final "e" is silent. It is not pronounced. The final silent "e" is a symbol that tells the reader to use the long vowel sound. Examples: Fat, fate; pin, pine.

7. **Two vowels together.** When a syllable has two vowels together, the first vowel is usually long and the second vowel is silent. Example: stain.

8. **Syllables ending with a single vowel.** When a syllable ends in a vowel, and it's the only vowel, that vowel is usually long. Examples: ba/ker, be/come, bi/sect, go/ing, fu/ture, my/self.

9. **R-controlled vowels.** When a vowel is followed by "r" in the same syllable, the vowel is neither long nor short. Examples: charm, term, shirt, corn, surf.

EDI-EL Reading

Word Reading

3. Use Phonics Rules Strategy

   A. Point to the word and explain the phonics rule.

   B. Generalize the phonics rule to other words.

   C. Check for Understanding.

When using phonics as a reading strategy, you facilitate the reading of new words by providing an appropriate phonics rule. It's important that you also generalize the rule so ELs can apply it to other words they encounter on their own. In this manner, ELs are improving their reading of many words rather than learning how to read one more word. When words don't follow phonics rules, you point this out also.

Use Phonics Rules Strategy Example 1

Learning Objective

Determine the main idea and key details in text.

> 3. Use Phonics Rules Strategy
> A. Point to the word and explain the phonics rule.

Students, look at this word main. *It has two vowels together: ai. Often in English when there are two vowels together the first vowel has the long sound, saying its name. And the second vowel is silent. Look at the word and listen while I read it. Main. I only say the "a," not the "i". Main.*

> B. Generalize the phonics rule to other words.

Here are some more words with two vowels together, and you only say the first vowel using the long vowel sound. Listen as I read them. The teacher quickly writes the words on the board and then reads them. *Train. Stain. Heat. Meat. Let's read them together. Train. Stain. Heat. Meat.*

> C. Check for Understanding.

The Checking for Understanding here includes the phonics rule. *Students, point to the word* main *in your handout and read it to your partner. Tell your partner how you know how to read the "ai" in* main. *Be ready to tell me if I call on you.* Call on non-volunteers to read the word and describe how they know how to read it.

Use Phonics Rules Strategy Example 2

> **Learning Objective**
>
> Describe the process and function of the digestive system.

> 3. Use Phonics Rules Strategy
> A. Point to the word and explain the phonics rule.

Students, look up here at the letter "g" in digestive. *The letter "g" has two sounds: a hard sound like gate or go and a soft sound that sounds like a "j" in words like giant or giraffe.*

Often when "g" is followed by an "e," "i" or "y," "g" uses the soft sound. So the "g" in digestive has the "j" sound. We say di-jes-tiv. Let's all read the word together. Digestive.

> B. Generalize the phonics rule to other words.

After writing words on the board so students can see the spelling, the teacher continues.

Here are some more words with a soft "g" sound. I will read them first, then you read them after me. Giant. Gym. Magic.

> C. Check for Understanding.

Students, point to the "g" in the word digestive *on your partner's handout and explain to your partner how to read the word. "A" partners go first and then "B" partners.* Call on non-volunteers to read "digestive" and to describe the "g" sound used.

From John: I just noticed something with the "digestive" example above. The last part of "digestive" does not follow the silent "e" rule. This leads to our next strategy.

English Words Don't Always Follow the Phonics Rules

ELs often misread words because they apply phonics rules to words that do not follow the rules, and in English many words do not follow the rules. In these cases, you preempt a possible mispronunciation by pointing out the exception to the phonics rule.

Use Phonics Rules Strategy Example 3

Learning Objective

Solve systems of linear equations.

The word *linear* is an exception to the silent "e" rule. It is also an exception to the two vowels together rule when the first vowel is long and the second vowel is silent.

> 3. Use Phonics Rules Strategy.
>   A. Point to the word and explain the phonics rule *exception.*

Teacher points to the Learning Objective on the board.

Solve systems of linear equations.

Students, look at this word in our Objective: linear.

The beginning letters are 1-i-n-e. You might think that it is read as line-ar. However, this word has its own pronunciation. The correct pronunciation is lin-e-ar. Let's say it together. Lin-e-ar. Again. Linear.

C. Check for Understanding.

In this case, the Checking for Understanding question cannot address a phonics rule because the word is an exception. Ask students to read the word or have them read the word in context.

From John: A few years ago I taught a middle school Algebra demo lesson on linear equations. I didn't pre-read the word *linear*. I was surprised when students pronounced it as line-ar. Now, I always pre-read or pre-pronounce.

Syllabication

Syllabication is the separation of a word into syllables. Syllables don't convey meaning; they make speech easier for the brain to process. Every syllable contains a vowel sound, so the number of syllables in a word is the same as the number of vowel sounds you hear.

Being able to break words into syllables makes it easier for ELs to read and pronounce new words. Content Standards call for syllabication instruction. However, syllabication can be used as a reading strategy in any lesson.

Rules of Syllabication

1. Every syllable must contain a vowel.

2. A one-syllable word is never divided **(cat, nest).**

3. Divide words at compound words, prefixes, and suffixes **(paint/brush, sun/glasses,** re/read, un/tie, **help/ful, mad/ly).**

4. When two or more consonants come between two vowels (VC/CV), the word is usually divided between the two consonants **(sum/mer, win/ter).**

5. When a single consonant comes between two vowels in a word, the word is usually divided after the consonant if the first vowel is not long **(fin/ish, par/ent).**

(Continued)

(Continued)

6. When a single consonant comes between two vowels in a word, the word is usually divided before the consonant if the first vowel is long **(ma/ker, ti/mer).**

7. When a vowel is sounded alone in a word, the vowel is a syllable itself (bi/ol/o/gy, i/tem).

8. When two vowels come together in a word and are sounded separately, divide the word between the two vowels **(po/et, cre/ate).**

9. When a word ends in *le* preceded by a consonant, divide the word before that consonant **(rat/tle, cra/dle).**

EDI-EL Reading

Word Reading

4. Syllabication Strategy

   A. Point to the word and explain the syllabication rule.

   B. Generalize the syllabication rule to other words.

   C. Check for Understanding.

You can often help ELs read a new word by referring to a syllabication rule. Then generalize the rule so they are not just learning to read one word, but can apply the rule to other words they read.

Syllabication Strategy Example 1

> **Learning Objective**
>
> Use symbolism to understand the author's meaning.

4. Syllabication Strategy

   A. Point to the word and explain the syllabication rule.

Look at this word: symbolism. You can see the word symbol *followed by the suffix "ism."*

When words have a suffix, the suffix is a separate syllable. Listen: symbol-ism. Symbol-ism. It is not symbo-lism. Let's read the word together. Symbolism.

B. Generalize the syllabication rule to other words.

Here is another word with a suffix: realism. You read the word real *and then the suffix "ism." It's read as real-ism, not rea-lism.*

C. Check for Understanding.

Students, explain to your partners how you know how to read words like symbolism *and* realism *that have a suffix.* Call on non-volunteers.

Syllabication Strategy Example 2

Concept Development

Hurricanes and tornadoes are examples of severe weather.

4. Syllabication Strategy

A. Point to the word and explain the syllabication rule.

Students, look at this word. It's hurricanes.
You can see the letters u-r-r-i *in hurricanes.* When two or more consonants come between two vowels, the word is usually divided between the two consonants. We read it as hur-ri-canes. Let's read it together. Hurricanes. Again. Hurricanes.*

B. Generalize the syllabication rule to other words.

This same rule applies to tornadoes. *We have two consonants between two vowels* o-r-n-a. *We divide the syllables between the "r" and the "n." We read it as tor-na-does, not as torn-a-does. It's tor-na-does. Let's read tornadoes together. Ready? Tornadoes.*

C. Check for Understanding.

What did I just show you that will help you read words like "hurricanes" and "tornadoes"? Point to the letters in the words and tell your partner, and be ready to tell me. Partner "A" go first, then partner "B." Call on non-volunteers.

> ### EDI-EL Reading
>
> *Word Reading*
>
> 5. Initial Letter Sounds Word Reading Strategy (for emergent readers)
>
>   A. Point to first letter in a new word.
>
>   B. Say the letter name. *Students say the name of the letter.*
>
>   C. Say the sound the letter makes. *Students say the sound.*
>
>   D. Say the new word, strongly emphasizing the initial sound. *Students say the word, emphasizing the initial sound, while looking at the word.*

Initial letter sounds can be used to support emergent readers and non-readers during a lesson. To do this, identify and name the first letter of a new word. Clearly state the letter name and the sound the letter makes. Have the students repeat with you. Now exaggerate and emphasize the initial letter *sound* as you clearly enunciate the entire word. Have students repeat the word, emphasizing the initial sound, while looking at the word and the initial letter in the word.

This strategy could be used, for example, in a lesson when students first read sequence words: *first, next,* and *last.* Just knowing the initial letter helps students read these new words.

In Chapter 7, Silvia describes using this strategy in the classroom.

WRITING

We've talked about Language Objective strategies for Listening, Speaking, and Reading. There's one more to cover—Writing.

In the classroom, you explicitly teach students to write using fully developed, well-crafted, well-delivered Explicit Direct Instruction writing lessons, as called for in language arts Standards. You explicitly teach students to write letters, words, sentences, paragraphs, and essays. Example EDI writing lessons include the following:

> ### Types of Writing
>
> #### Letter and Word Writing
>
> - Write uppercase and lowercase letters.
> - Write words.
>
> #### Sentence Level Writing
>
> - Write compound sentences.
> - Write complex sentences.
> - Write a topic sentence.

Paragraph Level Writing

- Write a paragraph with a topic sentence and supporting details.
- Revise writing to provide more descriptive details.
- Develop the topic with precise verbs, nouns, and adjectives to paint a clear picture in the mind of the reader.
- Provide transitional expressions that link one paragraph to another in a clear line of thought.
- Support claim(s) with clear reasons and relevant evidence, using credible sources and demonstrating an understanding of the topic or text. (Common Core Standards 6th grade)

Essay Level Writing

- Write a persuasive essay.
- Write about an autobiographical experience.
- Write a job application cover letter.
- Write a response to literature.
- Write a research report.

Writing as a Language Objective

Although writing is explicitly taught in language arts lessons, writing as a Language Objective refers to supporting student writing in the context of any lesson. You are not teaching writing directly but are facilitating students in writing specific words, phrases, or sentences that promote student use of the new vocabulary and language contained in the lesson.

Which Words to Write?

The words, phrases, or sentences selected for Writing Objectives should focus on student use of the new content and academic words directly related to the lesson.

Look at the two student responses below. The Content Vocabulary from the lesson is shown in **boldface**.

Learning Objective

Evaluate the author's argument by critiquing the relationship between generalizations and supporting evidence.

Skill Development

CFU: Is the author's argument credible?

Response 1

*The **author's argument** to reduce smoking is **credible** because he included **authoritative supporting evidence** on cancer deaths from the American Cancer Society and the National Cancer Institute.*

Response 2

*Yes. The **author** included information from the American Cancer Society saying "tobacco use was responsible for nearly 1 in 5 deaths or an estimated 440,000 deaths per year during 1997–2001." He also said that the National Cancer Institute found that cigarette smoking and exposure to tobacco smoke cause an average of 438,000 premature deaths each year in the United States.*

In Response 1, the student wrote a response that matches the Learning Objective, with extensive vocabulary taken from the lesson. This qualifies as a Writing Language Objective. In Response 2, the student writing entailed mostly copying information from the article.

From Silvia: At DataWORKS, we make a distinction between writing that promotes the use of the new content (productive writing) and writing that does not promote the use of the new content (unproductive writing). In productive writing, for example, students write information directly related to the new content. In unproductive writing, the students are mainly copying information.

The other day I saw a lesson on compound sentences. Twenty minutes of the class time was spent having students copy the sentences they were going to analyze. Important instructional time was lost while students copied information that could have been in a handout. Now I have a guideline: Don't use students as copy machines.

LANGUAGE STRATEGIES IN WRITING

At DataWORKS we refined and field-tested three strategies for Language Objectives in Writing that can be incorporated into any EDI lesson.

EDI-EL Strategies for Language Objectives in Writing

1. Write New Words on Whiteboards Strategy

2. Write Vocabulary-Based Answers on Whiteboards Strategy

3. Elaboration Writing Strategy

All of these strategies require students to write using vocabulary and content they are learning from the lesson. Remember, the fact that students are physically writing does not always count as a Language Objective in Writing. For example, ELs might write "Tom Sawyer" on their whiteboards to correctly answer the CFU question: Who was the main character? This is Checking for Understanding. However, it's not a Writing Objective because students are not trying to learn and use the words "Tom" and "Sawyer." Writing Objectives for language arts would have ELs writing words such as *main character, characterization, omniscient point of view,* and *flashback* on their whiteboards.

EDI-EL Writing

   I. Write New Words on Whiteboards Strategy

      A. Present new word (Listening, Speaking, Reading, Spelling).

      B. Students write new word on whiteboards.

      C. Check for Understanding.

Now let's go over the strategies. To start with, you can always just ask ELs to write a new word (spelled correctly) on their whiteboards. Pick important Concept and Academic words, especially ones that have unusual spelling or pronunciation. Include pair-shares and have students show their whiteboards.

Here is an example. (As you can see, Writing is often done in conjunction with Listening, Speaking, and Reading.)

   I. Write New Words on Whiteboards Strategy

      A. Present new word (Listening, Speaking, Reading, Spelling).

Students, put your finger on the bold word on the top of page 43. It's the most important word in today's lesson. Are you looking at the word? Listen while I say it: photosynthesis. One more time. Photosynthesis. Let's all say it together. Ready? Photosynthesis.

Look at the letters in photosynthesis. *Let's spell* photosynthesis *together. Ready? p-h-o-t-o-s-y-n-t-h-e-s-i-s.*

      B. Students write new word on whiteboards.

Students, write photosynthesis *on your whiteboard. Check that you spelled it correctly: p-h-o-t-o-s-y-n-t-h-e-s-i-s.*

> C. Check for Understanding.

I am going to call on some of you to read photosynthesis *and spell it. But first, turn to your partner and point to* photosynthesis *on your whiteboard. Read and spell* photosynthesis *to your partner. OK, hold up your whiteboards.* Call on non-volunteers to read and spell.

Another opportunity for ELs to write Content Vocabulary words is when responding to Checking for Understanding questions using whiteboards. Often, Checking for Understanding questions provide answer choices such as "a" or "b." In the example below, students are answering a CFU question.

Students, I have two sentences on the board. Which one is a compound sentence, sentence "a" or sentence "b"? Write "a" or "b" on your whiteboard. Then tell your partner how you know. I want you to say, "Sentence _____ is a compound sentence because . . ."

Rather than using multiple choice answers such as "a" or "b," you can rephrase CFU questions to require ELs to write a content word on their whiteboards, which is our next strategy.

> **EDI-EL Writing**
>
> 2. Write Vocabulary-Based Answers on Whiteboards Strategy
>   A. Ask a CFU question requiring a vocabulary-based answer.
>   B. Students write vocabulary-based answer on whiteboards.
>   C. Check for Understanding.

> A. Ask a CFU question requiring a vocabulary-based answer.

Students, I have two sentences on the board. Let's look at sentence "a" first. Is it a simple sentence or a compound sentence?

> B. Students write vocabulary-based answer on whiteboards.

Write "simple sentence" or "compound sentence" on your whiteboard.

> C. Check for Understanding.

Tell your partner how you know. I want you to say, "Sentence __ is a _____ sentence because . . ." Have students show their whiteboards. Then call on non-volunteers to justify their answers. Repeat for sentence "b."

Here are two more CFU examples that require ELs to write Content Vocabulary words using whiteboards. You cue students to spell the words correctly, and you call on non-volunteers to justify their answers.

A. Ask a CFU question requiring a vocabulary-based answer.

Students, what type of rock am I holding?

B. Students write vocabulary-based answer on whiteboards.

Write the word igneous, metamorphic, *or* sedimentary *on your whiteboards. Spell it correctly. The words are right here on the board.*

C. Check for Understanding.

Be ready to tell me orally how you know. I want you to say, "It is a ___ rock because . . ." Refer to the rock properties on your worksheet if you need to. After you have written your answers, partner "B" point to your whiteboard and convince partner "A" that you have the correct answer. Have students show their whiteboards. Call on non-volunteers to justify their answers.

Here's an example using Content Vocabulary from a math lesson.

A. Ask a CFU question requiring a vocabulary-based answer.

Students, which multiplication property is shown in Example 3 on page 54: commutative, associative, or distributive?

B. Students write vocabulary-based answer on whiteboards.

Write the name of the multiplication property on your whiteboard. Spell it correctly.

C. Check for Understanding.

Show your answer to your partner. Tell your partner how you know your answer is correct. Use a complete sentence, "It is the ____ property because . . ." Partner "A" go first. Have students show their whiteboard answers. Call on non-volunteers to justify their answers.

> **EDI-EL Writing**
>
> 3. Elaboration Writing Strategy
>   A. Teacher prompts for longer written answer.
>   B. Students write on paper.
>   C. Check for Understanding.

In this strategy, ELs are asked to write more than single-word answers. These longer answers are usually written into notes or used to answer a worksheet question that has a line for the answer. Sentences can also be written on whiteboards. However, long sentences or answers on whiteboards take time to write. And then when students erase, the information is gone. Also, when students hold up whiteboards with long answers, the answers are harder to read and analyze.

Note that the name of this strategy is *Elaboration* Writing Strategy. Students are not copying information; they are writing their own sentences.

You can provide sentence frames for written answers just as you do for oral answers. However, avoid having the sentence frame preprinted as part of an answer because the student writing will become a fill-in-the-blank exercise.

> 3. Elaboration Writing Strategy
>   A. Teacher prompts for longer written answer.

Students, now let's look at question 4 below the passage we have been analyzing. It asks about the credibility of the author's argument.

I want you to answer like this: The author's argument in the passage is credible because . . ." or "The author's argument in the passage is not credible because . . ."

> B. Students write on paper.

Write your answer on your worksheet in the space below the question.

> C. Check for Understanding.

When you are finished writing, read your answer to your partner and explain why you think your answer is correct. In a minute, I will call on some of you to read and explain your answers.

Directing students to paraphrase or summarize information can be used in any content area lesson. Have them write in their notes or on worksheets.

Students, in your own words write your own definition of

the commutative property
the rock cycle
First Great Awakening
Point to the definition you wrote and explain it to your partner. Be ready to read your definition if I call on you. Partner "B" go first.

Students, I have defined figurative language. I want you to write your own definition in your own words. Write it in your notes. Use a complete sentence like this, "Figurative language is . . ." When you are done, point to your definition and read it to your partner. I'll call on some of you in a minute to read your definition.

Students, I want you to write a short paragraph at the bottom of your Cornell notes to summarize what you learned today.
the significance of the Battle of Saratoga in 1777
how authors develop characterization
the general approach to solving quadratic equations
When you are done, read your summary to your partner. Partner "A" go first. Then I am going to call on a couple of you to read your summary.

> **From John:** After students write answers on paper and pair-share, I often have students hold up their papers as if they were whiteboards. Even though I can't always read all the answers, it encourages all students to participate and to have an answer ready. I call on non-volunteers to Check for Understanding.

SUMMARY: *LANGUAGE OBJECTIVES*

We covered a lot in this chapter about adding Language Objectives to all EDI lessons.

ELs need to learn content while simultaneously learning English. English and English language structures are explicitly *taught* in language arts and English Language Development lessons. However, English language acquisition for ELs is accelerated by explicitly adding Language Objectives in Listening, Speaking, Reading, and Writing in English to *all lessons in all content areas every day*. The focus is on supporting ELs in using the specific new English vocabulary and language structures already contained in the lesson, plus being able to generalize to similar language outside the lesson.

Listening and Speaking Objectives

EDI lessons include Listening and Speaking Language Objectives to support oral English language development for ELs. They need to be taught how to pronounce English sounds and words. They need to be able to differentiate between English sounds and words when presented orally.

Reading Objectives

English Learners need to be able to read English text quickly and accurately. EDI lessons include Reading Objectives to improve reading fluency for ELs. ELs are taught to read new words in every lesson every day and to generalize reading strategies to other text they read.

Writing Objectives

Language arts and English Language Development lessons teach writing directly. EDI Writing Language Objectives focus mainly on writing using the new vocabulary and ideas contained in the lesson.

We described 17 strategies for Language Objectives.

EDI-EL Language Objective Strategies

Listening and Speaking Strategies (With Reading)

1. Clear Enunciation Strategy

2. Physical Pronunciation Strategy

3. Connect to Known Sounds Strategy

4. Minimal Pairs Strategy

5. Word Chunking for Pronunciation Strategy

6. Backward Syllabication Strategy

7. Inflectional Endings Emphasis Strategy

8. Inflectional Endings Buildup Strategy

9. Pair-Share Strategy

Reading Strategies

Sentence Reading

1. Tracked Choral Reading Strategy

Word Reading

2. Read Whole Word Strategy

3. Use Phonics Rules Strategy

4. Syllabication Strategy

5. Initial Letter Sounds Word Reading Strategy

Writing Strategies

1. Write New Words on Whiteboards Strategy

2. Write Vocabulary-Based Answers on Whiteboards Strategy

3. Elaboration Writing Strategy

Now we are ready for the next chapter on Content Access strategies: how to make the English we use during the lesson easier to understand for English Learners.

6 Content Access Strategies

How to Make English Easier to Understand for English Learners

In the last two chapters, we described how to support English Learners in learning English by purposefully including Vocabulary Development and Language Objectives in every lesson. In this chapter, we will describe how to make the English you use during a lesson easier to understand.

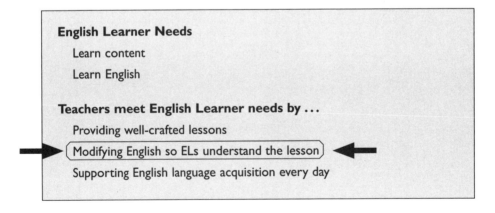

English Learner Needs

Learn content

Learn English

Teachers meet English Learner needs by ...

Providing well-crafted lessons

Modifying English so ELs understand the lesson

Supporting English language acquisition every day

WHAT ARE CONTENT ACCESS STRATEGIES?

Content Access Strategies are tools, techniques, or methods teachers use to make oral and written English easier to understand for English Learners. When English Learners understand more of the English used to deliver a lesson, they have greater access to the content being taught. Content Access Strategies do not change the content being taught. Instead, they address the English words used to teach the content.

Content Access Strategies fall into three areas, as shown in the box below. Note that these strategies that make English easier to understand focus mostly on the teacher. For example, the *teacher* speaks slowly and clearly. This is in contrast to Language Objectives, when the *students* Listen, Speak, Read, and Write during the lesson, and vocabulary development, when the *students* interact with the definition.

Content Access Strategies
to Make English Easier to Understand

I. Comprehensible Delivery

Increasing ELs' access to content by focusing on *known* words

II. Context Clues

Increasing ELs' access to content by providing meaning for *unknown* words

**III. Supplementary Materials and
       Adaptations of Existing Materials**

Increasing ELs' access to content by making *text* easier to understand

We will cover strategies for spoken and written English. Some of the strategies apply to both.

I. COMPREHENSIBLE DELIVERY

Comprehensible Delivery Strategies focus on making a lesson more accessible and comprehensible for English Learners by purposefully selecting and using English words they already know. Then you pronounce the known words clearly and slowly, so ELs don't *misunderstand* any of the words they, in fact, already know. Keep in mind that these initial strategies, such as speaking slowly and clearly, do not suddenly make an unknown word known. We'll have other strategies for unknown words. But it is important the ELs not miss any words they already know.

I. EDI-EL Comprehensible Delivery Strategies

Increasing ELs' access to content by focusing on *known* words

  A. Speaking Clearly Strategies
  B. Making Sentences Easier to Understand Strategies

C. Controlling Vocabulary Strategy

D. Connecting to Cognates Strategy

E. Defining Idioms Strategy

F. Replacing Pronouns with Nouns Strategy

G. Clarifying Passive Voice Strategy

Speaking Clearly

Our first strategies address oral speech, maximizing the clarity of spoken words. The goal is for ELs to recognize each individual word you are saying and not to misinterpret it as a similar-sounding word. This idea of ELs hearing words and then mistaking them for something else is called *acoustical approximations.* They hear *firstable* instead of *first of all.* ELs hear the teacher tell them they are going to read *Catch Her in the Right* instead of *Catcher in the Rye.* The effect occurs when ELs connect oral words with similar-sounding words they already know. Our speaking strategies below address providing clarity of speech and preventing acoustical approximations.

I. EDI-EL Comprehensible Delivery Strategies

A. Speaking Clearly Strategies

1. Speaking slowly

2. Using formal register when speaking

3. Inserting pauses between words

4. Extending vowels

5. Stressing consonants

6. Emphasizing each syllable

Our first strategy is to speak slowly. The average speech rate for English speakers in the United States is about 150–175 words per minute. This is too fast for many ELs, especially beginning and intermediates, to keep up with making meanings of the individual words. This lack of keeping up—even if ELs ultimately knew the meaning of the words—becomes lack of understanding of new content.

If you have ever learned a new language, you know how it seems that the native speakers are always talking fast. You wish they would slow down so you could understand more of what they're saying. Well, the English Learners are thinking the same thing, which leads us to our first strategy.

1. Speaking slowly
- Slow down speech rate for difficult or content-based sentences.
- Speak only slightly slower for familiar words and ideas.

Our first oral strategy is to just speak slowly. This allows ELs time for their brains to retrieve from long-term memory the meanings of the words you are saying. When you speak too rapidly, they are still processing words while you have moved on to additional words. They can't keep up.

Speaking slowly can be done anytime you are talking in a lesson. Slow your speech when you are describing new content. However, not all sentences need to be stated slowly. Sentences with familiar words and words used every day in class only need to be slowed slightly.

1. Speaking slowly
- Slow down speech rate for difficult or content-based sentences.

The teacher slows her rate of speech for this CFU question.
Students, I am going to ask you to tell me the definition of foreshadowing in your own words. What is foreshadowing? You should say, "Foreshadowing is . . ."

- Speak only slightly slower for familiar words and ideas.

Teacher speaks only slightly slower.
Tell your partner your definition. Use a complete sentence. Partner "A" go first.

2. Using formal register when speaking

Using the formal register means that you pronounce words clearly, crisply, and distinctly. You don't drop syllables or use slang variations of words. Formal register is especially important when you read text and students are following the words. You want them to hear the correct pronunciation of each printed word they are looking at.

Here is an example. You have a Learning Objective on the board: "We are going to identify characters in a story." Avoid pointing to it and reading it in a conversational register as "We're gonna 'den'ify characters inna story." Read it crisply, "We are going to identify characters in a story."

From John: When I coach classroom teachers, I often need to cue them to use the formal speaking register when they read the Learning Objective, Concept

Definitions, or other academic text. It's also important that you read text exactly as written when students are following along. Don't paraphrase while students are looking at the words.

3. Inserting pauses between words

Adding a slight pause between words ensures that each word has well-defined boundaries. When we talk quickly, we often connect or blend the end of one word to the beginning of the next word. For example, "Explicit Direct Instruction" becomes "Explicid Direc Tinstruction." This makes it difficult for ELs to comprehend what we are saying because they don't recognize the word *Tinstruction.*

Generally, you need to add space between all words to prevent the word blending effect. Read the Objective below aloud at a normal rate of speech.

Analyze the causes of World War II.

You might have blended the words *causes* and *of* and said, "Analyze the *Causesof* World War Two." You may have dropped the *d* from *World* and said, "Worl War Two." That's because "World War Two" is hard to say with the final *d* on *World.* The mouth movements are easier when you say "Worl War Two." However, when you add a little space after *World,* you tend to return the *d* to the end of the word.

It takes conscious effort to speak slower with a little space between words, but it helps ELs understand more, especially by preventing them from misunderstanding words they already know.

4. Extending vowels

With vowel extension, you deliberately attempt to elongate the vowels. When vowels are lengthened slightly, the words are pronounced more clearly.

Use regular verbs: *Uuuse reguular vuurbs.*

A triangle has three sides: *A triiiangle haas threeee siiides.*

5. Stressing consonants

Words become easier to understand when you stress consonants by over-emphasizing the movement of your tongue and lips when saying each word.

Say these words normally, and then say them again while really exaggerating your lip and tongue movements for each consonant. You can hear the increased clarity of the words

trapezoid	*trapezoid*
geologic	*geologic*
propaganda	*propaganda*

---
6. Emphasizing each syllable

You can make longer words easier to understand and slow down your speech by emphasizing individual syllables.

Stressing consonants and emphasizing syllables support each other. When you do one, you end up doing the other at the same time.

Read aloud the definition of the Kinetic Molecular Theory.

The Kinetic Molecular Theory explains gas properties by describing the behavior of the submicroscopic particles that make up a gas.

Now re-read it, emphasizing each syllable while stressing the consonants. Leave space between the words, but don't leave spaces between the syllables, or they will start to sound like separate words.

The Ki-net-ic Mo-lec-u-lar The-o-ry ex-plains gas prop-er-ties by des-crib-ing the be-hav-ior of the sub-mi-cro-scop-ic par-ti-cles that make up a gas.

Making Sentences Easier to Understand

We have just covered several strategies that make oral words clearer for English Learners. Now we are going to talk about making sentences more comprehensible for ELs.

The phrase "simple sentence" can have two meanings. One is the grammatical definition: a sentence that is an independent clause (subject-verb). The second meaning is a sentence that is not confusing, or is easy to understand. Generally, you can make sentences easier to understand (simpler) by making them simple (subject-verb) sentences.

You can purposefully create easier-to-understand sentences while you speak, but it's also important that ELs read text they can understand during a lesson. Below are strategies for simplifying sentence structures that apply to both oral and written sentences, along with an example of a teacher using the strategies.

I. EDI-EL Comprehensible Delivery Strategies

   B. Making Sentences Easier to Understand Strategies

      1. Breaking long sentences into several shorter sentences

      2. Simplifying sentences by rearranging and removing some of the dependent clauses

      3. Shortening sentences by removing unnecessary information
---

Sentences are easier to understand when they are shorter because there is less English for ELs to process at once. Shortening is accomplished by breaking longer sentences into shorter sentences.

Dependent clauses lengthen sentences and add linguistic complexity for English Learners. Revising to reduce dependent clauses improves comprehension.

Sentences often contain extra words or phrases that are not critical to the meaning of the sentence. These extraneous words can be removed, which shortens the sentence and improves comprehension.

Mrs. Chan is reviewing her lesson to "Interpret the connotative power of words." She is looking over her steps for Skill Development and Guided Practice. She wants to revise the steps to make them easier to understand for English Learners.

1. Breaking long sentences into several shorter sentences
2. Simplifying sentences by rearranging and removing some of the dependent clauses

Skill Development

Step 1. Read the sentence, paying close attention to the word that is in boldface.

She sees that Step 1 contains two ideas and includes the dependent clause "that is in boldface." She rewrites the sentence into two shorter sentences and revises to remove the dependent clause.

Step 1: Read the sentence. Pay close attention to the boldface word.

3. Shortening sentences by removing unnecessary information

Looking at Step 2 and Step 3 she realizes that she can shorten them by removing unnecessary information.

Step 2: Underline words ~~in the sentence~~ that give clues about the connotation.

Step 3: Circle the ~~type of~~ connotative feeling: positive or negative.

Controlling Vocabulary

With EDI for English Learners, you purposefully teach new words in *every* lesson (two or three new words for kindergarteners, up to four to seven new words per lesson by high school). Occasionally, if there are too many unknown words, you may need to remove or replace some new words that are not directly related to the new content. This strategy is called Controlled Vocabulary.

We have already talked about the three classifications of vocabulary words: Content, Academic, and Support Vocabulary. English Learners need to be taught the new Content and Academic Vocabulary that is directly related to the lesson. Usually, Support words are the ones to restrict or eliminate. Support words are words students need to understand in order to get meaning from a specific sentence, but the words themselves are not related to the new concepts being taught. Learning the meaning of Support Vocabulary words is not necessary for learning the specific Concepts and Skills you are teaching.

> ***From Silvia:*** In many classrooms, the idea of simplifying text is understood as removing all Academic and Content Vocabulary. Content Vocabulary cannot be removed. Learning new Content Vocabulary is the goal of every lesson, and English Learners need to be taught Academic Vocabulary throughout the school year.

I. EDI-EL Comprehensible Delivery Strategies

C. Controlling Vocabulary Strategy

   1. Deleting and Replacing Unnecessary Words Strategy

- Analyze the lesson for words not related to the purpose of the lesson.
- Delete or replace Support words first and then noncritical Academic words, to limit the number of unknown words.

Here's an example of Controlled Vocabulary.

Mr. Johnson is preparing a language arts lesson. He has his Learning Objective: Identify onomatopoeia. He will not replace the words *identify* (Academic Vocabulary) or *onomatopoeia* (Content Vocabulary). But he is rethinking the sentences he prepared that use onomatopoeia (words that sound like the sound they represent).

He looks over his first sentence.

1. Bees buzz as they fly around collecting pollen.

He sees the word *pollen.* Understanding the meaning of pollen contributes to the comprehension of the sentence about the bees, but it's not related to this lesson's Learning Objective: Identify onomatopoeia. If he were teaching a science lesson, *pollen* could be Content Vocabulary, and he would teach its meaning. But he doesn't want to stop to explain the meaning of *pollen* during this language arts lesson. The word *buzz* is onomatopoeia. He won't eliminate *buzz*. He rewrites the sentence deleting some of the words to control the vocabulary.

Original: 1. Bees buzz as they fly around collecting pollen.

Revised: 1. Bees buzz as they fly around.

He looks at each word in his next example sentence and replaces some of the words.

Original: 2. I like to hum as I do chores around the house.

Revised: 2. I like to hum as I clean the house.

Mr. Johnson studies his two sentences one more time. They still retain the onomatopoeia words *buzz* and *hum*. He has not compromised his Learning Objective whatsoever. In fact, he realizes that onomatopoeia will be easier to teach with his new sentences because he won't need to stop and explain *pollen* or *chores*. All he did was delete some of the Support words.

Cognates

Cognates are words that have a similar spelling, pronunciation, and meaning across two or more languages. The words are similar because they were derived from a common earlier language.

Referring to cognates is particularly helpful for students who speak Latin-based languages, such as Spanish, French, Italian, Portuguese, and Romanian, because many specialized words have common Latin roots. For example, in English the word *compare* shares the same root as the Spanish cognate, *comparar.*

When you are able to use cognates, you are supporting English Learners in using their home language as a resource for learning new academic words in English. Be careful when referring to cognates, however, because it's only effective when your English Learners already know the meaning of the related word in their own language.

From Silvia: Even though cognates have been found to help English Learners, educators need to be careful not to assume that English Learners already know related words in their primary language. For example, the other day, I saw a lesson that dealt with the Water Cycle. The teacher had carefully pre-selected some of the words and their Spanish cognates.

evaporation	evaporación
humid	húmedo
condensation	condensación
precipitation	precipitación
cycle	ciclo

The use of cognates was not successful for most of the English Learners because they did not already know the meaning of many of these cognates in their own language.

I. EDI-EL Comprehensible Delivery Strategies

D. Connecting to Cognates Strategy

1. Identify English words that are cognates.

2. Present the related word in the home language.

To Connect to Cognates, you analyze the lesson looking for opportunities to use cognates for words that English Learners *already* know in their home language. Then you provide the related word in their home language during the lesson.

From Silvia: One drawback to using cognates as an English Learner strategy is that the teacher needs to have some familiarity with the students' home language. Not every teacher can be expected to recognize words that have common roots. Also, it is hard to find cognates in languages that are not Latin-based. Although these languages often have English versions of many words (such as computer terms), these words are not cognates.

Besides identifying cognates for entire words, a related strategy is to use cognates for word parts. Look below and see how Mrs. Gomez does this.

Mrs. Gomez is defining *quadrilateral* during a math lesson. She points to her definition on the board and says, "Students, look at the word *quadrilateral*. The first part *quad* is similar to *cuatro* in Spanish, which means "four." The last part, *lateral* is the same in Spanish, which means "side." Look closely again at *quadrilateral*. It actually means "four sides." In fact, our definition says a quadrilateral is a four-sided figure."

She looks at her next definition: *rhombus*. The Spanish word is *rombo*. She decides not to connect *rhombus* to *rombo* because her students probably have not already been taught the meaning of *rombo*.

Idioms

"Idioms" are expressions in which the meaning of the whole expression has a different meaning from the meanings of the individual words. *It's raining cats and dogs* is an idiom. This idiom is understood by the English-speaking population to mean it is raining a lot. Idioms are difficult for ELs because they cannot use their knowledge of the meanings of the individual words to determine the meaning of the expression.

Defining Idioms as an EL strategy means you stop and define idioms as they come up in a lesson. Idioms might occur in a story students read, or they might be expressions you use yourself while talking.

From Silvia: Someone once told me to avoid using idioms in lessons with English Learners. However, one of our goals with EDI for English Learners—besides teaching grade-level content—is to advance their knowledge and use of English during every lesson. We do this by using words, phrases, and language structures already contained within a lesson. In EDI for English Learners, we don't avoid idioms. We define them as they naturally occur during a lesson.

As a matter of fact, a large proportion of language is not a collection of single words. Perhaps as high as 50% of language is composed of words that appear in multiword units, such as phrasal verbs ("run into"), social routines ("have a nice day"), collocations ("a quick shower"), and idioms ("raining cats and dogs"). English Learners need to be exposed to all of these.

I. EDI-EL Comprehensible Delivery Strategies

   E. Defining Idioms Strategy

      1. Be constantly alert for the use of idioms.

      2. Stop and explain the meaning of idioms when they occur.

Mrs. Harris is teaching a lesson on how to draw inferences. She has the definition written on the board.

An inference is something that you think is true based on the information that you have.

While elaborating on the definition, she adds, "Inferences are not written on the page. You have to figure out what the author is saying. You read between the lines."

She realizes that she has used an idiom and quickly adds an explanation, "Students, the phrase 'read between the lines' doesn't mean you actually look between the lines on the page." She points to the empty space between lines of text on the board and continues, "People use the phrase 'read between the lines' when they want to say that there is more information than just the words that were used."

Pronoun References

Pronoun references can be confusing for ELs. Often just changing pronouns to nouns can increase comprehension for English Learners. "Jose gave the pencil to Mike" is clearer than "He gave it to him." You should also continually use vocabulary words you are teaching, rather than allow pronouns to replace them. This is especially important for definitions. Definitions that use pronouns reduce the connection of the new word to its definition.

I. EDI-EL Comprehensible Delivery Strategies

   F. Replacing Pronouns with Nouns Strategy

      1. Replacing pronouns with nouns to increase clarity

      2. Replacing pronouns with nouns to reinforce use of new vocabulary

      3. Clarifying pronoun references explicitly

When you prepare your own materials, replace pronouns with nouns. Also, replace pronouns with nouns when speaking.

---

1. Replacing pronouns with nouns to increase clarity

Original text: **I** was working on my science project after school when Leanne called. **She wanted me** to go see an early movie with her.

Revised text: **Maria** was working on her science project after school when Leanne called. **Leanne wanted Maria** to go see an early movie with her.

In the example above, even the pronoun *I* was replaced with a name. Now it is easier for English Learners to follow and to analyze. "Maria must decide whether to go to the movies or work on her science project" is easier to discuss than "I (the person in the story) must decide whether to go to the movies or work on my science project."

2. Replacing pronouns with nouns to reinforce use of new vocabulary

A **linear equation** has variables raised to the first power.

It plots as a straight line.

The revision below reinforces the new vocabulary by providing more repetition of the Content Vocabulary *linear equation.*

A **linear equation** has variables raised to the first power.

A **linear equation** plots as a straight line.

The next example was revised for English Learners to increase clarity and the use of Content Vocabulary.

Original: The genes of the new offspring cell are genetically different from the parent cells. **They** have genes from both of **them**.

Revised: The genes of the new offspring cell are genetically different from the parent cells. The **offspring cell** has genes from both **parent cells**.

3. Clarifying pronoun references explicitly

Pronouns occur often in expository and narrative text. Even when you can't change the text, you clarify the pronoun reference orally to improve comprehension for English Learners.

Original text: **Linear equations** have variables raised to the first power. **They** plot as a straight line.

Oral explanation: *Students, "They plot as straight lines" refers to linear equations. So, the second sentence means* linear equations *plot as straight lines. Let's say that together. Linear equations plot as straight lines.*

In the next example, the teacher models the pronoun reference while looking for a context clue.

Original text: **The dress** was gorgeous. **It** was beautiful.

Oral explanation: *Students, I am trying to find out the meaning of the unknown word* gorgeous. *The second sentence gives me a clue. "It" in the second sentence refers to the dress. The second sentence means the dress was beautiful. Now, I have two sentences: The dress was gorgeous. The dress was beautiful. The second sentence shows that "gorgeous" means "beautiful."*

Passive Voice

Active voice means the subject performs the action. *I watched the football game. Passive voice* means the reverse. The subject receives the action. *The football game was watched by me.* Passive voice is often found in expository text, including scientific and technical writing.

Sentences in the passive voice are harder to process by English Learners who are still developing knowledge of English sentence structure. You improve comprehension when you use materials and oral sentences that use the active voice. However, ELs also need to understand passive voice sentence structure when they encounter it. We have two strategies.

I. EDI-EL Comprehensible Delivery Strategies

G. Clarifying Passive Voice Strategy

1. Strategically select or create active voice materials.
2. Explain passive voice when necessary.

1. Strategically select or create active voice materials.

When you are analyzing materials to use in a lesson, select text that is predominantly written in the active voice. It will be easier to understand. Alternatively, you can also change difficult passive voice sentences into active voice.

> Passive Voice: The baby bears were weighed by scientists every day. Then special food was prepared by the zoo keepers. At the end of the week, the growing bears were watched by students.
> Revised Active Voice: Scientists weighed the baby bears every day. Then zoo keepers prepared special food. At the end of the week, students saw the growing bears.

2. Explain passive voice when necessary.

When passive voice—which might be confusing for ELs—occurs during a lesson, stop and explain the sentence meaning.

Students, our definition says "a sentence containing two independent clauses is called a compound sentence."

Students, the words we are defining come at the end of the sentence. I can say this in another way: "A compound sentence contains two independent clauses." Now we have the important information at the beginning of the sentence: "A compound sentence contains two independent clauses."

II. CONTEXT CLUES

So far in this chapter on Content Access Strategies, we have been describing Comprehensible Delivery Strategies. These strategies, such as speaking clearly and controlling word choice, focus on using—and preventing the misunderstanding of—English words that ELs already know. Now, we are ready to discuss strategies you can use to provide meaning for words that ELs don't know, without actually stopping and teaching the meaning of every unknown word.

II. EDI-EL Context Clues Strategies

Increasing ELs' access to content by providing meaning for *unknown* words

    A. Contextualizing Definitions Strategy

    B. Facial Expressions Strategy

    C. Gestures Strategy

    D. Visuals Strategy

    E. Realia Strategy

    F. Analogies, Similes, and Metaphors Strategy

    G. Graphic Organizers Strategy

Information near an unknown word can often be used to figure out the unknown word. The nearby information is the context. Context Clues Strategies address using (or providing) nearby words, phrases, sentences, or other information to determine the meanings of words.

Providing Contextualized Definitions was already one of our vocabulary strategies in Chapter 4 for Support Vocabulary. In this section, we'll use the strategy to reinforce Academic and Content Vocabulary. Then we'll provide additional strategies that use context to provide meaningful information for English Learners.

II. EDI-EL Context Clues Strategies

A. Contextualizing Definitions Strategy (for Academic and Content Vocabulary)

1. Be on the alert for Academic and Content words.
2. Provide nearby contextual definitions.
3. Move on.

Most of the time when using contextualized definitions, you insert a definition as you talk.

Write the literal meaning of the word on line one.

Write the literal meaning of the word, the dictionary meaning, on line one.

Besides definitions, you can provide clarifying information, such as examples.

Felines are mammals.

Felines—such as cats, lions, and tigers—are mammals.

Lessons are more accessible for English Learners when you include additional contextual information that enables them to understand the meaning of the words in a lesson. There are several instances in which contextual definitions can provide meaning for Academic and Content words.

Use Context Clues if There Are Too Many Academic Words in a Lesson

Some Academic Vocabulary should directly be taught in every lesson. However, if there are too many Academic words to teach, contextualize some of them.

The population split into two groups: rural and urban.

The population split into two groups: rural people, who live in the country, and urban people, who live in cities.

Use Context Clues to Support Using a High Level of Academic Vocabulary

Sometimes Academic words are removed to simplify text. However, using Context Clues enables you to maintain a higher level of vocabulary without stripping out all the Academic words. Your Context Clues convey enough information that your students can still understand the gist of what you are saying even if they don't already understand every Academic word you use.

> Academic Vocabulary removed: The Manhattan Project was the American effort during World War II to *make* and *use* nuclear weapons.
>
> Academic Vocabulary reinstated using Context Clues: The Manhattan Project was the American effort during World War II to *develop* and *deploy* nuclear weapons. It was a project to *make* and *use* nuclear weapons.

Use Context Clues to Reinforce New Vocabulary

Context Clues is a great strategy to reinforce the definitions of new Academic and Content Vocabulary you have taught. The repetition helps students remember and provides a bridge while students learn the definitions.

Students, before I add these fractions, I am going to check the denominators, *the numbers on the bottom of the fractions, to see if they are the same.*

Now I want you to look at the denominators, *the numbers on the bottom of the fractions, in Example 2. Are they the same? Can we add the fractions?*

Students, I am going to identify the topic sentence *in the paragraph. I will identify the sentence that tells what the whole paragraph is about.*

Underline the verb, *the action word, in the sentence.*

Vocabulary Development Compared to Context Clues

Vocabulary Development and Context Clues appear to be similar. However, there are some differences. The purpose of Vocabulary Development is to teach students the meaning of specific new words. The primary purpose of Context Clues is to provide enough additional information, without stopping to teach the words, so that students understand the meaning of oral and written sentences. Context Clues also reinforce the definitions of words that have already been explicitly taught.

From Silvia: Another difference between Vocabulary Development and Context Clues is the amount of time involved and the student engagement.

With Vocabulary Development, the teacher provides a definition, and then students interact with the definition. They pair-share and answer Checking for Understanding questions.

Context Clues, on the other hand, are provided by the teacher, who then moves on without any student interaction regarding the word's meaning.

Vocabulary Development is done at the student level so they learn new words. Contextual Clues are done at the teacher level to convey information.

Additional Types of Context Clues

We have talked about using nearby words as Context Clues to provide meaning for unknown words. We can expand that definition to include any nearby information. We can use gestures, facial expressions, realia (real objects), analogies, similes, and metaphors to convey information.

II. EDI-EL Context Clues Strategies

B. Facial Expressions Strategy

  1. Make a facial expression that has universal meaning.

  2. Connect the facial expression to a word.

  3. Have students make the facial expression.

Facial expressions can be used to convey meaning because they are universal among humans. We reveal our emotions with our facial expressions, and we easily understand other people's emotions from their facial expressions. Table 6.1 lists universal emotions and the related facial expressions.

When you use facial expressions, connect them to a specific word. Then have students repeat the gesture.

Mrs. B is in front of the class reading from a short story. She reads, "Hector was *terrified* when the snake slid out from behind the rock." She uses the *fear* facial expression. She suddenly raises her eyebrows, opens her eyes wide, and drops her mouth open. She holds the facial expression for a few seconds. She say, "Students, show me a terrified look." The students show the fear facial expression. Then she continues reading.

II. EDI-EL Context Clues Strategies

C. Gestures Strategy

  1. Provide a description or definition.

  2. Add a gesture that clarifies the meaning.

  3. Have students make the gesture.

Table 6.1 Emotions and Facial Expressions

Emotion	Facial Expression
Happiness	raising and lowering of mouth corners
Sadness	lowering of mouth corners raise inner portion of brows
Surprise	brows arch eyes open wide to expose more light jaw drops slightly
Fear	brows raised eyes open mouth opens slightly
Disgust	Upper lip is raised nose bridge is wrinkled cheeks raised
Anger	brows lowered lips pressed firmly eyes bulging

"Gestures" are movements of the fingers, hands, arms, and shoulders. You can use gestures as visual representations of information you are describing. You provide a description or definition and then make a gesture that illustrates what you just described. It's important that you include a written or oral description so students connect the gesture to specific meaning. If you don't, students can misinterpret the meaning of the gesture and miss the meaning of the information you are presenting. After you've used and explained the gesture, have the students repeat the gesture.

From Silvia: One warning about gestures. Unlike facial expressions, which are universal, gestures—especially some hand gestures—do not always have consistent meanings in different cultures. I don't use gestures that are symbols for ideas. I craft gestures that are a physical representation that conveys information visually about what I am already describing.

Students, perpendicular lines cross at 90 degrees. The teacher raises her arms, crosses them in front of her to show perpendicular lines, and continues, *perpendicular lines cross at 90 degrees. Everyone, hold up your arms like I am and repeat with me, perpendicular lines cross at 90 degrees.*

Gestures Also Function as Cognitive Strategies

Cognitive Strategies are practices you add to lessons to help students remember information. Gestures can also be used as a Cognitive Strategy to help students remember. In many cases, gestures serve a dual role, providing contextual information and serving as a memory aid. To maximize the benefits of gestures, have the students make them with you.

> ***From John:*** I have taught several EDI demo lessons on predictions, what we think will happen in the future. (Wait. I just used a contextual clue. Go back and read the previous sentence. Do you see it? I defined what predictions are in the sentence. This is what makes contextual clues so powerful. The listener—or reader in this case—understands what I am saying even if they don't know every big word.) Back to gestures. Every time I add gestures to my predictions lesson, it makes the information click with the students. Gestures can go beyond providing just meaning. They help students remember. Below is how I use gestures in this lesson.

Students, we use two things to make predictions. We use clues from the text—written words on the page—and prior knowledge—what we already know. Students, look at my hands. We use clues from the text . . . I hold my hands together chest high as if I am reading a book . . . and prior knowledge. I raise both hands up and point to my temples. Students, turn to your partners and tell them what we use to make predictions. And use your arms to show your partners. I am going to call on some of you to tell me, and I want you to say, "To make predictions, we use . . ." Partner B go first this time. Students, I want to see all of your arms up as you talk.

> ***From Silvia:*** When John and I make classroom visits, we distinguish between "talking with your hands," gestures used as Context Clues, gestures used as cognitive strategies, and gestures that serve as both. We do this because we need to discuss the nuances of the specific benefits to the students. Teachers are often told to "use gestures," but gestures are more beneficial to students when they are added to achieve a specific effect—to provide information, to remember information, or both. For ELs, of course, gestures must be coupled with definitions to convey meaning.

> D. Visuals Strategy
>
>   I. Written text
>
>   • Provide a text-based lesson.

Most teachers are familiar with the idea of using visuals for English Learners. However, one of the most important visuals for ELs is *written text.* Interacting with text in every lesson improves reading fluency and facilitates English language acquisition.

There are many opportunities to include text-based visuals in the EDI lessons. The EDI lesson components should always be text based: for example, written Learning Objective, written Concept Definitions, written reasons the lesson is important to learn, and written Skill Development steps.

Other text-based visuals include graphic organizers, semantic maps for text structure, word walls with written definitions, sentence strips, flip charts, and so forth.

> 2. Picture with definition
>
>   • Provide a definition.
>
>   • Show a picture to clarify.

Pictures clarify ideas. However, they need to be presented along with a definition. Students don't always know exactly what to look for in a picture or what it is. In the dirigible example below, if there is no definition, some students looking quickly at the photo might think that a dirigible is another name for a football.

In the story, the two men rode in a dirigible. A "dirigible" is a big balloon that rises up in the air and carries people. There's a picture of a dirigible above. The men rode in the box at the bottom of the dirigible.

II. EDI-EL Context Clues Strategies

E. Realia Strategy

1. Show realia to illustrate concepts and ideas.

"Realia" refers to using real items or objects. Realia such as animal teeth, rocks, flags, and so forth can be used to illustrate and clarify vocabulary and ideas. When you use realia, your students see—and often touch—what you are explaining.

Mrs. Robertson is teaching a science lesson. She reaches down and picks up an object off her desk and says, *Students, we just read the definition of sedimentary rocks. This is a sedimentary rock that I am holding. You can see it has layers.*

She carefully points to the layers while rotating the rock. *I am going to pass this sedimentary rock around so all of you can see it and touch it.* She hands the rock to the student in the first row who slowly turns the rock, looking at the layers, before passing it to the next student.

From Silvia: The EL strategies we are describing here are used to provide meaning for unknown words. It is not necessary to use realia to define English words that students already know. For example, holding up bananas and pencils as realia is only suitable for a beginning English Language Development class.

II. EDI-EL Context Clues Strategies

F. Analogies, Similes, and Metaphors Strategy

1. Connect new words to related known ideas.

Analogies, similes, and metaphors are comparisons that can be used to convey information. For English Learners, these comparisons connect unknown words to ideas they already know.

A radius is a line drawn from the center of a circle to the edge. A radius [new word] *of a circle is like a bicycle spoke* [known idea] *on a bicycle tire. Each bicycle spoke is a radius, going from the center of the tire to the outside edge.*

Mitosis *is the process in which cells divide to make two identical daughter cells. Mitosis* [new word] *is like a photocopying machine* [known idea], *which duplicates papers.*

Students, quotation marks [new words] *are like a book cover* [known information]. *The first quote is the front cover, and the last quote is the back cover.*

Students, during the Cold War the Soviet Union wanted a buffer zone *between them and Western Europe. A buffer zone* [new information] *is an area that provides protection. For example, air bags* [known information] *in a car provide a buffer zone between you and hitting the windshield in a car crash. Well, the Soviets wanted a buffer zone of friendly nations between them and the countries in Western Europe.*

II. EDI-EL Context Clues Strategies

G. Graphic Organizers Strategy

1. Organize to show the relationships between ideas.
2. Include information such as definitions and visuals to convey the meaning of words that are difficult to understand.

Graphic organizers reduce linguistic demands for English Learners because you reduce large amounts of information to key ideas that are placed strategically in an organizer. Graphic Organizers for ELs should provide additional language support by including definitions, contextual information, and pictures (see Table 6.2).

Learning Objective

Describe how plants and animals have levels of organization for structure and function.

Table 6.2 first organizes information as called for in the Learning Objective, including description, structure, and function. The graphic organizer also defines some of the words and provides a visual to help students make meaning of what they are learning. The specific information to fill out

Table 6.2 Plants and Animals Graphic Organizer

		Description (details)	Structure (form)	Function (job)
	Cells			
	Tissues			
	Organs			
Digestive System	Organ Systems			
	Whole Organism			

Source: © 2013 DataWORKS Educational Research.

the organizer—descriptions, structures, and functions of cells, tissues, organs, organ systems, and whole organisms—will be explicitly taught during the lesson.

We just described Context Clues Strategies that focused on providing additional information for unknown words. Now we will talk about strategies for instructional materials that make them more accessible for English Learners.

III. SUPPLEMENTARY MATERIALS AND ADAPTATIONS OF EXISTING MATERIALS

"Supplementary Materials" are *additional* materials that you bring into a lesson. "Adaptations of Existing Materials" refers to modifications you make to your *existing* materials.

Teachers often bring in materials or modify existing materials. Often districts purchase supplemental materials for classroom instruction. However, as an EL strategy, you supplement or adapt for the purpose of making your lesson more accessible *linguistically* for English Learners. This distinction is important. You are modifying to address language. Generally, you make the text more readable, or you provide additional visuals, pictures, manipulatives, realia, or multimedia to clarify English text.

> Teach English Learners grade-level content. Only the linguistic demands of the materials used are reduced.

When you supplement or adapt, you still teach the same lesson. You only reduce the linguistic demands of the materials. You don't reduce the grade level of the lesson or the thinking required in the lesson.

> *From John:* This last idea is so important that I am going to repeat it. Actually, it's one of the premises of this book. You never reduce the grade level of the content you are teaching English Learners. You only address the difficulty of the language you use to teach the lesson.

Let's look at the Supplementary Material and Adaptations of Existing Materials strategies. We have three.

III. EDI-EL Supplementary Materials and Adaptations of Existing Materials

Increasing ELs' access to content by making *text* easier to understand

A. Selecting Text and Passages with Suitable Readability Levels

B. Using Simplified Text

C. Using Elaborated Text

A. Selecting Text and Passages with Suitable Readability Levels

1. Analyze the readability levels of the text.

2. Select text with lower readability level without compromising the intent of the lesson.

Difficult text can be challenging for ELs. You can select easier-to-read materials without compromising the rigor of the content you are teaching. For expository text, select easier-to-read passages that cover the same content. For narratives, use easier-to-read stories that contain the same literary elements you are teaching.

For example, if your Learning Objective is to "Compare characters from two different stories," you can locate two stories that are easier to read. However, you still teach your students to *compare* characters from the two different stories. You don't reduce the lesson from *comparing* characters to *identifying* characters. Remember, English Learners always get the same content. Only the linguistic demands of the materials used are reduced.

Mr. Owen is looking over his high school language arts book list, which also includes each novel's readability level. He knows that readability is based on factors such as average sentence length and average number of syllables per word. It does not reflect the grade level of the students who should read the book. He notes that John Steinbeck's *Of Mice and Men* has a fourth- to fifth-grade readability level. *War and Peace* has a 12th-grade readability. He selects *Of Mice and Men*.

Note: The Common Core standards are using Lexile levels to measure text complexity. Lexile levels of specific books can be used to help select suitable reading materials. Information on Lexiles can be found at www.lexile.com.

Strategies That Make Text Easier to Read and Easier to Understand

We have already talked about strategies that increase comprehension for English Learners—strategies such as controlling the number of new words, shortening and simplifying sentences, restricting use of passive voice, and defining idioms. Now we are going to apply those same strategies to larger reading selections, ranging from paragraphs and passages all the way to entire textbooks.

"Simplified Text" is the term used to describe text that already incorporates the easier-to-understand strategies. When preparing lessons, select passages for ELs that use Simplified Text. You can also use the Simplified Text strategies as criteria for identifying suitable supplemental materials and text book adoptions.

From Silvia: Many textbooks come with simplified text versions of passages to use for re-teaching. Simplified text also works well for an initial EDI lesson to teach a new concept.

III. EDI-EL Supplementary Materials and Adaptations of Existing Materials

B. Using Simplified Text
1. Reduce the quantity of difficult words.
2. Reduce sentence length.
3. Simplify sentences.

Below is original text and simplified text for a science lesson using expository text. Content Vocabulary is retained in both versions. The bold-face words are Academic Vocabulary words (related to the Concept) that will be kept. The underlined words indicate areas for simplification.

Learning Objective

Distinguish between asexual and sexual reproduction.

Original text: Reproduction is the **process** by which plants and animals produce offspring. Reproduction may be asexual or sexual. Asexual reproduction occurs when a **single** cell divides to form two daughter cells that are genetically **identical** to the parent cell. Sexual reproduction <u>involves</u> the <u>union</u> of an egg (female sex cell) and sperm (male sex cell) to <u>produce</u> a cell <u>that is</u> genetically different from the parent cells.

Below is the simplified text version of the same content. Some words are replaced and dependent clauses are rewritten. The content remains the same. Content Vocabulary is retained (reproduction, daughter cells, parent cell, egg, sperm). Academic words closely related to the concept of reproduction are retained (process, single, identical). Academic words not closely related to reproduction are replaced (produce, occurs, form, involves, union). Some long sentences are broken into shorter sentences.

Reproduction is the process plants and animals use to make offspring. Reproduction may be asexual or sexual. In asexual reproduction, one cell divides to make two daughter cells. The daughter cells are genetically the same as the parent cell. In sexual reproduction, an egg (female sex cell) and a sperm (male sex cell) join together to make a new cell. The new offspring cell is genetically different from the parent cells.

Caution: Make sure that simplified text does not remove all the Academic Vocabulary from a lesson. Here's what happened to John when he taught a history lesson.

From John: I taught a history lesson on the Cold War—the state of hostility without actual warfare—between the U.S. and the Soviet Union from the end of World War II until the collapse of the Soviet Union in 1991.

I incorporated a state-released test question for this standard in the lesson. Many students could not answer it at the end of the lesson. Here's why:

During the lesson, I described the Cold War as a war that never had any "direct fighting" between the U.S. and the Soviet Union. The test question used the term "armed conflict." I described how the U.S. wanted to expand capitalism, under which people own the means of production. The Soviets wanted to expand Communism, under which the state owns the means of production. The released question used the phrase "competition for political influence." During the lesson, I stated that the Soviet Union wanted friendly countries between themselves and Europe to reduce the possibility of future invasions. Another released question I studied used the term "defensive buffer zone."

During EDI lessons, you don't teach students the answers to specific sample test questions. (Once released, the question won't be used again.) However, you need to teach and use vocabulary at the level that will be used in test questions.

Below is the sample test question. I have underlined some vocabulary words. This is the level of vocabulary that needs to be incorporated into lessons as part of the two to seven new words defined and taught in every lesson. It's the type of vocabulary you define and use with sentence frames for students to use while pair-sharing and answering questions during lessons.

Which of the following was a <u>primary</u> cause of the <u>Cold War</u> between the United States and the Soviet Union?

A. a <u>*competition*</u> for <u>*political influence*</u> over other countries

B. direct, <u>*armed conflict*</u> between the two nations

C. a deep <u>*reduction*</u> in <u>*military expenditures*</u>

D. the <u>*founding*</u> of the United Nations

Content Vocabulary related to history and the Cold War. Define with written definitions and footnotes.

Cold War

political influence

armed conflict

military expenditures

Academic Vocabulary used across content areas. Define with footnotes and Contextualized Definitions.

primary

competition

reduction

founding

III. EDI-EL Supplementary Materials and Adaptations of Existing Materials

C. Using Elaborated Text

1. Make implicit information explicit.

2. Use clear text structure.

3. Add Context Clues.

Elaborated text—often called "student-friendly text"—clarifies, elaborates, and explains *implicit* information to make it *explicit.* Elaborated text incorporates clear *text structures*—such as main idea and supporting details or compare and contrast—to explicitly show students the relationships between pieces of information. Transition words are used to emphasize relationships or to alert the reader that the next piece of information is coming.

Unlike simplification, elaborated text often adds words and Context Clues to increase comprehension. In practice, most text adaptations involve a combination of simplification and elaboration. For example, you can simplify difficult sentences in text and, at the same time, add Context Clues and additional clarifying information.

Below is elaborated text. The text structure is emphasized by the title and the sentence "There are two types of reproduction: asexual and sexual." The key concepts are identified using boldface. The word *process* is defined with a footnote. The phrases "genetically identical" and "genetically different" are followed by contextualized information.

> **The Differences Between Asexual and Sexual Reproduction**
>
> Reproduction is the process[1] by which plants and animals produce offspring. There are two types of reproduction: asexual and sexual.
>
> In **asexual reproduction,** a single cell divides into two cells. The two cells are called daughter cells. The daughter cells are genetically identical to the parent cell. The daughter cells have the same genes as the parent cell.
>
> In **sexual reproduction,** a male cell and a female cell combine to make a new cell. The two parent cells are an egg (a female sex cell) and a sperm (a male sex cell). The genes of the offspring cell are genetically different from the parent cells. The offspring cell in sexual reproduction has genes from both parent cells.

---

[1]process: steps or method

SUMMARY: CONTENT ACCESS STRATEGIES

We covered three major Content Access Strategies in this chapter. The goal is to increase English Learners' access to grade-level content through the use of strategies that make the English used during a lesson easier to understand.

First, we discussed Comprehensible Delivery: how to make the spoken English more clear and how to make English sentences more understandable.

Second, we covered Context Clues: how to provide and use information near unknown words to facilitate meaning.

And, third, we discussed Supplementary Materials and Adaptations of Existing Materials: strategies that increase ELs' access to content by making text-based English easier to understand and comprehend.

Now we're ready to start creating well-crafted EDI lessons and incorporating EL strategies—Vocabulary Development, Language Objectives, and Content Access Strategies. We'll start in the next chapter.

Below is a list of all the Content Access Strategies that were described in this chapter.

Content Access Strategies to Make English Easier to Understand

I. Comprehensible Delivery

Increasing ELs' access to content by focusing on known words

A. Speaking Clearly Strategies
  1. Speaking slowly.
  2. Using formal register when speaking.
  3. Inserting pauses between words.
  4. Extending vowels.
  5. Stressing consonants.
  6. Emphasizing each syllable.

B. Making Sentences Easier to Understand Strategies
  1. Breaking long sentences into several shorter sentences.
  2. Simplifying sentences by rearranging and removing some of the dependent clauses.
  3. Shortening sentences by removing unnecessary information.

C. Controlling Vocabulary Strategy
  1. Deleting and replacing unnecessary words.

D. Connecting to Cognates Strategy
  1. Identify English words that are cognates.
  2. Present the related word in the home language.

E. Defining Idioms Strategy
  1. Be constantly alert for the use of idioms.
  2. Stop and explain the meaning of idioms when they occur.

F. Replacing Pronouns with Nouns Strategy
  1. Replacing pronouns with nouns to increase clarity.
  2. Replace pronouns with nouns to reinforce use of new vocabulary.
  3. Clarifying pronoun references explicitly.

G. Clarifying Passive Voice Strategy

    1. Strategically select or create active voice materials.

    2. Explain passive voice when necessary.

II. Context Clues

Increasing ELs' access to content by providing meaning for *unknown* words

A. Contextualizing Definitions Strategy

    1. Be on the alert for Academic and Content words.

    2. Provide nearby contextual definitions.

    3. Move on.

B. Facial Expressions Strategy

    1. Make a facial expression that has universal meaning.

    2. Connect the facial expression to a word.

    3. Have students make the facial expression.

C. Gestures Strategy

    1. Provide a description or definition.

    2. Add a gesture that clarifies the meaning.

    3. Have students make the gesture.

D. Visuals Strategy

    1. Written text

    2. Picture with definition

E. Realia Strategy

    1. Show realia to illustrate concepts and ideas.

F. Analogies, Similes, and Metaphors Strategy

    1. Connect new words to related known ideas.

G. Graphic Organizers Strategy

    1. Organize to show the relationships between ideas.

    2. Include information such as definitions and visuals to convey the meaning of words that are difficult to understand.

III. Supplementary Materials and Adaptations of Existing Materials

Increasing ELs' access to content by making *text* easier to understand

A. Selecting Text and Passages with suitable readability levels

    1. Analyze the readability levels of the text.

    2. Select text with lower readability level without compromising the intent of the lesson.

B. Using Simplified Text

   1. Reduce the quantity of difficult words.

   2. Reduce sentence length.

   3. Simplify sentences.

C. Using Elaborated Text

   1. Make implicit information explicit.

   2. Use clear text structure.

   3. Add Context Clues.

Part III

Integrating Strategies for English Learners Into EDI Lessons

7 How to Present a Learning Objective to English Learners

Remember our discussion from Chapter 2? English Learners learn in the same manner as native English speakers. They first need a well-crafted lesson. Then you add EL strategies to your well-crafted lesson. Since English Learners are in the process of learning English, you add Language Objectives (Listening, Speaking, Reading, and Writing) and Vocabulary Development (two to seven new words in every lesson), and use Content Access Strategies to make the English you use in the lesson easier to understand.

In the next few chapters, we will describe how to teach the well-crafted lesson, describing each EDI lesson design component while incorporating EL strategies, but first a note about using text.

PROVIDE TEXT-BASED LESSONS FOR ENGLISH LEARNERS

Reading academic text is especially beneficial for English Learners to support their language acquisition and reading fluency. English Learners need to see, read, and interact with academic text every day in every lesson in every content area.

> English Learners need to see, read, and interact with academic text every day in every lesson in every content area.

EDI lessons for English Learners are always text-based lessons—not just the passages ELs read, but the lesson itself. For example, the Learning Objective, Concept Definitions, lesson Importance, and Skill Development strategic steps are always presented visually as text. You can project them using PowerPoint, a document camera, or an overhead projector, or you can write directly on a flip chart or the board. The important part is that your students— from kindergarten to 12th grade—interact with written academic text.

Ideally, students have their own copy of the text that matches word for word what the teacher is using. Besides supporting reading fluency, having their copy of important parts of the lesson text provides a resource to refer to during and after a lesson. Oral presentations only allow ELs one chance to get it.

Now back to our EDI lesson components. We are starting with the Learning Objective.

LEARNING OBJECTIVE

A Learning Objective is a written statement describing what your students will be able to do successfully and independently by the end of a specific lesson as a direct result of your teaching. Notice that last part: "as a direct result of your teaching." With EDI, you are explicitly and directly teaching students exactly how to do something. Here are some Learning Objectives.

Language Arts

Retell familiar stories, including key details.

Explain how authors use reasons and evidence to support points in a text.

Determine the connotative meaning of words as used in a text.

Provide an accurate summary of text distinct from prior knowledge or opinions.

Math

Add mixed numbers.

Solve word problems involving money.

Graph exponential and logarithmic functions.

Science

Describe the properties of rocks (hardness, luster, color).

Describe the causes of genetic disorders.

Calculate density.

Social Science

Describe the early explorations of the Americas.

Describe the 13th, 14th, and 15th Amendments and analyze their connection to Reconstruction.

Describe the effects of the major battles of World War II.

Learning Objectives come directly from content standards. In fact, content standards themselves are a collection of Learning Objectives. Here's a standard from the Common Core first-grade standards:

Describe characters, settings, and major events in a story, using key details.

Many standards contain multiple Objectives, so the standards are deconstructed into Learning Objectives for specific lessons. There are three Learning Objectives in the standard above.

1. Describe characters in a story, using key details.

2. Describe settings in a story, using key details.

3. Describe major events in a story, using key details.

These three Objectives could be taught individually or combined. For example, characters and setting could be taught in one lesson. A culminating lesson could combine all three. Breaking standards into individual, teachable Learning Objectives such as these is called "deconstructing the standards."

Skills, Concepts, and Context

Content standards and Learning Objectives contain specific components: Skills, Concepts, and sometimes a Context.

A "Skill" is something done (an action). In EDI lessons, Skills are described using measurable verbs such as *identify, describe, compare and contrast, analyze, critique, solve, calculate,* and so forth.

A "Concept" is something known (an idea). Concepts are the main ideas in a lesson. Concepts are usually described using nouns such as *theme, point of view, figurative language, fraction, quadrilateral, density, mitosis, Manifest Destiny, supply and demand,* and *Great Depression.*

Some standards contain a "Context," which is a limiting condition or is a specific method of executing a standard. Examples of a Context include "in expository text," "in poetry," "by graphing." When standards include a Context, make sure you use the proper methodology or the proper instructional materials so you match the intent of the standard.

Although Concepts are usually described using nouns, verbs can occasionally be used to describe Concepts, such as in this kindergarten standard: *Add by counting objects.* This standard's Concept is not *objects.* The Concept to teach is *addition. Students, addition means finding out how much we have altogether.* The Context—the method of adding—is "by counting objects."

In the Common Core Learning Objectives shown below, the *Skill* is in italics, the **CONCEPT** is in bold uppercase, and the Context is underlined.

Compare and contrast the overall **TEXT STRUCTURE** of information in two or more texts.

Determine the meaning of **FIGURATIVE LANGUAGE** in poetry or drama.

Solve **QUADRATIC EQUATIONS** by completing the square.

Find the **AREA OF A RECTANGLE** with whole number side lengths by tiling (placing tiles over the rectangle and counting the number of tiles to determine the area).

In the example below, the Skill and the Concept are interrelated. The Concept is "what adding mixed numbers represents," and the Skill is the algorithm used to add the mixed numbers.

ADD MIXED NUMBERS with like denominators.

Learning Objectives Are Important

Clear Learning Objectives drive an entire lesson and make it coherent. First, they define the purpose of a lesson. For example, if the Objective is

"Describe the setting in a story," you now have a purpose for the entire lesson. You have boundaries for what to teach and what not to teach. During Concept Development, you teach students what a setting is. During Skill Development, you provide a methodology to identify and describe the setting. You model identifying and describing the setting in a passage yourself, and then you guide your students in identifying and describing the setting in a different passage. You strategically select passages or stories that have clearly defined settings so there are plenty of examples to use during the lesson and for Independent Practice afterward.

Another reason it's important to use clear Learning Objectives is to make sure the Independent Practice your students complete at the end of the lesson matches the Objective. You may need to modify the Independent Practice or be selective and only use the parts that match the Objective. In essence, you're checking that you are not asking students to do something that you did not teach them.

> Make sure the Independent Practice your students complete at the end of the lesson matches the Objective.

Third, clearly written Objectives ensure that lessons are on grade level, matching a grade-level standard. This may be the most important reason for ELs—teaching on grade level provides equal opportunity to learn for English Learners when they are taught new grade-level concepts and skills each year. Also, ELs who are not taught on grade level have a difficult time answering grade-level test questions.

As schools across the country implement the Common Core State Standards, it will become even more important to teach on grade level to provide equal access for English Learners to participate in the new standards and to include them on the path of success in life and career.

Fourth, having clear Learning Objectives prevents lessons from becoming activities. For example, they redirect a lesson away from "Today, we will use manipulatives" toward a standards-based Objective such as "Today, we will identify place value using manipulatives." Clear Objectives refocus the purpose of the lesson away from "Answer the questions at the end of the chapter" to "Analyze the author's use of figurative language in expository text."

Finally, Learning Objectives are important because they focus the students' attention when presented to the class. Your reading of the Objective, followed by students' choral reading, directs students' attention to the lesson and displaces other distractions they might be thinking about at the beginning of class.

> ***From John:*** This idea of having a Learning Objective to direct classroom teaching is very, very important. In fact, when Silvia and I conduct classroom observations, one question we ask is "What is the Learning Objective?" If the observers cannot determine the Learning Objective from watching the teaching, the lesson is usually not effective. And just having an Objective written on the board is not enough.

HOW TO PRESENT A LEARNING OBJECTIVE TO ENGLISH LEARNERS

Now we're going to go over how to present a Learning Objective. You aren't teaching the content yet, just presenting the Objective to your students so they know what it is and so they can read and pronounce the new words. Students learn the full meaning of the Objective over the course of the lesson.

While presenting the Objective, you intentionally incorporate EL Language Objectives (Listening, Speaking, and Reading), Vocabulary Development, and EL Content Access Strategies (slow speech, clear enunciation).

The presentation of the Learning Objective sets the stage for the lesson and provides the initial Listening, Speaking, and Reading for ELs. Let's go over the steps.

How to Present a Learning Objective to English Learners

Using a written Learning Objective,

1. Teacher pre-teaches.
   - **Teach pronunciation** of difficult-to-pronounce words. (EL Listening and Speaking)
   - **Define** Academic Vocabulary embedded in the Learning Objective (but not the Concept itself, which is explicitly defined during Concept Development). (EL Vocabulary Development)

2. **Teacher pre-reads** the Objective slowly with clear enunciation while students look at the words. (EL Listening and Reading)

3. **Students chorally read** the Objective. (EL Speaking and Reading)

4. **Pair-share.** Students read the Objective to each other. (EL Listening, Speaking, and Reading)

5. **Check for Understanding.** Students state or read the Objective. (EL Speaking and Reading)

Presenting the Learning Objective using only Steps 2 through 5 works much of the time: (2) teacher pre-reads the Objective, (3) students chorally read the Objective, (4) pair-share—students read the Objective to each other, and (5) Check for Understanding—non-volunteers state the Objective. These steps incorporate multiple Listening, Speaking, and Reading opportunities. However, you can add more language support for ELs by including Step 1, the pre-teach.

During the pre-teach, you teach ELs how to pronounce and read new or difficult words in the Objective, words such as *cite, analyze, evidence, character, fraction, irrational numbers, Pythagorean Theorem, photosynthesis,* and so forth. Use one of the EDI-EL Language Strategies such as Backwards Syllabication or Connect to Known Sounds. If necessary, add a Check for Understanding for pronunciation by calling on non-volunteers to pronounce difficult words.

The Learning Objective pre-teach is also an opportunity to define any new Academic Vocabulary words contained in the Learning Objective. (Warning: Don't define Concepts while presenting the Learning Objective. Concepts are explicitly taught during Concept Development with written definitions followed by examples and non-examples and extensive Checking for Understanding questions.)

Start by showing a written Learning Objective that ELs can see. (EDI-EL Visuals: Written Text) You can use PowerPoint or write the Objective on the board.

We are going to show four examples of presenting Learning Objectives. Read them carefully. There is a rhythm to teaching English Learners—pronouncing words, defining words, pre-reading, choral reads, pair-shares, Checking for Understanding. We'll build upon this basic technique later in the lesson as you teach new content.

> **From John:** I taught a demo lesson during which the observing teachers wrote down each strategy I used. When their turn came to teach, they had a hard time following all their detailed notes. Suddenly, one teacher "got it" and exclaimed, "There's a rhythm to this. I don't need all these notes."

Now let's listen to Silvia describe how she presents a Learning Objective, starting with the pronunciation and vocabulary pre-teach.

Learning Objective Example 1

1. Teacher pre-teaches.

   A. Teach pronunciation of difficult-to-pronounce words. (EL Listening and Speaking)

> B. Define Academic Vocabulary embedded in the Learning Objective (but not the Concept itself, which is explicitly defined during Concept Development). (EL Vocabulary Development)

Learning Objective ▶

Today, we will interpret[1] idioms.

1 interpret—explain the meaning of something

CFU ▶

What are we going to do today?

EDI always uses text-based lessons so ELs can see and work with text. I've used PowerPoint, overhead transparencies, sentence strips, flip charts, and document cameras. In this lesson, I use PowerPoint with matching handouts for students. As I walk in, the students are sitting in widely spaced rows, so I have the students slide their desks together to facilitate pair-shares.

I start with a pre-teach for pronunciation. Looking at the Objective, I anticipate that ELs might misread *idioms* using a long *i* sound, as *eye-dioms*. As a Spanish speaker myself, I understand how some Spanish-speaking English Learners might use a Spanish vowel pronunciation, *ee-dioms*. I use the EDI-EL Connect to Known Sounds Strategy. I grab a marker and write *idiot* on the board and point to it.

Students, you already know how to read this word, idiot.

I don't like using the word *idiot* in the classroom. However, it is a perfect spelling and sound match, and students probably already know the word.

I point to the word *idiom* in the Learning Objective on the PowerPoint screen.

Our new word, idiom, *does not mean "idiot," but has the same sound at the beginning of the word. Listen, idiot, idiom. Let's say both words: idiot, idiom. Now just our new word, idiom. Say idiom two more times. Idiom, idiom.*

I don't define *idiom* while presenting the Learning Objective. *Idiom* is the lesson's Concept. I'll teach its meaning during Concept Development. I'm only teaching how to read and pronounce *idiom* during the Learning Objective.

The Academic word *interpret* first shows up in the lesson during the Learning Objective. I define it now, starting with Listening and Speaking. I know students sometimes mispronounce *interpret* as *interpert*. I pre-empt this by emphasizing the correct pronunciation using the EDI-EL Stressing Consonants Strategy. I say *interpret*. I have students imitate and repeat after me.

Now I define *interpret*. *Interpret* is a multiple-meaning word. ELs probably already know interpret as "translate from one language to another," so I use the EDI-EL Multiple-Meaning Words Strategy. In the paragraph below, I use strikethrough to show where I use the EDI-EL Replace Pronouns With Nouns to Increase Clarity Strategy.

Students, look at this word, interpret. *You may already know that* ~~it~~ *"interpret" means to translate from one language to another. For example, when you interpret for someone, you might translate sentences from English to Spanish.*

Interpret has a new meaning in today's lesson.

I point to the definition, read it, and then follow with an example.

"Interpret" means to explain the meaning of something. For example, when you interpret a drawing, you explain the meaning of ~~it~~ *the drawing. So in today's lesson, when we interpret idioms, we will explain what* ~~they~~ *idioms mean.*

I could ask the students the definition of *interpret,* and they would read the definition back to me. I can only spend a couple of minutes here, but I want a higher-order question.

What would be another way of saying, "I am going to explain the meaning of a poem" using our new word interpret?

I have students pair-share, telling their sentence to their partners, and I call on a few non-volunteers.

I've pre-taught how to read and say *idiom* and *interpret.* I taught the definition of the Academic word, *interpret.* I'm ready to read the Objective.

> **2. Teacher pre-reads the Objective slowly with clear enunciation while students look at the words. (EL Listening and Reading)**

The second step in presenting a Learning Objective is for the teacher to read the entire Objective while having students *look* at the words as they're being read. You do this by directing your students to track the words on a handout with their fingers as you read (EDI-EL Tracked Choral Reading Strategy). If there is no handout, have your students look up at the board. Point to each word as you read, so students are connecting oral words to printed, written words. For young students, you can use "air tracking": they point to the words on the board as you read them.

Your pre-reading needs to be done slowly so you are not reading faster than students' decoding rate. If you read too fast, students are not following the individual words. You want your students to be looking at each word as you say it.

When you present a Learning Objective, include EDI-EL Content Access Strategies. Use a formal register (analyzing, not analyzin') while speaking, enunciating clearly and not slurring words together. Extend vowels, stress consonants, and emphasize each syllable in new words. Read the exact words that are in the Objective so ELs connect oral words to the written words.

Students, track on your page while I read the Objective. Look at your partner. Everyone's finger should be on the word today. Track and listen. Today, we will interpret idioms.

3. Students chorally read the Objective. (EL Speaking and Reading)

After the teacher reads the Objective, students read it chorally. If the words are difficult, have students read the Objective more than once to practice. If the text is easy, just read it once.

Students, let's read together. Today, we will interpret idioms.

4. Pair-share. Students read the Objective to each other. (EL Listening, Speaking, and Reading)

Direct students to read the Objective to their partner. Cue the listening partner to follow along, checking the words.

Read the Learning Objective to your partner. Partner A go first. Partner B follow the words on your page. Then switch.

5. Check for Understanding. Students state or read the Objective. (EL Speaking and Reading)

Call on non-volunteers to read the Objective. The class is pre-paired. You have taught them how to read and say the words. They have practiced chorally and in pair-shares.

Remember, you are only asking students to read the Learning Objective at this point. You aren't asking students about the meanings of the Concepts in the Objective.

I am going to select someone to tell me what we are going to do today. What is our Learning Objective?

Now, John will describe how he recently presented a language arts Learning Objective.

Learning Objective Example 2

I. Teacher pre-teaches

    A. Teach pronunciation of difficult-to-pronounce words. (EL Listening and Speaking)

    B. Define Academic Vocabulary embedded in the Learning Objective (but not the Concept itself, which is explicitly defined during Concept Development). (EL Vocabulary Development)

Learning Objective

Today, we will distinguish[1] among the connotative meaning of words with similar denotations.

1 distinguish—tell the difference between

CFU

What are we going to do today?

There are three new words in this Learning Objective that might be difficult for English Learners: distinguish, connotative, and denotations. I preteach, starting with Listening, Speaking, and Reading. I step toward the screen and point to the word *distinguish.*

Students, look up here where I am pointing.

I want students to be looking at new words while pronouncing them so they are developing printed word recognition, not just pronunciation.

I use EDI-EL Content Access Strategies: Slow Speech, Extended Vowels, and Stressed Consonants. I slow my rate of speech as I switch between giving directions ("Look up here.") to providing content. I use the EDI-EL Word Chunking Strategy for the word *distinguish.* The oral chunking syllables (dis-sting-gwish) are a better representation of the actual pronunciation than the spelling syllables (dis-tin-guish).

As I say *distinguish,* I drag out the vowels and emphasize the consonants, *dis-sting-gwish.* I repeat *distinguish* so students can hear it multiple times, and then I have them say it chorally.

Students, this word is distinguish. *Listen carefully: dis-sting-gwish, dis-sting-gwish. Let's say it together. Disstinggwish.*

I saw that some of you did not say distinguish. *We will all say it again. Ready? Distinguish. Again. Distinguish.*

I repeat until all students are participating. This is an effective classroom management practice.

Connotative and *denotation* are the new Concepts. I'll teach them during Concept Development with definitions, examples and non-examples, and Checking for Understanding questions. *Distinguish,* however, is Academic Vocabulary. I have already identified *distinguish* as a word to teach. The meaning of *distinguish* can't be defined with a one-word synonym, so I use the EDI-EL Vocabulary Definition Strategy.

Students, if you look on your page you will see a footnote with the definition of distinguish. Distinguish means "to tell the difference between."

After having the students read the definition, I elaborate, generalizing the definition to other situations.

For example, I can distinguish between a pencil and a marking pen. I can tell the difference between them.

I need a Checking for Understanding question. I include a sentence frame.

Students, tell your partner what distinguish means. I want you to say, "The word distinguish *means . . ." Partner "A" go first.* The students turn to their partners and repeat the definition.

I don't call on any of the students. Instead, I have the students apply the definition. This will also help them generalize the meaning of the word.

Students, I want you to use distinguish *in your own sentence that shows you know its meaning. Here's a sample sentence: I can distinguish between cats and dogs because dogs bark and cats meow. Create your own sentence using* distinguish. *Tell your partners and be ready to tell me. Partner "B" go first, then "A."*

I wait while all students tell their partners their sentences. Then I reach into my can of Popsicle sticks with student names. I pull a stick to select a non-volunteer.

Nicole, tell me your sentence.

Nicole: *I can distinguish between my backpack and my sister's backpack. My backpack is green. Hers is yellow.*

I use the EDI-EL Contextualized Definitions Strategy to reinforce the meaning of distinguish.

Good job. You can distinguish, or tell the difference between, the two backpacks.

I call on one more student to respond.

For *connotative* I start with the EDI-EL Connect to Known Sounds Strategy, showing students that *native* is a word they already know that sounds like *connotative.* I have students say *native* and *connotative.*

I use the same strategy for *denotations,* which has the ending sound of *ation.* I have the students say *nation, denotation.* I then add the plural *denotations* (EDI-EL Inflectional Endings Buildup Strategy). I have the students pair-share, pointing to *connotative* and *denotations* and reading the words to their partners (EL Listening, Speaking, and Reading).

> 2. Teacher pre-reads the Objective slowly with clear enunciation while students look at the words. (EL Listening and Reading)

Students, follow along on your handout as I read. I slow my rate of speech. *Today, we will distinguish among the connotative meaning of words with similar denotations.*

> 3. Students chorally read the Objective. (EL Speaking and Reading)

Everyone read. Today, we will distinguish among the connotative meaning of words with similar denotations.

> 4. Pair-share. Students read the Objective to each other. (EL Listening, Speaking, and Reading)

Read the Objective to your partner. "B" partner, go first. Check that your partner is pronouncing the words correctly.

> 5. Check for Understanding. Students state or read the Objective. (EL Speaking and Reading)

I pull sticks for two non-volunteers to read the Objective to the class. The second student stumbles on the word *denotations.* I have the entire class repeat the word twice and ask him to read the Objective again (EDI-EL Implicit Language Correction Strategy).

My students now have the Learning Objective and the words *distinguish, connotative,* and *denotations* in their working memories and are ready to continue the lesson. The presentation of a Learning Objective usually takes less than two minutes. This one took a little longer because of the pre-teaching.

Here's a math example. You can hear the rhythm: Pre-pronouncing words, defining vocabulary, pre-reading, choral reads, pair-shares, Checking for Understanding.

Learning Objective Example 3

> 1. Teacher pre-teaches
>
> A. Teach pronunciation of difficult-to-pronounce words. (EL Listening and Speaking)
>
> B. Define Academic Vocabulary embedded in the Learning Objective (but not the Concept itself, which is explicitly defined during Concept Development). (EL Vocabulary Development)

> **Learning Objective**
>
> Today, we will apply the Pythagorean Theorem to solve real-world problems[1]
>
> 1 real-world problems—problems that could happen on the job or in life
>
> **CFU**
>
> What is our Objective?
>
> What are we going to solve today and how?

Pronunciation

Teach ELs how to pronounce the words *Pythagorean Theorem* before reading the Learning Objective. You can use the EDI-EL Backwards Syllabication and Stress Consonants strategies.

Students, this word is "Pythagorean." The last part is orean; *say* orean, orean. *The first part is* pythag. *Say* pythag. *Now let's say the whole word: Pythag-orean. Pythagorean.*

Students, this word is "theorem." Listen carefully. It has an m *on the end of the word, theorem. Say theorem. Theorem.*

Now, say Pythagorean Theorem to your partner twice.

Vocabulary Development

The word *apply* is Academic vocabulary that first shows up in this lesson in the Learning Objective. Teach ELs its meaning while presenting the Learning Objective. Since *apply* has an easy synonym, use the EDI-EL Synonym Strategy including the EDI-EL Cross-Reference the Brain Strategy to help students remember. Contextualize the meaning of *apply* after defining it, in order to reinforce the definition.

Students, this word is "apply." Let's read this word together. Apply. The word apply *means "use." So, today's Objective means we will use the Pythagorean Theorem. I want you to remember the meaning of "apply." When I say "apply," you say "use." When I say "use," you say "apply." Apply, use. Use, apply. Apply, use. Today, we will apply, or use, the Pythagorean Theorem.*

The word *theorem* first shows up in this lesson in the Learning Objective. (In math, a theorem is a math statement that can be proven to be true.) However, in this case, the definition would be more meaningful if defined during Concept Development, where the formula representing the Pythagorean Theorem could be referred to. In this case, define *theorem* during Concept Development.

The phrase *real-world problems* is defined during the Learning Objective.

Students, you can see the definition for "real-world problems" in the footnote below the Learning Objective. Let's read the definition together.

Real-world problems: problems that could happen on the job or in life. So today's problems will not be just math problems. They will represent problems that could occur out of school, at a job, or when you build or design something."

> 2. Teacher pre-reads the Objective slowly with clear enunciation while students look at the words. (EL Listening and Reading)

Read the Learning Objective using EDI-EL Comprehensible Delivery Strategies such as Speaking Slowly, Inserting Pauses Between Words, and Emphasizing Each Syllable.

Students, track while I read. Today, we will apply the Pythagorean Theorem to solve real-world problems.

> 3. Students chorally read the Objective. (EL Speaking and Reading)

Students, your turn to read. Go. Today, we will apply the Pythagorean Theorem to solve real-world problems.

> 4. Pair-share. Students read the Objective to each other. (EL Listening, Speaking, and Reading)

Students, read the Objective to your partner. Partner B, go first.

> 5. Check for Understanding. Students state or read the Objective. (EL Speaking and Reading)

What are we going to do today? I am going to call on two people to read the Objective.

In the next example, Silvia uses the EDI-EL Initial Letter Sounds Reading Strategy to present a kindergarten Learning Objective. She supports emergent readers by having her students use letter sounds they already know.

> *From Silvia:* The Common Core State Standard for my kindergarten lesson is "With prompting and support, identify characters, settings and major events in a story." I deconstruct the standard and will only teach setting during this lesson. I do not include the words "with prompting and support" in my Objective presented to the students. These words are the Objective's Context—in this case, directions for the teacher, for me.

For the stories, I use several short excerpts of two to three sentences with some picture support. The goal is to interact with the text, not just use the pictures.

The kindergarteners are sitting on the carpet in front of me. The Learning Objective is written on poster board placed on an easel on my right side.

Learning Objective Example 4

> ### Learning Objective
>
> Identify[1] setting in a story.
>
> I identify—look for
>
> ### CFU
>
> What are we going to do today?

I point to the *s* alphabet card on the wall and start with Listening and Speaking.

Students, this is the letter s. *What letter is this? The students respond:* s.

Look up on the wall, students. Here is Sammy the Snake on the s *card. The letter* s *makes the /s/ sound. Let's all hiss like a snake and say the* s *sound, /s/.* The students smile while hissing like snakes.

I point to the letter *s* at the beginning of the word *setting* in the Learning Objective.

All eyes up here. Students, this is the letter s. *What sound does it make?* The students all hiss again.

I use the EDI-EL Stress Consonants Strategy for the consonant *s.* I purposefully stress the *s* sound while speaking.

Students, this word is sssetting. It starts with the /s/ sound. Listen again, sssetting. Let's all say this word, sssetting.

Now, I am going to read the entire sentence.

I use the EDI-EL Tracked Choral Reading Strategy and have the kinders Air Track.

Students, point up here at each word and listen while I read.

I wait a moment until all students are pointing. I read very slowly while pointing individually to each word and emphasizing the *s* sound.

Identify . . . sssetting . . . in . . . a . . . ssstory. Listen again. Identify . . . sssetting . . . in . . . a . . . ssstory.

I use the EDI-EL Contextualized Definitions Strategy for the meaning of *identify.*

Students, the word identify *means "look for." So, today we will identify, or look for, the setting in a story.*

I add a gesture (EDI-EL Gestures Strategy). I curl my fingers on both hands, raising them to my eyes like binoculars and repeat.

Today, we will identify setting in a story. Students, put your hands up like mine and let's read our Objective one more time. The students raise their hands.

I cue a couple of students to use their hands. The students and I read together as I point to the words.

Today we will identify setting in a story.

I have the students tell the Learning Objective to each other.

Students, turn to your partners. Partner A, tell Partner B what we are going to do today.

After waiting a few moments,

Now, partner B tell partner A.

I am ready to call on non-volunteers to tell me the Objective.

In the classroom, proficient readers can always refer to a written Objective to answer the CFU question "What are we going to do today?" However, emergent readers cannot read well enough to refer to the text. In these cases, when students can only recall part of the Objective, I have them repeat the entire Objective after me while I point to the words.

I call on the first non-volunteer student.

Student: *Identify setting.*

I elaborate: *That's right. We will identify setting in a story.*

One student responds with only one word: setting. I echo the entire Objective again and ask her to repeat with me.

Identify setting in a story.

SUMMARY: HOW TO PRESENT A LEARNING OBJECTIVE TO ENGLISH LEARNERS

How to Present a Learning Objective to English Learners

Using a written Learning Objective,

1. Teacher pre-teaches.

- **Teach pronunciation** of difficult-to-pronounce words. (EL Listening and Speaking)
- **Define** Academic Vocabulary embedded in the Learning Objective (but not the Concept itself, which is explicitly defined during Concept Development). (EL Vocabulary Development)

2. **Teacher pre-reads** the Objective slowly with clear enunciation while students look at the words. (EL Listening and Reading)

3. **Students chorally read** the Objective. (EL Speaking and Reading)

4. **Pair-share.** Students read the Objective to each other. (EL Listening, Speaking, and Reading)

5. **Check for Understanding.** Non-volunteers state or read the Objective. (EL Speaking and Reading)

We have described how to present an EDI Learning Objective with embedded Language Objectives and Vocabulary Development. We emphasized teaching grade-level lessons for English Learners. We laid out some of the basic lesson delivery principles of *EDI for English Learners,* including pre-pronouncing words, embedded Vocabulary Development, teacher pre-reading of text, student choral reading, pair-shares, and Checking for Understanding. These practices are used throughout EDI lessons.

We're ready to go to the next chapter, How to Activate Prior Knowledge for English Learners, where you connect something students already know to the new content you are going to teach them.

Note: The Appendices contain additional important information. Appendix F discusses teaching English Learners on grade level. Appendix G describes creating standards-based pacing guides, and Appendix H describes how to design standards-based Learning Objectives.

8 How to Activate Prior Knowledge for English Learners

Now we're ready for the second component of a well-crafted lesson. When you Activate Prior Knowledge (APK) during an EDI lesson, you explicitly reveal a connection between something your English Learners already know and what you are going to teach them in the new lesson. What you're really doing is moving some information from students' long-term memory into their working memory. Now it's available to build upon.

Students, today we are going to identify complex sentences. Before we start, I want to review a type of sentence we already know: compound sentences.

EDI lessons include Activating Prior Knowledge to facilitate the brain's natural tendency to build upon, or connect to, something already known and contained in long-term memory. Students might not recognize the connection between what they already know and what they are going to learn, so you do it for them. You explicitly retrieve pertinent information from students' long-term memory and place it into their working memory, ready to use during the lesson. When students don't have prior knowledge, you quickly provide some.

There are two methods to Activate Prior Knowledge: Subskill Review and Universal Experience. No matter which method you select, Activating Prior Knowledge should be limited to about five minutes so the bulk of the lesson is spent on the *new* learning.

Activate Prior Knowledge is a long phrase to say over and over, so we often just shorten it to APK.

ACTIVATE PRIOR KNOWLEDGE WITH A SUBSKILL REVIEW

A Subskill Review is a re-teaching of something academic learned at school. In EDI you don't *quiz* students to see whether they remember something taught at school in the past; you *re-teach* it. Students then answer Checking for Understanding questions about the information you just provided.

Students often have various gaps in their academic knowledge. You don't need to address all of the gaps at once. During a Subskill Review, you identify specific information pertinent to the new lesson and quickly re-teach it to help students be successful during the new lesson.

Students, before we start using syllabication rules, let's review vowels and consonants.

Generally, computational-based lessons such as mathematics (and some science lessons) use a Subskill Review to re-teach a *specific* subskill that students will use later while solving problems during Skill Development. Following the Subskill Review, the remainder of the lesson concentrates on the new learning.

Students, before we multiply two-digit numbers by two-digit numbers, let's review regrouping when multiplying two-digit numbers by one-digit numbers. Watch while I work a problem.

For some students, the Subskill Review triggers their memory on how to do something they were taught in the past. For other students, the APK Subskill Review serves as a mini remediation session so they can participate in the new lesson.

The Subskill Review itself can be below grade level. That's fine. You only spend about five minutes during APK. It's a quick re-teach of a specific subskill used in the new lesson. The bulk of the lesson focuses on teaching the new grade-level content.

And remember, Activating Prior Knowledge is not an assessment to measure whether students remember something from the past. Generally, you work a problem first to remind students how to do it, and then you have the students work a matching problem. We call this the "Rule of Two," which will be used extensively during Skill Development and Guided Practice.

The box on page 166 describes how to Activate Prior Knowledge for English Learners using a Subskill Review.

How to Activate Prior Knowledge for English Learners Using a Subskill Review

1. **Identify a subskill** (or something previously taught at school) that prepares students for the new lesson.

2. **Teacher works a problem first.** Include reading. (EL Reading, Content Access Strategies: Slow, Clear Speech)

3. **Optional Pair-share, Check for Understanding.** If the problem is difficult, have students pair-share and ask non-volunteers to describe how the problem was solved. If the problem is simple, omit CFU to speed up APK. (EL Listening and Speaking)

4. **Students work matching problem** (whiteboards).

5. **Non-optional Pair-share. Check for Understanding.** Students explain to each other how they solved the problem. Call on non-volunteers. (EL Listening and Speaking)

6. **Explicitly tell students the connection to the new lesson.**

Here's an example of a Subskill Review for a mathematics lesson showing the EL strategies used.

Activate Prior Knowledge Example 1: Subskill Review

1. Identify a subskill (or something previously taught at school) that prepares students for the new lesson.

Students have already had a lesson on representing parts of a whole as a fraction (part of a pizza, ½ of a pizza). This will become the Activate Prior Knowledge for the new lesson, which is *Represent parts of a group as a fraction* (6 of 12 students is ½ of the students).

2. Teacher works a problem first. Include reading. (EL Reading, Content Access Strategies: Slow, Clear Speech)

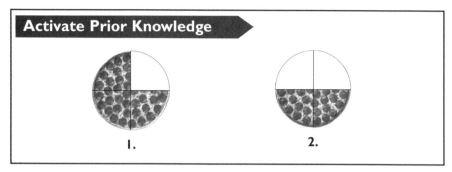

Activate Prior Knowledge

1.

2.

What is the fraction for each pizza?

Source: Pizza image from Thinkstock/Brand X Pictures.

(Language Objectives: Listening and Reading; ED-EL Tracked Choral Reading Strategy.) There is one sentence to read: "What is the fraction for each pizza?" English Learners probably know what a pizza is. However, they might mispronounce the word *pizza* while reading since the first *z* is pronounced like *t, peetsuh. Pizza* is Support Vocabulary, so time won't be spent teaching its meaning. The Content Vocabulary in the sentence is *fraction.* The teacher pre-reads the question before the students read chorally.

Students, look up here where I am pointing at a question. The question says, "What is the fraction for each pizza?" Let's read the question. Go. "What is the fraction for each pizza?"

(Content Access Strategy: EDI-EL Contextualized Definitions.) This Activate Prior Knowledge addresses something students have been recently taught. However, the teacher uses Contextualized Definitions for *numerator* and *denominator* to provide meaning for these important Content Vocabulary words. For engagement, he has the students count the number of pieces with him, chorally.

Watch, while I do the first example. For a fraction, the numerator represents the number of equal parts we have. The numerator is the number on the top of a fraction. Let's count the number of pizza slices. Let's count together. One. Two. Three. The numerator is three.

The denominator, the number on the bottom of the fraction, is how many equal pieces there were all together. One piece is missing, but I am going to count all the parts there would be in a whole pizza, even the missing piece. Look at the board while I point and let's count together. One. Two. Three. Four. The denominator is four.

(Language Objectives: Listening and Speaking; EDI-EL Inflectional Endings Emphasis Strategy.) The fraction "three-fourths" has an inflectional ending *s* and ends with four consonants, *rths,* which might be hard for ELs to pronounce. The teacher has the students practice saying *three-fourths*, emphasizing the ending *s*.

Now I can write my fraction: ³⁄₄. *We say this as three-fourths. Listen carefully. There is an* s *on the end, three-fourthssss. Let's all say it together. Three-fourths. One more time, three-fourths. Say three-fourths to your partner two times.*

> 3. Optional Pair-share, Check for Understanding. If the problem is difficult, have students pair-share and ask non-volunteers to describe how the problem was solved. If the problem is simple, omit CFU to speed up APK. (EL Listening and Speaking)

(Language Objectives: Listening and Speaking; Pair-Share.) As English Learners pair-share, describing how the teacher determined the fraction, they are discussing mathematics and using the words *numerator* and *denominator.*

Students, I want you to write the fraction ¾ next to Example 1 on your handout. Partner A, point to partner B's paper and explain how I came up with the fraction three-fourths. And I want you to use the words numerator *and* denominator *as you explain.*

This example included a pair-share—"point to partner's paper and explain"—without a CFU question. If the problem is harder, call on non-volunteers to explain how you solved the problem. When the APK example is very easy, just have the students work the second example after they have watched you do one.

> 4. Students work a matched problem (whiteboards).
>
> 5. Non-optional Pair-share. Check for Understanding. Students explain to each other how they solved the problem. Call on non-volunteers. (EL Listening and Speaking)

(Language Objectives: Listening and Speaking; Pair-Share.) English Learners pair-share, describing how they solved the second problem. The teacher includes sentence frames to support using the words *numerator* and *denominator.* It's a higher-order question.

Students, I want you to write the fraction for Example 2 on your whiteboard. When you are done, explain to your partner how you did it. B goes first. And I want you to use the words numerator *and* denominator *when you describe your fraction to your partner. You should say, "The fraction of the pizza is ___. The numerator is ___ because ___. The denominator is ___ because ___."*

Call on non-volunteers to respond in complete sentences. The pair-share is important to maximize Activating Prior Knowledge because all students orally describe their thinking.

> 6. Explicitly tell students the connection to the new lesson.

Students, I can see that you remember how to write fractions that are part of a whole. You wrote one-half on your whiteboards to show that Example 2 shows one-half of a pizza. Of the whole pizza, one-half is shown.

Today's fractions will be similar, but we will write fractions that represent part of a group. We could have a group of four apples, eat one, and then three-fourths of the group is left. Turn to the next page where I have the definition.

APK for Declarative Knowledge Lessons

Declarative knowledge (factual information) lessons can use a Subskill Review. Although there are no actual problems to solve, you can still facilitate students' remembering information already taught at school. In a history lesson, for example, students can review information they were already taught, using notes, graphic organizers, or other materials. The pair-share is important so all students discuss the previous information. Also, as individual students report out during the Checking for Understanding, all students are hearing more information. The example below includes EDI-EL Listening, Speaking, and Reading.

Activate Prior Knowledge Example 2: Subskill Review—Declarative Knowledge

Students, get out your notes from yesterday. Partner A, describe the first Reconstruction Amendment, Amendment 13, to your partner. Partner B, describe the 14th Amendment to your partner.

In a minute, I will call on some of you to report out. Then, today we will describe the 15th Amendment and its connection to Reconstruction after the Civil War.

Activating Prior Knowledge With a Universal Experience

The second method of Activating Prior Knowledge is to use a Universal Experience. A Universal Experience APK reveals something from students' daily lives that is useful for learning the new content. In this case, the APK does not address something academic that was taught at school. Instead, you facilitate a short discussion of something your students have experienced in their own lives—a Universal Experience—that reveals that they already do know something about the new content. Students answer Universal Experience questions from their own background knowledge. Activating Prior Knowledge with a Universal Experience is often a foreshadowing of the lesson's Concept Definition.

Activate Prior Knowledge of Ideas, not Vocabulary Words

Avoid asking students what they already know about specific Content Vocabulary words before defining them. If you ask students to write on their whiteboards *how* they know the scary part of the movie is about to happen, they will all write words like "the music," "the lighting." If you ask students to write on their whiteboards what they *know* about the word *foreshadowing,* you will be looking at many blank whiteboards.

So, for an effective Universal Experience APK, don't Activate Prior Knowledge of a new Content Vocabulary *word.* Activate Prior Knowledge of the *meaning* of the new word. Then make the connection to the new lesson by revealing that there is a name for an idea students already know. During Concept Development, you provide the formal written definitions of the new Content Vocabulary.

Students, you just explained to me that you all know that movies and television shows use music as a hint to tell you that something is about to happen. Well, authors do the same thing. They write clues in their stories to give you hints about what is going to happen next. We call these hints foreshadowing clues. *Let's read the definition of* foreshadowing clues. *It's on the top of the next page.*

From Silvia: We have found that Activating Prior Knowledge is sometimes misapplied. Students are being asked what they already know about the Learning Objective before any teaching has taken place. For example, the Learning Objective is on the board: Describe the ideas of three major figures during the Reformation in the 1500s. Students are then asked, "Who knows some of the figures during the Reformation, and what were their ideas that led to the Reformation?"

Invariably, this type of forward questioning—asking questions before teaching—leads to many students not being able to contribute much to the discussion. The only students whose prior knowledge is activated are those few who already know the new content before it is taught. Also, when students provide incorrect guesses, other students listening to the incorrect responses are sometimes learning them.

ACTIVATE PRIOR KNOWLEDGE WITH A UNIVERSAL EXPERIENCE

How to Activate Prior Knowledge for English Learners Using a Universal Experience

1. **Present a scenario or question.** Have students read the question. The choral reading of the APK question is mainly for engagement. If the text is difficult, pre-read first.

2. **If necessary, give your own response first to focus student responses.**

3. **Ask students to provide a response from their own personal experience.**

4. **Pair-share.** Students share their responses.

5. **Check for Understanding.**

6. **Explicitly tell students the connection to the new lesson.**

Activating Prior Knowledge with a Universal Experience should focus on the activation process. Avoid difficult text or vocabulary words that you need to stop and define. English Learners should be able to participate in Activate Prior Knowledge with little or no language support. Students should still read any text used. If necessary, pre-read for emergent readers, but easy text should be used during APK.

Here is an example of teaching APK using a Universal Experience. Students interact using their own personal experiences.

Activate Prior Knowledge
Example 3: Universal Experience

1. Present a scenario or question. Have students read the question.

Students, I have a question on the board. Let's read it together: Has anyone ever given you a present or a gift? What was the present?
The teacher does not pre-read. This is conversational English. A contextualized definition is included for *present.*

> **2. If necessary, give your own response first to focus student responses.**

My grandmother gave me a jacket for my birthday.
The teacher provides an example first. This is not always necessary, but now ELs know what type of answer is being asked for.

> **3. Ask students to provide a response from their own personal experience.**

Get out your whiteboards and write down a present and the name of the person who gave it to you. For example, did you get a gift for Christmas or your birthday? Write your answers on your whiteboards—the present you received and who gave it to you. You can see that I wrote "jacket" and "Grandmother" on my whiteboard.
Now the students provide their own response. The teacher showed her own whiteboard to clarify what the students should do.

> **4. Pair-share. Students share their responses.**

Describe the present and who gave it to you to your partner. Partner "A" go first. Use a complete sentence, such as "_____ gave me a _____."
During this pair-share, all students recall and verbalize their experience. The teacher provides a sentence frame so students use complete sentences.

> **5. Check for Understanding.**

Students, chin-it. Hold up your whiteboards. I am going to call on some of you to tell me your present and who gave it to you.
The teacher scans the whiteboards and calls on a couple of students to report out. Avoid getting into a long discussion with many students describing their specific presents in detail.

> **6. Explicitly tell students the connection to the new lesson.**

All of you have received presents in the past. Today, we will write a letter thanking the person who gave you a present. We are going to write a thank you letter. Track on your paper while I read our Learning Objective: Today, we will write a thank you letter. Let's read together.
The teacher now explicitly states the connection between the students' prior knowledge and the new learning. She then refers to the Learning Objective.

Pair-Share During APK

The student pair-share is important when Activating Prior Knowledge because it allows all students to verbalize their personal experience even if they aren't called on by the teacher. This maximizes Activating Prior Knowledge for all students because each student brain needs to come up with an example and verbalize the example during the pair-share.

From Silvia: This is one of the few examples of pair-shares that do not qualify as Language Objectives for Listening and Speaking. That's because this pair-share is conversational English using words students already know. Language Objectives for English Learners focus on English language acquisition in which ELs use new words.

Here is another example of Universal Experience APK.

Activate Prior Knowledge
Example 4: Universal Experience

Mr. Johnson is preparing a lesson. He has his Learning Objective: calculate the unemployment rate. He could go over some arithmetic regarding percentages and decimals as a Subskill Review APK. However, this is a high school social science lesson. He wants his students to start thinking about employed and unemployed people.

Mr. Johnson decides to use a universal experience familiar to his students, namely jobs. He writes three sentences in his lesson notes.

1. Raise your hand if you have a job after school, if you work somewhere.

2. Raise your hand if you want a job but can't find one.

3. Raise your hand if you have given up looking for a job.

The class will read each question chorally. He will ask his students to explain to their partners their experience for each question. He will call on a few students to report out after each question. Following the questions, he will connect to the new lesson by explicitly telling his students they are already familiar with having a job, not having a job, and not looking for a job. He will state that information just like this is used to calculate the unemployment rate for groups of people, or even for an entire nation. During Concept Development, he will present the definitions and formulas for calculating unemployment rates.

M... ... ... as Universal Experience because students ... ... onal experiences. He includes student interac... ... he lesson.

H... ... es (EDI-EL Simplified Text). Most of them ... ... ls using the new Content Vocabulary *emplo...* ... *nt rate* before teaching. He will define these ... ... ent, and students will use them extensively ... ... on. Although English Learners will be talking ... ... re using conversational English they alread...

[Handwritten note: While activating prior knowledge I was able to identify misconceptions that could interfere with understanding.]

SUMMARY: ACTIVATE PRIOR KNOWLEDGE

- The Activate Prior Knowledge lesson component is used to connect students' existing knowledge to new learning.
- There are two methods:

  1. Subskill Review. re-teach a pertinent subskill that's used in the lesson.

  2. Universal Experience. Connect to students' personal experiences.

- Don't start APK using the new vocabulary. The students haven't been taught it yet.
- Reveal the connection of prior knowledge to the new lesson.

How to Activate Prior Knowledge for English Learners Using a Subskill Review

1. **Identify a subskill** (or something previously taught at school) that prepares students for the new lesson.

2. **Teacher works a problem first.** Include reading. (EL Reading, Content Access Strategies: Slow, Clear Speech)

3. **Optional Pair-share, Check for Understanding.** If the problem is difficult, have students pair-share and ask non-volunteers to describe how the problem was solved. If the problem is simple, omit CFU to speed up APK. (EL Listening and Speaking)

4. **Students work matching problem** (whiteboards).

5. **Non-optional Pair-share. Check for Understanding.** Students explain to each other how they solved the problem. Call on non-volunteers. (EL Listening and Speaking)

6. **Explicitly tell students the connection to the new lesson.**

How to Activate Prior Knowledge for English Learners Using a Universal Experience

1. **Present a scenario or question.** Have students read the question. The choral reading of the APK question is mainly for engagement. If the text is difficult, pre-read first.

2. **If necessary, give your own response first to focus student responses.**

3. **Ask students to provide a response from their own personal experience.**

4. **Pair-share.** Students share their responses.

5. **Check for Understanding.**

6. **Explicitly tell students the connection to the new lesson.**

Here is Silvia's rule for APK:

Connect all students. Keep it short (5 minutes).

We've discussed Learning Objectives and Activating Prior Knowledge—the Student Preparation portion of an EDI lesson. Now we are ready to start teaching new content. In the next chapter, we describe Concept Development, teaching students the big ideas in a lesson using Critical Attribute Concept Development.

As we continue, we'll maintain our focus on language, ensuring that ELs understand the English used in the lesson while simultaneously supporting English language acquisition through embedded vocabulary development, listening, speaking, reading, and writing in every lesson.

9 How to Teach Concepts to English Learners

Concept Development

During Concept Development, you teach students the definitions and meanings of the concepts—big ideas—in the lesson. The specific concepts you teach in a given lesson are derived from the lesson's Learning Objective. For example,

Describe **Manifest Destiny**.

Calculate the **circumference** of a circle.

Describe the causes of **genetic disorders**.

Describe the **setting** in a story.

Make **inferences** about text.

CONCEPT DEFINITIONS

EDI Concept Development is built upon written, bulletproof Concept Definitions. *Written* definitions are important for EDI Concept Development. First, it forces you to have a very clear understanding and definition of what you are teaching. Second, it provides a written reference for English Learners (as opposed to just hearing an oral definition). And, finally, it provides academic text for English Learners to read during the lesson.

"Bulletproof" means definitions are accurate, containing the critical attributes—the features, qualities, properties, and characteristics—that define the concept. Knowing the critical attributes is important because you use them to teach the definition.

Below are some concept definitions with the critical attributes underlined.

Manifest Destiny was the <u>belief</u> that the <u>expansion of the United States throughout the American continents</u> was both <u>justified</u> and <u>inevitable</u>.

Circumference is the <u>distance around</u> a <u>circle</u>.

A **genetic disorder** is an <u>abnormal condition</u> <u>inherited through genes or chromosomes</u>.

The **setting** is <u>where the story takes place</u>.

Concept Definitions don't need to be stated in one sentence. Often you need additional sentences to provide clarity or additional information.

An **inference** is something that <u>you think is true,</u> <u>based on information</u> that you have.

- An **inference** is <u>not written</u> in the text.
- To make an **inference**, use <u>evidence from the text</u> and <u>prior knowledge</u>.

In EDI, you explicitly provide Concept Development by defining a concept and explaining what the definition means using examples that illustrate the critical attributes of the definition. Then you help students remember and ask questions to Check for Understanding.

> ***From John:*** Often when I coach teachers during Concept Development, I cue them, "Just declare what this means. Tell the students what it is." In language arts lessons, I often add, "Don't refer to the story yet. Just declare the meaning of the concepts you are teaching, such as setting, foreshadowing, figurative language, or characterization. Later, during Skill Development, open the story and start identifying or analyzing."

Critical Attribute Concept Development

In EDI, you teach Concept Development by presenting a written concept definition and then explaining and elaborating on what the concept means using examples that illustrate the definition. This is called Critical Attribute Concept Development. The breakthrough idea here is teaching concept definitions by pointing back and forth between an attribute contained in the written definition and exactly the same attribute contained in the examples on page 178.

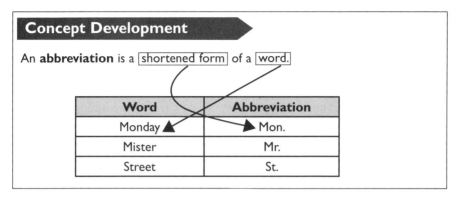

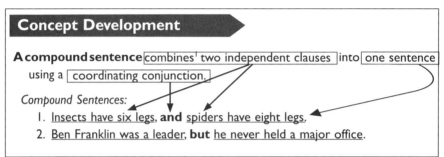

Work the Page

> Work the Page by pointing back and forth between written definitions and examples that show ELs exactly what the written definitions mean.

We have a name for the pointing back and forth. We call it Work the Page. During EDI Concept Development, you Work the Page, pointing back and forth between written definitions and examples that show exactly what the definitions mean.

For this back-and-forth pointing to work most effectively, students need to be able to see everything at once. For example, if you use a PowerPoint presentation, the definitions and the examples need to be visible at the same time. If the definition is on one slide and the examples are on the next slide, followed by a Checking for Understanding question on another slide, students have a hard time connecting the information. Ideally, students have matching handouts (or textbooks) so they can interact with their own copy of the text and have it available as a reference during the lesson.

Concept Development Is Important for Students

Concept Development is important for all students, including English Learners. When ELs understand concepts, they can generalize concepts to examples and relate examples to concepts. For example, when ELs are taught to capitalize months and days of the week, they learn a concept, a general rule they can apply without referring to a list of days and months to capitalize.

> EDI Goal: 100% of students learn new Concepts.

The goal for EDI is 100% of students learning new Concepts in every EDI lesson, even if they can't solve a specific problem. In other words, 100% of students know what setting is (where the story takes place), even if they are poor readers. One hundred percent of students write a properly *constructed* persuasive essay (position statement, supporting reasons with transition words, counterargument, closing statement) even if their grammar, spelling, or punctuation is not perfect.

In mathematics, 100% of students know what a square root is even if they can't calculate one. One hundred percent of students know the relationship between the lengths of the sides of a right triangle (Pythagorean Theorem: $a^2 + b^2 = c^2$) even if they can't do the arithmetic.

When lessons do not have effective Concept Development, students mechanically manipulate information without understanding it. For example, students correctly add the sides of a polygon, but they do not know that they are calculating the perimeter, the distance around the polygon. Kindergarteners can point to the name of the author on the cover of a book, but they do not know that the author wrote the story.

Concept Development Is Important in Mathematics

In mathematics, students need to be taught concepts. They can't just manipulate numbers using algorithms. They need to know what their answers represent. The Common Core State Standards for mathematics have a strong focus on conceptual knowledge, as shown in the mathematics "shifts" below.

Some Common Core "Shifts" in Mathematics

- Teachers focus deeply on foundational knowledge and deep **conceptual understanding.**
- Students demonstrate deep **conceptual understanding** of core math concepts by **applying** them to new situations, as well as **writing** and **speaking** about their understanding.

(Continued)

(Continued)

- Teachers provide opportunities at all grade levels for students to apply math **concepts** in "**real world**" situations.
- Students are **practicing** (skills) and **understanding** (concepts); both are occurring with intensity.
- Students can **decontextualize** problems—represent a situation symbolically.
- Students can **contextualize** problems—interpret what the answer means.

Source: Based on http://engageny.org/wp-content/uploads/2011/08/common-core-shifts.pdf

From Silvia: We often observe classrooms with minimal Concept Development. The other day John saw a lesson in which students were calculating simple interest. During the lesson, John asked the students a question: Who received the interest payment, the bank or the borrower? The students were baffled. It turns out that they were multiplying numbers together but didn't understand conceptually what the answer meant. Always include well-developed Concept Development in every lesson.

Concept Development is also important for students because concepts are assessed on state tests. Although assessments have not been released yet for the Common Core Standards, the test questions are surely going to include concept-based questions, including those for mathematics, where students are expected to apply conceptual knowledge to real-world problems.

HOW TO TEACH CONCEPTS TO ENGLISH LEARNERS

How to Teach Concepts to English Learners

Using written Concept Definitions,

1. **Present written Concept Definition** (Use a text-based visual presentation)
   - **Teach** pronunciation of difficult-to-pronounce words. (EL Listening and Speaking)

- **Read** the written Concept Definition while students look at the words. (Include Content Access Strategies: Slow, Clear Speech)
- **Students chorally read** the Concept Definition. (EL Speaking and Reading)

2. **Explain the Concept Definition.** (Include Content Access Strategies: Clear Speech)

- **Point** to examples and non-examples while explaining what the Concept Definition means.
- **Define** any new Academic Vocabulary. (EL Vocabulary Development)
- **Define** words in the examples, if necessary. (EL Vocabulary Development)
- **Include** physical demonstration, if applicable.

3. Help students remember.

4. Check for Understanding.

- Ask **higher-order** questions.
- Provide **sentence frames** using new vocabulary.
- Have students **pair-share** using complete sentences. Cue both partners to explain. (EL Listening and Speaking)

Concept Development is taught using four broad steps. You can see that the teaching has the same EL teaching rhythm that we used for a Learning Objective—pronouncing words, defining words, pre-reading, choral reads, pair-shares, Checking for Understanding. The big difference for Concept Development here is Step 2, Explaining the meaning of the Concept.

1. Present written Concept Definition (Use a text-based visual presentation)

 A. **Teach** pronunciation of difficult to pronounce words. (EL Listening and Speaking)

 B. **Read** the written Concept Definition while students look at the words. (Include Content Access Strategies: Slow, Clear Speech)

 C. **Students chorally read** the Concept Definition. (EL Speaking and Reading)

You always start Concept Development by presenting a written Concept Definition. You use the general EDI-EL approach while presenting the written Concept Definition: teach ELs how to pronounce individual words (if necessary), pre-read while students track and look at the words, and then have students read chorally (EDI-EL Tracked Choral Reading Strategy). Although they may appear to be repetitive, the tracking and choral readings are important Listening, Speaking, and Reading practice for ELs. Don't skip them. Include EDI-EL Content Access Strategies such as Speaking Slowly and Clearly.

This first step of presenting the written Concept Definition implements EDI-EL Language Objectives: Listening, Speaking, and Reading, but you have not provided any meaning yet.

> 2. Explain the Concept Definitions (Include Content Access Strategies: Clear Speech)
>
> A. **Point** to examples and non-examples while explaining what the concept definition means
>
> B. **Define** any new Academic Vocabulary (EL Vocabulary Development)
>
> C. **Define** words in the examples, if necessary (EL Vocabulary Development);
>
> D. **Include** physical demonstration, if applicable

Use examples and non-examples to explain what the Concept Definition means. Work the Page, pointing back and forth between the critical attributes in the written definition and the same attributes illustrated by the examples, while you explain.

Although non-examples are not appropriate for all lessons, they can really add clarity to Conceptual knowledge. Non-examples are non-examples because they don't match all the attributes in the Concept Definition. The classic non-example is for similes. Similes are figurative language that compares two unlike objects using like or as. For example, *Joe is as tall as a telephone pole.* The non-example of a simile is *Joe likes ice cream.* It has the word *like* but is not a simile because two unlike objects are not being compared. Non-examples are effective because they preempt common errors students might make and clarify specific attributes of a Concept.

We have been describing text-based Concept descriptions and examples. However, physical objects are integral to many lessons. If you are teaching a lesson that uses objects or manipulatives, Concept Development is generally when you introduce them. In science, for example, after you read the written description of the three types of rocks, you hold up each type of rock and point to the attributes in the rock that you just described in the written, bulletproof definition. Pass the rocks around for the students to hold. The physical objects become the example of what the written concept definition means.

> 3. Help students remember.

During Concept Development, add Cognitive Strategies. "Cognitive Strategies" are techniques you use to help students remember information.

The most basic Cognitive Strategy is repetition—having students repeat information—to help the brain remember. The EDI-EL pre-reading, choral reading, and pair-shares provide repetition and contribute to long-term retention of Concept Definitions. The repetition also enables ELs to practice and internalize new language, including sentence structure and new vocabulary words.

Repetition is also how students remember rote information such as the alphabet, counting, addition facts, and multiplication facts. Repetition is important for retention because it changes the chemistry of the brain by creating and strengthening neural pathways to retrieve information.

Besides repetition, teachers can use highlighting and memory aids that help students remember information, such as mnemonics and gestures. The example below uses the letters in the words themselves as a memory aid.

Fables use animals to teach a lesson or moral.

Myths use gods to explain nature or how the earth was formed.

Students, here is how to remember the difference between fables and myths. Fables usually include animals. The word fable *contains the letter "a," which is the first letter in* animal. *Myths often tell how the earth was formed. Look at the word* myth. *Myth has a "th" at the end of the word, just like the word* earth. *Partner A, point to the definitions of fable and myth and explain to your partner how you can remember* fable *and* myth *by looking at letters in the words.*

Gestures can help students remember. Quite often gestures act out the meaning of an idea. Students remember the motion which, in turn, triggers the meaning. (Humans can remember gestures much faster than phrases or sentences.) Gestures also add kinesthetics (movement) to a lesson.

A third way to help students remember is to use graphic organizers. Graphic organizers compress large amounts of information and show the relationships among the ideas. Graphic organizers can be used in any lesson, but they are particularly effective for showing relationships among declarative information in social science and science lessons. Relationships can include cause and effect, problem and solution, compare and contrast, and so forth.

4. Check for Understanding.

   A. Ask **higher-order** questions.

   B. Provide **sentence frames** using new vocabulary.

   C. Have students **pair-share** using complete sentences. Cue both partners to explain. (EL Listening and Speaking)

Intersperse Checking for Understanding questions as you present your bulletproof Concept Definition and examples and non-examples. These questions are important to verify that students are learning. Student responses provide information for you to make instructional decisions such as *Do I need to re-teach?*

Use sentence frames to support English Learners in answering questions in complete sentences that incorporate Academic and Content Vocabulary words from the lesson. And, of course, use pair-shares so ELs practice using the proper vocabulary and are ready to answer if called upon. Cue for which partner goes first so all students respond.

Ask Higher-Order CFU Questions During Concept Development

EDI focuses on using higher-order questions—questions that cannot be answered by merely reading back a sentence off the page. ELs are included in higher-order questions because ELs can think at high levels even if they cannot compose a complete response in English.

Below are sample higher-order questions for Concept Development that can be used in any lesson. The questions require students to paraphrase definitions in their own words, to apply definitions to examples and non-examples, and to justify their answers. Provide sentence frames so students answer in complete sentences using the new vocabulary.

Additional higher-order questions are discussed in Appendix A under Constructed Response Questions.

Sample Higher-Order Questions for Concept Development

- In your own words, what is _____?
- Why is this an example of _____?
- Why is the non-example a non-example?
- Why is _____ not an example of _____?
- Which one is an example of _____? Why?
- What is the difference between the example and the non-example?
- Match the examples to the definitions of _____. Explain your answer.
- Which (picture/poster/object) shows an example of _____. Explain why.
- Give an example of _____. Explain your answer.
- Draw an example of _____. Explain your answer.

Generally, students should describe Concept Definitions in their own words. However, some definitions are hard to paraphrase. For example, in kindergarten: *Students,* add *means to find out how much we have altogether.* This is hard for students to restate in their own words. So, depending on the grade level and the specific definition, it's not always practical to have students paraphrase definitions.

Be careful when asking students to create an example. Don't ask students to do something they have not been taught to do yet. For example, if you have just defined similes, don't ask students to write their own simile.

EXAMPLES OF HOW TO TEACH EDI CONCEPT DEVELOPMENT TO ENGLISH LEARNERS

As described in the previous pages, to teach Concept Development, you present a written Concept Definition. You use examples to show English Learners what the written definition means. You help students remember and then Check for Understanding including pair-shares.

Now let's look at some examples of Concept Development EDI-EL style, while emphasizing Language Objectives, Content Access Strategies, and Vocabulary Development.

Concept Development With English Learner Strategies Example 1: Abbreviations

I. Present written Concept Definition. (Use a text-based visual presentation)

  A. **Teach** pronunciation of difficult-to-pronounce words. (EL Listening and Speaking)

  B. **Read** the written Concept Definition while students look at the words. (Include Content Access Strategies: Slow, Clear Speech)

  C. **Students chorally read** the Concept Definition. (EL Speaking and Reading)

Use the general EDI-EL approach: teach pronunciation, if necessary; pre-read while English Learners look at the words; have students chorally read. You're focusing on EL Listening, Speaking, and Reading.

In the example on page 186, pronunciation for the word *abbreviation* would have already been taught during the Learning Objective. The word *shortened* could be a difficult word to pronounce. It has an *ed* inflectional ending, which could be hard for ELs. Pronunciation can be taught using the EDI-EL Word Chunking for Pronunciation and EDI-EL Inflectional Endings Buildup.

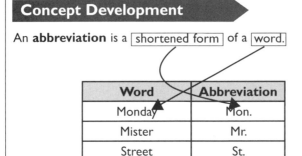

Concept Development

An **abbreviation** is a shortened form of a word.

Word	Abbreviation
Monday	Mon.
Mister	Mr.
Street	St.

Abbreviations are read as whole words.

Mr. Smith is my teacher.

Read as

Mister Smith is my teacher.

CFU

1. Which sentence uses an abbreviation? How do you know?

   A. Monday is the first day of school.

   B. Mon. is the first day of school.

2. How do you read abbreviations? How do you read Mr.?

3. What is an abbreviation? What is the difference between a word and an abbreviation of a word?

   The difference between a word and an abbreviation is _____.

Students, look where I am pointing and listen carefully. Short-ened. Shortened has the word short *in it. Say short. Short. Here is the next part. Short-en. Say short-en. Short-en. Now listen carefully for the full word. There is an* ed *at the end, short-en'd. Listen again, short-en'd. Say short-ened. Shortened.*

After pre-pronouncing individual words, you are ready to pre-read the Concept Definition. Use the EDI-EL Tracked Choral Reading Strategy. Read the definition while students track, looking at each word. While pre-reading, read slowly, clearly enunciating each word. After you have pre-read, ELs are prepared to read. Have them read the Concept Definition chorally with you. The tracked reading implements EL Language Objectives Listening, Speaking, and Reading.

Students, look at your handouts. See where it says "An abbreviation"? Put your finger under the word An. *Track while I read. An abbreviation is a shortened form of a word. Let's read together. An abbreviation is a shortened form of a word.*

2. Explain the Concept Definition. (Include Content Access Strategies: Clear Speech)

    A. **Point** to examples and non-examples while explaining what the Concept Definition means

    B. **Define** any new Academic Vocabulary. (EL Vocabulary Development)

    C. **Define** words in the examples, if necessary (EL Vocabulary Development);

    D. **Include** physical demonstration, if applicable

After you and your students have read the definition, you are ready to provide meaning for the definition and the words contained in the definition. You Work the Page, pointing back and forth between the definition and the examples, explaining and defining words contained in the definition. In the box on page 186, the arrows show where to point while explaining.

Students, we just read the definition of an abbreviation. Let me explain what the definition means. An abbreviation is a shortened form of a word. Students, circle the word short *inside the word* shortened. *(Teacher points.) You already know the meaning of short as "not tall." Today, short means "small." So, a shortened form of a word means a smaller way of writing a word.*

Look right here at the word Monday. *(Teacher points.) Next to the word* Monday *is the abbreviation for Monday, M-o-n. (Teacher points.)*

You can see that the abbreviation is shorter, smaller. It has only three letters, M-o-n. (Teacher points to the words "shortened form" in the definition and to the abbreviation, Mon.)

(Continue with abbreviations for Mister and Street.)

The definition of *shortened* is provided using a combination of the EDI-EL Multiple-Meaning Words Strategy (short means not tall; short means smaller) and the EDI-EL Word Morphology Strategy (short, shortened). You point and explain that an abbreviation is a "shortened form" of a word. You point back and forth between the written definition and the examples while doing this.

You continue using EDI-EL Tracked Reading (pre-read and choral read) for "Abbreviations are read as whole words." Then you elaborate on what this means, pointing to the example sentence, "Mr. Smith is my teacher."

Students, we read the abbreviation "Mr." as the whole word, "mister." So this sentence is read as "Mister Smith is my teacher." Let's read the sentence together, reading the abbreviation as "Mister." Mr. Smith is my teacher.

Non-examples are included in EDI Concept Development when they clarify the Concepts, but non-examples are not effective in all lessons. In this lesson, non-examples of abbreviations (such as contractions) would not add clarity. Non-examples are not used.

> **3. Help students remember.**

In this lesson, a gesture can be used. Hold up your hands about two feet apart horizontally, palms facing each other, and then move them together while repeating the definition.

Students, look at my hands while I read. (Hands two feet apart.) *An abbreviation is a shortened* (move hands together) *form of a word. Students, raise your arms like mine. Let's read and move our hands at the same time. An abbreviation is a shortened form of a word.*

> **4. Check for Understanding.**
>
> A. Ask **higher-order** questions.
>
> B. Provide **sentence frames** using new vocabulary.
>
> C. Have students **pair-share** using complete sentences. Cue both partners to explain. (EL Listening and Speaking)

In EDI lessons, Checking for Understanding questions are usually located at the bottom of Concept Development. However, the questions are meant to be interspersed while teaching. The first CFU question can be asked after teaching the definition of *abbreviation* and explaining the three examples.

1. Which sentence uses an abbreviation? How do you know?

   A. Today is Monday.

   B. Today is Mon.

Students, look at sentences A and B. (Point to sentences.) *Which sentence uses an abbreviation? Write A or B on your whiteboard and tell your partner how you know which sentence uses an abbreviation.*

> ***From Silvia:*** Caution! At this point, you can't ask students about an abbreviation such as Dec. (December) that has not already been taught. In this lesson, every abbreviation to be used must be presented during the lesson. You can't expect students to already know the abbreviations before the lesson is taught. An abbreviation table is provided to teach the abbreviations. The teacher pre-reads and then students chorally read all the abbreviations.

The next CFU question is asked after explaining that abbreviations are read as whole words.

2. How do you read abbreviations? How do you read Mr.?

The final CFU questions can be asked to wrap up Concept Development. There are two questions. The first one is a recall question, and the second is a higher-order question. Asking students to paraphrase what abbreviations are, in their own words, is not practical in this lesson.

3. What is an abbreviation? What is the difference between a word and an abbreviation of a word?

Now students, I want you to pair-share with your partner. What is the difference between a word and an abbreviation of a word? Point to the list of abbreviations and explain the difference. And say, "The difference between a word and an abbreviation is ____."

Concept Development With EL Strategies Example 2: Pythagorean Theorem

Now we have a sample math lesson along with a description of EL strategies used to teach it. Notice the extensive focus on language and literacy, even in a math lesson.

Learning Objective

Use the Pythagorean Theorem to solve problems.

Concept Development

The **Pythagorean Theorem**[1] describes the relationship[2] among the length of the sides of a **right triangle**.

1 theorem—statement that can be proven mathematically

2 relationship—how things are connected and affect each other

The **Pythagorean Theorem** states that if a triangle is a right triangle, then the square of the first leg plus the square of the second leg is equal to the square of the hypotenuse.

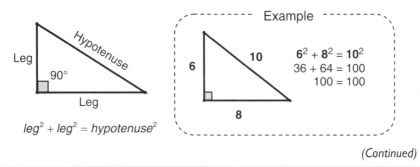

Example

$$6^2 + 8^2 = 10^2$$
$$36 + 64 = 100$$
$$100 = 100$$

$$leg^2 + leg^2 = hypotenuse^2$$

(Continued)

(Continued)

CFU

1. (whiteboards) For which triangle can you apply, or use, the Pythagorean Theorem? Why?
The Pythagorean Theorem applies to triangle _____ because_____.

2. In your own words, what relationship is described by the Pythagorean Theorem? What is that relationship?
The Pythagorean Theorem _____.

Let's look at the first sentence in Concept Development.

The Pythagorean Theorem[1] describes the relationship[2] among the length of the sides of a right triangle.

1. theorem: statement that can be proven mathematically

2. relationship: how things are connected and affect each other

Language Objectives: Listening, Speaking, and Reading

How to pronounce and read the words *Pythagorean Theorem* would have been explained during the Learning Objective using the EDI-EL Backwards Syllabication Strategy: *orean, Pythag-orean.* Use the EDI-EL Stress Consonants Strategy to emphasize that *Pythagorean* ends with an *n* and *Theorem* ends with an *m.*

Students, listen carefully to the ending of the words. Pythagorean Theorem.

Use the EDI-EL Tracked Choral Reading Strategy. Pre-read and then have the students chorally read the entire definition.

Vocabulary Development

- *Pythagorean Theorem* is Content Vocabulary taught with written definitions.
- The word *theorem* itself is Content Vocabulary. It is defined in a footnote: "a statement that can be proven mathematically." Define *theorem* in context while defining the Pythagorean Theorem. Then connect the meaning of *theorem* to *Pythagorean Theorem.*

Students, a theorem is a statement that can be proven mathematically. The Pythagorean Theorem is a statement about right triangles that can be proven mathematically. (Point and explain.)

- The word *relationship* appears in the Pythagorean Theorem definition. *Relationship* is Academic Vocabulary. This word is not math specific. A footnote definition is provided, but you can include the EDI-EL Multiple-Meaning Words Strategy.

Students, you already know that relatives are members of your family: brothers, sisters, parents, uncles. Today, the word relationship *refers to how any group of things is connected to each other, not just families. Let's read the definition. Relationship: how things are connected and affect each other. The relationship we are talking about today is how the sides of a right triangle are related to each other.*

You could also note that *ship* on the end of the word *relationship* is not referring to a boat. Use the EDI-EL Word Morphology Strategy, pointing out to students that the ending *ship* shows a "state or condition." Relationship, the state of being related. Musicianship, the state of being a good musician.

Language Objective: Writing

After the Pythagorean Theorem has been explained, a CFU question can present the opportunity to write the new words. Use the EDI-EL Write New Words on Whiteboards Strategy.

Students, you probably have never written the words Pythagorean Theorem before, so I have an easy question. What is the name of the specific theorem we are studying today? Write the name on your whiteboards and spell it correctly. Read your spelling to your partner. Check that your partner spelled it correctly and be ready to show me.

Now let's look at the second sentence in Concept Development.

The Pythagorean Theorem states that if a triangle is a right triangle, then the square of the first leg plus the square of the second leg is equal to the square of the hypotenuse.

Language Objectives: Listening and Speaking

The word *states* might be mispronounced as *estates* by some Spanish-speaking students. Pre-empt this using the EDI-EL Physical Pronunciation and Inflectional Endings Emphasis Strategies.

Students this word is states, *not estates. Listen to the hissing* s *sound at the beginning and the ending of the word* states. *My tongue is up in the front of my mouth hissing, states. Say states. One more time, states.*

Vocabulary Development: Academic Vocabulary

The word *states* is an Academic word that can be used in multiple content areas. Define it using the EDI Multiple-Meaning Words Strategy.

You already have heard of states as in the United States. We all live in a state. Today, state has another meaning. State means "say or tell." For example, to state your name means to say your name. Our sentence, "The Pythagorean Theorem states . . ." means "The Pythagorean Theorem says . . ."

Work the Page. Teach the definitions incorporating EL strategies as you point back and forth between the written definitions and the examples and graphics, explaining what the definitions mean. Present the general formula $leg^2 + leg^2 = hypotenuse^2$, pointing back and forth between the general formula, the written definition, and the triangle example.

How to remember: For the formula $leg^2 + leg^2 = hypotenuse^2$, show students that the two legs go together on one side of the formula, $leg^2 + leg^2$. The hypotenuse, which is the longer side, goes by itself, $hypotenuse^2$.

Check for Understanding (Listening and Speaking)

Integrate Checking for Understanding questions, providing sentence frames for students to use. Have students point to the graphics on the page while explaining the Pythagorean Theorem to their partners using complete sentences. Call on non-volunteers. Cue students—and require them—to use complete sentences in pair-shares and when answering questions (theorem, relationship, legs of a triangle, hypotenuse, right triangle).

Concept Development With EL Strategies Example 3: Compound Sentences

Below is an example of Concept Development for compound sentences. The written definition of "compound sentences" is followed immediately by examples of compound sentences that you use to illustrate the attributes contained in the written definition.

When teaching, you Work the Page, pointing back and forth while explaining what the attributes contained in the Concept Definition look like in the examples. You explain why the non-examples are not compound sentences. You integrate higher-order Checking for Understanding questions as you teach.

In describing this example, we'll focus on the possible EL Strategies. In the box on page 193, the arrows show where to point while you Work the Page. You physically connect the definitions to the examples for English Learners using a text-based, visual presentation from PowerPoint, a document camera, transparencies, or something written directly on the board.

Learning Objective

An **independent clause is** a group of words with a subject and a verb, a simple sentence.

> *Dogs bark at cats.*

Coordinating conjunctions are words that connect[2] independent clauses.

> *for, and, nor, but, or, yet, so* (FANBOYS)

A **compound sentence** combines[1] two independent clauses into one sentence using a coordinating conjunction.

Compound Sentences:

1. Insects have six legs, **and** spiders have eight legs.

2. Ben Franklin was a leader, but he never held a major office.

Not Compound Sentences:

3. Flies **and** ants are both insects.

4. Ben Franklin and Thomas Jefferson signed the Declaration of Independence.

1 combine—work or exist together
2 connect—to join together

CFU

1. Why is sentence 2 a compound sentence? Point to sentence 2 and explain.

   Sentence 2 is a compound sentence because _____.

2. Why is sentence 4 not a compound sentence? Point to sentence 4 and explain.

   Sentence 4 is not a compound sentence because _____.

3. In your own words, what is a compound sentence?

   A compound sentence ____.

Language Objectives: Listening, Speaking, and Reading

Teacher pronounces, pre-reads, and then students read the definitions of *compound sentences, coordinating conjunction,* and *independent clauses.* Students read the seven coordinating conjunctions chorally. Use EDI-EL Strategies such as Extending Vowels, Stressing Consonants, and Emphasizing Each Syllable (co-or-di-na-tion, con-junc-tion, com-pound).

Vocabulary Development: Content Vocabulary

Compound sentence, coordinating conjunction, and *independent clauses* are explicitly defined using the EDI-EL Develop Concept Strategy with written definitions and examples and non-examples. Point out that an independent *clause* is not Santa *Clause* or animal *claws* (EDI-EL Multiple-Meaning Words Strategy and EDI-EL Homophone Strategy).

Vocabulary Development: Academic Vocabulary

"Combine" means to work or exist together. "Connect" means to join together. There are subtle differences between these words. Teach using footnotes with written definitions.

A compound sentence combines two independent clauses into one sentence.

Students, "combine" means to work or exist together. The two independent clauses are together in the compound sentence. (Point to a sample compound sentence and explain.)

Coordinating conjunctions are words that connect independent clauses.

Students, "connect" means join together. Look at the example sentence. (Point.) *You can see where the coordinating conjunction "and" joins the two independent clauses together into one sentence.*

A Cognitive Strategy is included to help students remember the coordinating conjunctions: for, and, nor, but, or, yet, so are the FANBOYS.

CONCEPT DEVELOPMENT FOR DECLARATIVE KNOWLEDGE

Concept Development for procedural knowledge (how to do something) lessons can include multiple examples. However, purely declarative knowledge lessons, such as many history and science lessons, cover a fixed set of facts. But the technique of elaborating on attributes can still be used. Below is the Concept Development for the Oregon Trail.

Concept Development With EL Strategies Example 4: Oregon Trail

> **Concept Development**
>
> The **Oregon Trail** was one of the main overland routes on the North American continent traveled by pioneers[2] to settle new parts of the United States.
>
> 2 pioneers—first people to travel to a new area and begin living there

In 1800, America's |western border reached only as far as the Mississippi River.| Following the Louisiana Purchase in 1803, the country nearly |doubled in size| , pushing the |nation's western edge past the Rocky Mountains.|

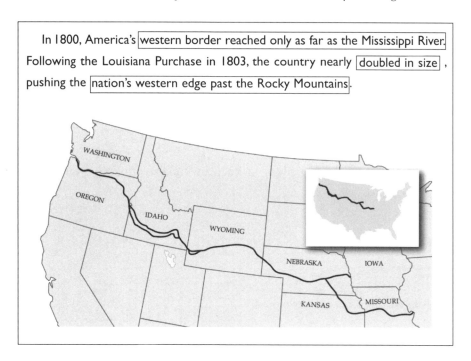

For this example, there are several words to address for ELs. Definitions can be provided using written, superscripted, and contextualized definitions.

1. Oregon Trail. Pronounce *Oregon.* Have students imitate you (EDI-EL Clear Enunciation, Students Imitate Strategy). *Oregon Trail* is Content Vocabulary and is defined in writing.

2. Overland. Teach this word using the EDI-EL Word Morphology Strategy: *over* and *land.* Point to the map and explain *overland.*

3. Continent. Use a contextualized definition. *A continent is a large amount of land surrounded by oceans.* Point to a world map (visual).

4. North American Continent. Point to a world map and show the North American Continent (visual).

5. Pioneer. This is defined with a footnote definition.

6. "pushing the nation's western edge." Contextualize to provide meaning. *The western edge of the nation moved all the way to the Pacific Ocean.* Point to the map (visual).

There are several attributes in the Oregon Trail definition to elaborate upon. During Concept Development, you Work the Page, pointing between the text and the map showing the route. It was overland as opposed to oceanic routes. You point to the Mississippi River area to show that this used to be the western border of the United States. You point to the map insert and show that the United States doubled in size, expanding past the Rocky Mountains to the Pacific Ocean. For a pair-share, you have students point to the map and explain the Oregon Trail to their partners.

SUMMARY: CONCEPT DEVELOPMENT

Here are some of the big ideas to keep in mind every time you teach a Concept.

How to Teach Concepts to English Learners

Using written Concept Definitions,

1. **Present written Concept Definition** (Use a text-based visual presentation)

   - **Teach** pronunciation of difficult-to-pronounce words. (EL Listening and Speaking)
   - **Read** the written Concept Definition while students look at the words. (Include Content Access Strategies: Slow, Clear Speech)
   - **Students chorally read** the Concept Definition. (EL Speaking and Reading)

2. **Explain the Concept Definition.** (Include Content Access Strategies: Clear Speech)

   - **Point** to examples and non-examples while explaining what the Concept Definition means.
   - **Define** any new Academic Vocabulary. (EL Vocabulary Development)
   - **Define** words in the examples, if necessary. (EL Vocabulary Development)
   - **Include** physical demonstration, if applicable.

3. **Help students remember.**

4. **Check for Understanding.**

   - Ask **higher-order** questions.
   - Provide **sentence frames** using new vocabulary.
   - Have students **pair-share** using complete sentences. Cue both partners to explain. (EL Listening and Speaking)

1. The Concepts to teach during Concept Development are derived from the Learning Objective, which comes from a content standard.

2. Provide written, bulletproof Concept Definitions that contain critical attributes.

3. Provide text-based lessons to support language acquisition for English Learners and to serve as a reference in case they miss something you say.

4. Provide examples and non-examples to show students what the written definitions mean.

5. Use Critical Attribute Concept Development to teach. Work the Page by pointing back and forth between the attributes in the written definition and the attributes illustrated in the examples. Provide physical demonstrations if appropriate.

6. Help students remember. Provide students with methods of remembering what you taught.

7. Intersperse Checking for Understanding, using higher-order questions.

8. Incorporate English Learner strategies throughout.
   - Vocabulary Development (Content, Academic, Support). Identify new vocabulary to teach. During Concept Development, you explicitly teach the meaning of the lesson's Content Vocabulary. Contextualize or define other Academic and Support words.
   - Language Objectives (Listening, Speaking, Reading, Writing). Pre-read and then have ELs read Concept definitions. Have English Learners pair-share, explaining definitions and examples to each other. Provide sentence frames so ELs answer CFU questions in complete sentences using new vocabulary.
   - Content Access Strategies (make English easier to understand). For example, speak clearly and slow down for academic language.

We're ready to turn the page to the next chapter on Skill Development and Guided Practice. This is the part of an EDI lesson when you explicitly show English Learners how to solve problems (or answer questions). Then you guide them step by step as they solving matching problems—usually on whiteboards so you can see their work.

10

How to Teach Skills to English Learners and Provide Guided Practice

This chapter describes Skill Development and Guided Practice together because in EDI they are taught together. Let's start with Skill Development.

> When you model, you explicitly state out loud the thinking processes you use to solve a problem.

SKILL DEVELOPMENT

"Skill Development" is explicitly teaching students how to execute the skill contained in the Learning Objective. Remember, skills are described by verbs such as *identify, describe, determine, compare and contrast, analyze, evaluate, calculate, solve,* and *write.* During Skill Development, you provide written steps to accomplish the skill. Then you model, using the steps yourself. When you model, you explicitly state out loud the thinking processes you use to solve a problem. Modeling is very effective for students because they are "hearing" your thinking.

After modeling, you ask CFU *process* questions that ask students to describe the thinking process you used to execute the skill. Note that you ask questions related to *how* you solved the problem, not just what the answer is. In other words, you don't ask, "What is the answer to the problem I just solved?" Instead, you ask, "*How* did I, the teacher, solve the problem?"

For example, suppose your Learning Objective is *Compare and contrast the most important points and key details presented in two texts on the same topic.* Skill Development is the part of the lesson during which you provide a set of steps, a methodology, that will enable English Learners to compare and contrast any two texts discussing the same topic. You model your own thinking process while using the steps to compare and contrast two texts. As you model, you ask CFU process questions about how you did it. Students pair-share their answers before you call on non-volunteers.

From Silvia: I must add a clarification here. We often see students being asked to restate the steps. (What is Step 1? Step 1 is subtract the ones column. Regroup, if necessary.) The CFU questions following teacher modeling should address the thinking and decision making used in applying the Skill Development steps, not just restating the steps themselves. (How did I know I needed to regroup?)

Skill Development Is Important

Skill Development is important for students. First, you always provide a methodology (steps) that enables students to successfully execute skills and solve problems. Students are not asked to do something without your modeling a method. Second, when you model your thinking, your students hear from you the internal thinking they need to use to solve the problem.

GUIDED PRACTICE

After the teacher has modeled solving problems during Skill Development, it's the students' turn. During Guided Practice, the teacher directs the whole class to work problems step by step under close guidance. This is usually done with whiteboards. You have students work a step on their whiteboards, pair-share their answers, and then hold the whiteboards up so you can see their work. As you progress through the steps, all students are working all the steps under your supervision, and you are checking that all students have executed each step correctly.

During Guided Practice, you can Check for Understanding in three areas. First, check for correct answers to determine whether students executed the steps correctly. Generally, you do this by scanning the room, looking directly at the raised whiteboards. If less than 80% are correct, then re-teach the whole class.

Second, after looking at the whiteboards, call on non-volunteers to read and describe their answers in complete sentences using Academic and Content Vocabulary. You ask students to interpret their answer, defend their answers, or explain what the answer means.

Third, you ask higher-order thinking process questions. These questions ask students to describe how they obtained their answer.

Teach Thinking Processes

Note that both Skill Development and Guided Practice use higher-order thinking process questions. During Skill Development, the process question is generally "Students, how did I, the teacher, solve the problem?" During Guided Practice, the process question is "Students, explain how you solved the problem."

During Skill Development and Guided Practice, you are not just solving problems. You teach students the thinking processes to use and include Checking for Understanding questions related to the thinking processes.

Guided Practice Is Important

Guided Practice is important. When you have students work problems step by step, you can correct errors at each step. By the time the steps are completed, everyone has the correct answer.

EDI RULE OF TWO: COMBINED SKILL DEVELOPMENT AND GUIDED PRACTICE

From John: Originally, during EDI Skill Development, I would work several problems while students watched. Then I would have students get out whiteboards and work several problems.

Silvia would be watching and telling me, "John, you're droning. You're talking too much. The students need to do something." And then the final comment, "John, you are teaching yourself how to do it, not the students. You need more student interaction."

Meanwhile, Silvia started asking her students to work a problem immediately after she did the first one. Wow! So, we sat down and wrote up the Rule of Two to enhance EDI.

Work matched problems. You do the first one, and the students do the second one. Then repeat, using matched pairs for each problem variation in the lesson.

The EDI Rule of Two combines Skill Development and Guided Practice in an interlaced manner. You provide matched problems in pairs. ("Matched" means that the thinking required to solve the problem is the same.) First, you solve a problem. Then you have your students solve a matched problem on their whiteboards. Then you do a slightly different variation. Students do a similar one on whiteboards. In the box below, the first set of problems subtracts with regrouping in the ones place. The second pair is a different variation. It uses regrouping through zero in the tens column.

Matched Problems

Subtraction with regrouping

1. (teacher) $\begin{array}{r} 463 \\ -235 \\ \hline \end{array}$ 2. (student) $\begin{array}{r} 674 \\ -348 \\ \hline \end{array}$

Subtraction with regrouping through zero

3. (teacher) $\begin{array}{r} 903 \\ -157 \\ \hline \end{array}$ 4. (student) $\begin{array}{r} 604 \\ -438 \\ \hline \end{array}$

This combined Skill Development and Guided Practice continues until you have taught all the variations of problem types that you will ask students to do later during Independent Practice.

As you work a problem, you ask process questions about how you (the teacher) are solving it. As students work a problem—usually on their whiteboards—you ask CFU questions about what the answer is, what the answer means, and how they determined their answer.

Slowly Release Students as You Work Additional Problems

As you progress through the matched pairs during Skill Development and Guided Practice, you start to release students to do more of the work on their own. For example, you don't need to call on students to explain every step, especially steps they have successfully done several times. During the Guided Practice release, students can work two or more steps at once, and your CFU questions now address the unique aspects of the latest variation.

From Silvia: It is important to recognize different problem variations. We often see classes in which students are sent to Independent Practice too soon.

Recently, I saw ELs being taught how to solve word problems with subtraction. Only one example was provided.

Ryan had five birds and two flew away.

How many birds does Ryan have now?

The students were told that the answer was three. Immediately, the ELs were asked to start working the next problems on their own.

After a few minutes, 80% of the students were raising their hands to request assistance. I was told by a frustrated teacher that it was hard to believe the students were having such a difficult time doing these simple problems.

Here's why the students asked for help. There were actually three different problem types and wording, and all the variations were not modeled for the students.

Three word problem variations of $5 - 3 = 2$

1. Ryan had five birds. Three birds flew away. How many birds does Ryan have now? $5 - 3 = ?$

2. Emily had some marbles. She lost three, and she still has two marbles. How many marbles did Emily start with? $? - 3 = 2$

3. Ashley had five dolls. She gave some to Mia. Ashley has two dolls left. How many dolls did Ashley give to Mia? $5 - ? = 2$

During EDI Skill Development and Guided Practice, students are explicitly taught—and then practice how to solve—each problem type that will show up in the Independent Practice. This match should be confirmed before the lesson is taught.

PROCEDURAL AND DECLARATIVE KNOWLEDGE

Before we go any further, let's review the two types of knowledge taught in EDI lessons—procedural knowledge (how to do something) and declarative knowledge (knowing facts about something). It is important to recognize the difference because EDI lessons are designed differently depending on the type of knowledge being taught. Let's start with Procedural Knowledge.

Procedural Knowledge

Procedural Knowledge is knowing how to do something. In Procedural Knowledge lessons, you teach your students *how* to do something, for example,

How to add fractions.

How to solve a quadratic equation.

How to calculate markups and discounts.

How to determine the main idea of a text.

How to determine the meaning of figurative and connotative words and phrases in text.

How to use sensory details to convey experiences and events precisely.

How to calculate density and buoyancy.

How to calculate acceleration of an object when a force is applied.

How to calculate the probability of inheriting a genetic trait using a Punnett Square.

Procedural Knowledge can be applied over and over. For example, students can add many different fractions. They can determine the main idea of numerous passages.

Skill Development and Guided Practice for Procedural Knowledge

Now, let's look at how to implement the Rule of Two for Procedural Knowledge. First, you develop steps. There are two types of steps—direction steps and strategic steps.

Direction steps direct students to do something, but they don't provide any methodology to use. The Skill Development steps below are directions.

Learning Objective

Determine main idea and supporting details in text.

Skill Development/Guided Practice   *These steps are directions.*

Step 1. Read the paragraph.

Step 2. Circle the main idea.

Step 3. Underline sentences that are supporting details.

As you can see, these steps tell students what to do, but they don't include any strategies or information on how to do it. Also, notice that the verbs in Steps 2 and 3 are mechanical directions: *circle, underline.*

Strategic steps include strategies for the students to use. They're the steps during which you model your thinking processes. The same steps rewritten with strategies added in bold are shown below. Also, the verbs in Steps 2 and 3 are now cognitive—*determine, identify.* The directions to *circle* and *underline* have been moved to the end of the sentences. Compare these steps to the ones on page 203. Now they're strategic and teachable.

Learning Objective

Determine main idea and supporting details in text.

Skill Development/Guided Practice *These steps include strategies.*

Step 1. Read each sentence carefully.

Step 2. **Determine** the main idea, **the one sentence that tells what the other sentences are about**. (circle)

Step 3. **Identify** the supporting details that **give information about the main idea.** (underline).

Teaching Procedural Knowledge

The box below shows the general approach for teaching Skill Development and Guided Practice for Procedural Knowledge. Using the Rule of Two, you work a problem first and ask students how you did it. Then the students work a matching problem, and you ask them how they did it. You continually include Content Access Strategies (speaking slowly and clearly), Vocabulary Development (defining new words), and Language Objectives (Listening, Speaking, Reading, and Writing).

How to Teach Skill Development and Guided Practice for Procedural Knowledge to English Learners

Using Matched Problems, written Skill Steps, and Rule of Two

1. Skill Development: Teacher works a problem first.

    A. **Teacher and students read a step.** Pre-pronounce and pre-read, if necessary. Define any new words. Use visual text.

    B. **Teacher executes a step**, modeling the thinking required. Pre-read text, if necessary. Define any new words. Speak slowly and clearly.

C. **Teacher asks a Checking for Understanding question** about the thinking required to execute the step.

- **Pair-share. Students explain** to each other how the teacher executed the step and the thinking required. Provide sentence frames using new vocabulary. Have students pair-share using complete sentences. Cue both partners to explain.
- Call on non-volunteers. Provide corrective feedback on content and language. Re-teach, if necessary.

2. Guided Practice: Students work a matching problem step by step (usually on whiteboards).

   A. **Teacher pre-pronounces, pre-reads, and defines** any new words ELs are going to encounter.

   B. **Students execute steps** one at a time under teacher's direction.

   C. **Students answer Checking for Understanding questions**, describing their intermediate answers and final answer and explaining how they determined their answer.

   - Students pair-share using complete sentences. Provide sentence frames using new vocabulary. Cue both partners to explain.
   - Call on non-volunteers. Provide corrective feedback on content and language. Re-teach, if necessary.

Now let's look at some examples.

Skill Development/Guided Practice Example 1: Locate Information in the Periodic Table of the Elements

Our first example is a science lesson: locating information in the Periodic Table of the Elements. There are three problem variations for locating information: (1) using the element name, (2) using the atomic symbol, and (3) using the atomic number.

Applying the Rule of Two, the teacher models locating information for rows 1, 3, and 5 (Skill Development) in the box on page 206. Students locate corresponding information for rows 2, 4, and 6 (Guided Practice).

Take a moment to look over the example lesson. (Although the lesson is a science lesson, the instructional practices apply to any lesson.) Before we go on, look over the lesson and read the Skill steps, the matched teacher-student problems (rows 1–2, 3–4, and 5–6), the CFU questions that go with the Skill steps, and the example teacher dialog shown below the CFU questions.

Learning Objective

Locate information in the Periodic Table of the Elements.

Skill Development/Guided Practice

Step 1. Use the given information to locate the element on the Periodic Table of the Elements.

Step 2. Use the Periodic Table of the Elements to provide the missing information.

	Element name	Atomic Symbol	Atomic Number	(Rule of Two)
1.	potassium			(teacher)
2.	phosphorus			(students whiteboards)
3.		Na		(teacher)
4.		Cl		(students whiteboards)
5.			17	(teacher)
6.			10	(students whiteboards)

CFU (Teacher works odd rows.)

Step 1. How did I locate the element on the Periodic Table?

(pair-share) *Partner A, show your partner where the element is located in the Periodic Table of the Elements and explain how I, the teacher, found it.*

Step 2. How did I locate the missing information in the Periodic Table?

(pair-share) *Partner B, point to your partner's Periodic Table of the Elements and explain how I, the teacher, located the missing information. Students, copy the information into your own organizers.*

CFU (Students work even rows.)

Step 1. How did you locate the element on the Periodic Table?

Partner B, show your partner where the element is located in the Periodic Table of the Elements and explain how you located it. Be ready to tell me.

Step 2. (whiteboards) Students, write the missing information on your whiteboard. How did you locate the missing information?

Partner B, point to the Periodic Table of the Elements and explain to your partner how you found the information. Be ready to tell me the information in a complete sentence. For example, the atomic symbol for phosphorus is _____. Be ready to tell me how you located the information.

Now, let's go over this example of Skill Development/Guided Practice, using the Rule of Two while emphasizing English Learner strategies.

> I. Skill Development: Teacher works a problem first.
>
>   A. **Teacher and students read a step.** Pre-pronounce and pre-read, if necessary. Define any new words. Use visual text.

(EDI-EL Language Objectives: Reading) Have students read the Skill Development/Guided Practice step chorally. You usually don't need to pre-read steps because ELs have already read and been taught the words during the Learning Objective and Concept Development (EDI-EL Tracked Choral Reading Strategy).

(EDI-EL Language Objectives: Listening, Speaking, Reading) Pre-pronounce and have students say the element names, *potassium* and *phosphorus.* For the word *phosphorus,* use the EDI-EL Phonics Rule Strategy. Point out that *ph* in English is pronounced as an *f* sound. Now you are providing a generalizable rule that ELs can apply to other words they read, such as *photon.*

(EL Vocabulary Development) Use EDI-EL Contextualized Definitions. For Step 1, contextualize the phrase *given information* (the information that is already in the organizer). Point to the organizer and show the "given information." Contextualize *locate* (to find).

> I. Skill Development: Teacher works a problem first.
>
>   B. **Teacher executes a step**, modeling the thinking required. Pre-read text, if necessary. Define any new words. Speak slowly and clearly.

While modeling, incorporate the new vocabulary: *I have used the given information to locate the atomic symbol for potassium on the Periodic Table of the Elements. The atomic symbol—the abbreviation—for potassium is* K. These sentences are rich in Academic Vocabulary (given information, locate) and Content Vocabulary (atomic symbol, potassium, Periodic Table of the Elements). These rich sentences are much more beneficial for ELs than hearing, "I have found the answer. It's K." One sentence also contextualized the definition of atomic symbol: "abbreviation."

For Skill Development/Guided Practice Step 2, define *provide* contextually (to give, to make available). Define *missing information* contextually (the information that is not there). Point to the missing information in the organizer.

(Content Access Strategies: Slow Speech, Clear Enunciation, Insert Spaces Between Words, Visual Presentation.*)* Model, stating your internal thinking, as you locate missing information. Speak clearly while pointing to a visual of the Periodic Table that ELs can see.

1. Skill Development: Teacher works a problem first.

   C. **Teacher asks a Checking for Understanding question** about the thinking required to execute the step.

   - **Pair-share.** Students explain to each other how the teacher executed the step and the thinking required. Provide sentence frames using new vocabulary. Have students pair-share using complete sentences. Cue both partners to explain.
   - Call on non-volunteers. Provide corrective feedback on content and language. Re-teach, if necessary.

Now you ask Checking for Understanding questions about how the missing information was located.

(Vocabulary Development, Speaking) Use sentence frames and have students pair-share and answer in complete sentences. *The atomic number for potassium was determined by* _____. Call on non-volunteers. Provide corrective feedback on content and language. Re-teach, if necessary.

2. Guided Practice: Students work a matching problem step by step (usually on whiteboards).

   A. **Teacher pre-pronounces, pre-reads, and defines** any new words ELs are going to encounter.

   B. **Students execute steps** one at a time under teacher's direction.

   C. **Students answer Checking for Understanding questions,** describing their intermediate answers, final answer, and explaining how they determined their answer.

   - Students pair-share using complete sentences. Provide sentence frames using new vocabulary. Cue both partners to explain.
   - Call on non-volunteers. Provide corrective feedback on content and language. Re-teach, if necessary.

For Guided Practice, have the students locate information for the next row. Have them write their answers on their whiteboards and pair-share, pointing to the Periodic Table and explaining to their partners how they obtained their answer. Call for students to raise their boards. Call on non-volunteers to explain their answers in complete sentences. Provide content and language feedback, if necessary.

Repeat the Rule of Two process, alternating between you and the students in locating the required information from the Periodic Table of the Elements.

Skill Development/Guided Practice
Example 2: Determine Main Idea and
Supporting Details in Text

Now let's look at another example, determining the main idea and supporting details. (The circles and underlines on page 210 show how the paragraphs will look *after* the students analyze them during the lessons.)

There are two paragraphs. Note: At DataWORKS, if we create our own passages for a lesson, we number the sentences to make it easier for English Learners to locate or refer to specific sentences during a lesson. *Students, why is Sentence 3 a supporting detail? You should say, "Sentence 3 is a supporting detail because ____."* Students can also rapidly identify information by writing just the sentence number on their whiteboards rather than the entire sentence. *Students, which sentence is the main idea in the paragraph? Write on your whiteboards the number of the sentence with the main idea. Explain to your partner why you think that sentence is the main idea. You should say, "Sentence ___ is the main idea because ____."*

From Silvia: Caution. When students copy a sentence to a whiteboard (e.g., to show a main idea or supporting detail), this does not meet the criteria of a Writing Language Objective. Writing Language Objectives focus on English Learners writing using new vocabulary or original writing, not copying.

Learning Objective

Determine[1] main idea and supporting details in text.

1 determine—figure out

Skill Development/Guided Practice

Step 1.   Read each sentence carefully.

Step 2.   Determine the main **idea, the one sentence that tells what the other sentences are all about.** (circle)

Step 3.   Identify the supporting details that **tell more about the main idea.** (underline)

(Continued)

(Continued)

1. The blue whale is the largest animal on Earth. 2. The blue whale can measure 100 feet in length. 3. It can weigh as much as 30 elephants. 4. The heart of the blue whale is the size of a small car. 5. Blue whales live in the ocean.

CFU

Step 2. (pair-share) How did I (the teacher) determine which sentence is the main idea?

Step 3. (pair-share) How did I (the teacher) identify supporting details?

(pair-share) Why is sentence 5 not a supporting detail?

1. Water can have three forms. 2. Water can be liquid. 3. In freezing temperatures, water becomes ice. 4. Water can also become a gas when it boils. 5. Water is used for drinking.

CFU

Step 2. (whiteboards) Write the number of the sentence that is the main idea on your whiteboard. How do you know? (sentence frame) "Sentence ___ is the main idea because..." (pair-share)

Step 3. Underline a supporting detail in the paragraph. (whiteboards) Write the number of a sentence that has a supporting detail. How do you know? (sentence frame) "Sentence ____ is a supporting detail because...." (pair-share) Why is sentence 5 not a supporting detail?

Let's look at the EL practices.

Skill Development Steps

(EDI-EL Language Objectives: Reading) Students have already been taught the meanings and how to read the words contained in the steps during the Learning Objective and Concept Development. For example, the word *determine* was defined in the Learning Objective. Have students chorally read each step. If you hear reading or pronunciation errors during the choral read, then pre-read before the choral read. If you have emergent readers, pre-read each Skill Development/Guided Practice step (EDI-EL Tracked Choral Reading Strategy).

First Paragraph: Blue Whales

The first paragraph in this lesson describes the blue whale. Using the Rule of Two, model this paragraph, determining the main idea, identifying the supporting details, and asking students to describe how you did it.

The purpose of the lesson is to determine relationships between sentences in expository text, in this case between the main idea and supporting details. While reading the paragraph, you provide meanings for words and phrases in the paragraph. However, you are not teaching ELs the characteristics of a blue whale. For example, you don't ask students to describe the blue whale. You ask them how you determined the main idea and why a specific sentence is a supporting detail.

(EDI-EL Language Objectives: Reading) Have the students chorally read the sentences in the paragraph. Pre-read individual difficult words (such as *elephant)* before reading a sentence, or pre-read the entire sentence (EDI-EL Tracked Choral Reading Strategy).

(EL Vocabulary Development) Use the EDI-EL Contextualized Definitions Strategy to define the Academic Vocabulary *measure* and *length.*

Provide meaning by paraphrasing individual sentences. For example, in Sentence 2, the blue whale can measure 100 feet long. *Students, this sentence is telling how long the blue whale is. One hundred feet would be from here across the lawn to the flag pole.* Sentence 4 states that the heart of the blue whale is the size of a small car. *Students, our heart is the size of our fist.* (Hold up fist.) *The blue whale's heart is the size of a car. Look out the window. The blue whale's heart would be the size of one of those cars.*

(Content Access Strategies: Slow Speech, Clear Enunciation, Insert Spaces Between Words, Visual Presentation.) Speak slowly and clearly throughout the lesson. Point to visuals of a blue whale and an elephant.

(EDI-EL Higher-Order Questions, Vocabulary Development, Speaking) Provide sentence frames and call on non-volunteers to answer higher-order Checking for Understanding questions in complete sentences. *Sentence ___ is the main idea because ___. Sentence __ is a supporting detail because___.* Have students pair-share so they are all speaking and verbalizing their answers.

Second Paragraph: Water

The second paragraph is for the students to analyze. Again, the focus is on determining the main idea and supporting details in the paragraph, not teaching about water. However, you still support ELs in understanding the words and ideas about water that are used in the passage.

(EDI-EL Language Objectives: Listening, Speaking, Reading) There are several words that ELs might recognize orally, but not as written text: *liquid,*

freezing, temperatures, and *boils.* Pre-read these words or pre-read the entire sentence before having students read chorally. Have students pronounce the *s* ending of *temperatures* and *boils* (EDI-EL Inflectional Endings Emphasis Strategy).

(EDI-EL Vocabulary Development) Provide contextualized definitions of *forms, liquid, ice,* and *gas.*

(Content Access Strategies) Speak slowly and clearly. Provide meaning by paraphrasing individual sentences.

(EDI-EL Higher-Order Questions, Vocabulary Development, Speaking) Have students use their whiteboards to show the sentence number of the main idea and later the supporting details. Direct students to explain their whiteboards to their partners using complete sentences. *Sentence ___ is the main idea because ___ . Sentence ___ is a supporting detail because___ .*

New in This Edition: EDI Internal Rule of Two

The EDI Rule of Two describes how a teacher works a problem and then the students work a matching problem. However, there's an enhancement that makes the Rule of Two even more effective and engaging for students when doing repetitive practices. It's the *Internal* Rule of Two. Here's how we developed it.

In this lesson, Silvia modeled determining the main idea in the first paragraph and asked a question about how she did it. She modeled finding the first supporting detail and asked a question about how she did it. Then—and this is the new part—she immediately asked the students to find the next supporting detail in the *same* paragraph. This worked because she had already modeled finding the first supporting detail. What Silvia did was determine the main idea and the first supporting detail. Then she immediately asked the students to identify the remaining supporting details inside the same paragraph. Hence, the Internal Rule of Two. Plus, the students were quickly involved in the process rather than watching her analyze the entire paragraph by herself.

> **From Silvia:** One caution here on Internal Rule of Two. You can't always expect to do every other sentence. Depending on the text, sometimes you need to work one or two sentences and then have the students do one or two. Blindly analyzing every other sentence will not work with most text.

When a Skill Development problem involves repetitive processes, use the EDI Internal Rule of Two: Have students immediately perform a repetitive process after you have modeled it first. You don't need to have students wait until the entire next problem before you have them do something. But here's the guideline: Students can immediately perform a process only after *your modeling* has provided enough information that they know how to do it. Let's look at the first paragraph of Example 2 again and apply the Internal Rule of Two.

1. The blue whale is the largest animal on Earth. *2. The blue whale can measure 100 feet in length. 3. It can weigh as much as 30 elephants. 4. The heart of the blue whale is the size of a small car.*

Students, I already identified the main idea in the paragraph. It is Sentence 1: "The blue whale is the largest animal on Earth." I also identified a supporting detail in Sentence 2 that says the blue whale can measure 100 feet in length. This sentence is a supporting detail because it gives more information about how large the blue whale is.

Now I want you to tell me whether Sentence 3 is a supporting detail. Let's read it together. "It can weigh as much as 30 elephants." The word "it" refers to the blue whale. The blue whale can weigh as much as 30 elephants. Students, write "supporting detail" or "not a supporting detail" on your whiteboards. Is Sentence 3 a supporting detail? Show your whiteboard to your partners and explain why you wrote your answer.

In the example above, the teacher orally applied the EDI-ED Replace Pronouns With Nouns to Increase Clarity Strategy. *"It" means the blue whale.* The EDI-EL Write Vocabulary-Based Answers on Whiteboards Strategy was also used. *Students, write "supporting detail" or "not a supporting detail" on your whiteboards.* This provided an opportunity for students to write Content Vocabulary.

Skill Development/Guided Practice Example 3: Add Polynomials

Learning Objective

Add polynomials.

Skill Development/Guided Practice

Step 1. Remove parentheses.

Step 2. Group like terms in order with the highest exponent first.

(Continued)

(Continued)

Step 3.　Combine like terms.

Step 4.　Interpret[1] the sum.

1 interpret—tell what something means

   1. $(3x^3 - 2x^2 - 4) + (4x^3 - 3x^2 + 2)$

   2. $(4p^3 - 3p^2 - 9) + (5p^3 - 2p^2 + 6)$

CFU

(Teacher works problem 1.) After each step, pair-share. *How did I, the teacher, . . . ?*

(Students work problem 2.) After each step, pair-share. *How did you, the student, work the step?* (Students show whiteboards for teacher to see their work. Call on individual students to read their whiteboards and explain how they did each step.)

This example shows the general approach for Skill Development and Guided Practice that can be used for any math lesson.

Rule of Two. You, the teacher, model your thinking solving Problem 1. Interpret what the answer means. Ask CFU questions about how you solved it. Direct students to work Problem 2 step by step on their whiteboards. Check the whiteboards at each step. Ask students to describe what they did.

(EDI-EL Language Objectives: Reading) Have students read the Skill Development steps chorally.

(EL Vocabulary Development) These Skill Development steps contain extensive mathematics Content Vocabulary (*parentheses, group like terms, exponent,* and *combine like terms).* These words should have already been defined during Concept Development. However, you can use the EDI-EL Contextualized Definitions Strategy to restate and reinforce their definitions as you say the words while executing the steps. Define *interpret* during Step 4. There is a footnoted definition (EDI-EL Definition Strategy).

(EDI-EL Listening and Speaking, TAPPLE Effective Feedback) Using complete sentences, students pair-share and answer CFU questions about how the teacher solved Problem 1 and about how they solved Problem 2 on their whiteboards. As you check the whiteboards at each step, provide corrective feedback until all students have correct intermediate answers and final answer on their whiteboards. Include language error corrections (EDI-EL Explicit, Implicit, and Elicit Language Correction Strategies), if necessary.

Declarative Knowledge

Now let's switch to Declarative Knowledge. Declarative knowledge is knowing about something. It addresses facts and information. Unlike procedural knowledge, which can be applied to multiple situations, declarative knowledge addresses one set of facts that doesn't change. Declarative knowledge lessons include the following:

Describe geographical feature in the local region.

Analyze the limitations on government contained in the Bill of Rights.

Analyze the effects of the economic policies of the New Deal.

Describe the position of the sun in the sky during the day and how it changes from season to season.

Explain the sequence and function of the digestive system.

Describe how energy in sunlight is transferred into chemical energy through photosynthesis.

How to Teach Declarative Knowledge: Literacy Approach

EDI uses the literacy approach for teaching declarative knowledge. (The literacy approach means students learn content from written text.) This approach is one of the foundational shifts in the Common Core Standards—students learning directly from text. This is a movement away from oral lectures. Common Core lessons include teacher-supported purposeful reading of text to extract, organize, and analyze specific relevant information that matches the Learning Objective. The text used is the course textbook or related passages and readings. The box below shows some of the shifts in the Common Core State Standards.

Some Common Core "Shifts" in English Language Arts

- Elementary school classrooms are places where students access the world—science, social studies, the arts, and literature—through text. (K–5th)
- Content area teachers outside of the English Language Arts classroom emphasize literacy in their instruction. Students learn through domain-specific texts in science and social studies classrooms. (6–12th)

(Continued)

(Continued)

- Students read text around which instruction is centered. Teachers provide scaffolding and support so that it is possible for students reading below grade level to succeed.
- Classroom experiences connect to text on the page. Students provide evidentiary arguments based on text.

Source: Based on http://engageny.org/wp-content/uploads/2011/08/common-core-shifts.pdf

Declarative knowledge lessons can almost always be taught using graphic organizers that capture the intent of the Learning Objective. In EDI literacy-based lessons, students read text during Skill Development and Guided Practice in order to complete graphic organizers. Reading text, however, means that you guide students through reading selections, providing vocabulary, pronunciation, and reading support. Students are not just assigned to read on their own.

EDI Literacy Approach Supports
Language Acquisition for English Learners

The EDI Literacy Approach is very effective for English Learners because they are increasing their reading fluency and use of English in every lesson as they interact with written text. When lessons are presented orally, the lesson is actually oral comprehension; ELs are only listening. Also, oral lessons tend to use more conversational English, as opposed to a text, which uses more Academic Vocabulary.

EDI lessons are already text based—for example, the written Learning Objective and Concept definitions—but with the literacy approach you integrate textbook selections directly into the lesson.

In literacy-based lessons, you teach an overview of the ideas during Concept Development. Then, during Skill Development and Guided Practice, you get out the textbook to read about the same information in greater detail. In essence, you front load information during Concept Development that students will read about during Skill Development and Guided Practice. Using the Rule of Two, you alternate with the students, analyzing groups of sentences or paragraphs in the text. Although important Content Vocabulary is covered during Concept Development, you provide pronunciation and meaning for additional new words that show up in the text.

Teaching Declarative Knowledge

The Declarative Knowledge Literacy Approach is shown in the box below.

How to Teach Skill Development and Guided Practice for Declarative Knowledge to English Learners

Literacy Approach

1. **Provide an overview of the new information during Concept Development.**

2. **During Skill Development and Guided Practice, go into greater detail using text.**
   - Read from text to extract pertinent information to place in a graphic organizer that shows relationships between ideas.
   - Pre-read text, if necessary. Define any new words. Speak slowly and clearly.

3. **Rule of two.**
   - Steps mainly address the directions for completing the organizer.
   - Model extracting information from text and placing it in the organizer.
   - Have students extract information and place it in the organizer.

4. **Checking for Understanding**
   - Ask questions about where the information goes in the organizer and why.
   - Ask summarizing and compare and contrast questions about the information in the completed or partially completed organizer.
   - Provide sentence frames using new vocabulary. Have students pair-share using complete sentences. Have students point to information in text. Cue both partners to explain.
   - Call on non-volunteers. Provide corrective feedback on content and language. Re-teach, if necessary.

This method of pre-teaching during Concept Development, before reading, works very well. English Learners can read above their reading levels when they are already familiar with the content. In fact, the content is actually covered twice, once during Concept Development and a second time in greater detail while reading during Skill Development and Guided Practice. You incorporate EL strategies while working with the text, focusing on pronunciation, reading, and definitions of new words.

Below is a literacy-based history lesson using a graphic organizer. You teach an overview of Hamilton's and Jefferson's economic ideas during Concept Development. Then, during Skill Development and Guided Practice, you use the textbook to provide information to place in the graphic organizer. The graphic organizer shows relationships among the ideas you are teaching. This approach implements Common Core State Standards shifts: *Students access the world through text. Students learn through domain-specific texts. Students provide evidentiary arguments based on text.*

Skill Development/Guided Practice Example 4: Declarative Knowledge

Learning Objective

Compare the economic ideas of Hamilton and Jefferson.

Skill Development/Guided Practice

Step 1. Scan the organizer to identify the required information.

Step 2. Read the selected paragraphs from the textbook. Write pertinent[1] information in the proper location in the organizer.

1 pertinent—directly related to what you are looking for

Compare Economic Ideas

	Hamilton	Jefferson
Tariffs (taxes on goods coming in or out of a country)		
War Bonds (government promise to pay back money borrowed to finance war)		
Central Bank (bank that regulates money in a nation)		

CFU

Step 1. Why did I scan the organizer first? (*So I know exactly what information I am looking for.*)

Step 2. How did I decide where to place the information in the organizer? Why did I not use some information in the text? (*Because it does not match the organizer.*)

Skill Development Steps

(EDI-EL Language Objectives: Reading) Have students read the steps chorally as you use them. Note: Steps in Declarative Knowledge lessons are mostly directions in how to complete the reading. There are some words to address in these steps.

(EDI-EL Vocabulary Development) Define *pertinent* (EDI-EL Definition Strategy). Contextualize *scan* (EDI-EL Contextualized Definitions Strategies).

(Context Access Strategies) The organizer includes definitions for English Learners—*tariffs, war bonds,* and *central bank* (EDI-EL Graphic Organizer Strategy).

English Learners Read

(Language Objective: Reading; EDI-EL Vocabulary Development) During Skill Development and Guided Practice, you and your English Learners read the textbook (or other suitable written text) as a resource of information for the graphic organizer. For difficult text, pre-read before ELs read using the EDI-EL Tracked Choral Reading Strategy. Define new words using one of the EDI-EL vocabulary strategies such as Contextualized Definitions, Multiple-Meaning Words, Synonyms, and Word Morphology. For easier text, pre-pronounce and define individual new words without pre-reading all the text.

(Supplementary Materials and Adaptations of Existing Materials) When selecting text for English Learners to read, use the criteria described for Simplified Text and Elaborated Text.

English Learners Write

(Language Objective: Writing) English Learners write pertinent information in their organizers. They paraphrase and summarize content-related information. The information they write is the information they are learning. The writing also serves as a Cognitive Strategy to help them remember the new content.

Rule of Two

With literacy-based declarative knowledge lessons, you model first, extracting some information and placing it in the proper location in the organizer. Then the students extract some additional information and place it in the organizer. As the lesson progresses, students can extract information on their own and with their partners. However, before students are asked to read additional paragraphs by themselves, pre-pronounce and define any difficult words.

Check for Understanding for both Literacy and Content

The Checking for Understanding questions in literacy-based EDI lessons address two areas: Literacy and Content.

Literacy-based questions address the process of identifying relevant information from a text for placement in specific parts of an organizer, including identifying why some information in the text is not included (because it is extra information not pertinent to the Learning Objective and the organizer). The fact that every detail is not included forces students to think about what they are reading and to interact deeply with the text as they distinguish between pertinent information and information that is not relevant to the organizer.

The literacy-based CFU questions shown in the Hamilton-Jefferson lesson above address the literacy component of the lesson—what information is important in the text, and where it goes in the organizer. But you also include content-based questions.

Content-based questions address the content itself. Now you are asking questions about the specifics of the content. In the example above, you could ask questions such as "What was Hamilton's view on War Bonds?" However, you can use the structure of the organizer as a basis for creating CFU questions.

Checking for Understanding for Graphic Organizers

When using graphic organizers, student interaction and Checking for Understanding questions can be built around the structure of the organizer. For example, you can ask students to (1) summarize rows or columns or (2) compare and contrast rows or columns, depending on the specific organizer (see Table 10.1). You intersperse these CFU questions as students complete the organizer.

Students, I want you to summarize Jefferson's and Hamilton's economic ideas. Partner "A," summarize Hamilton's economic ideas. Partner "B," summarize Jefferson's economic ideas. Summarize to your partner. In a minute, I will call on some of you to report out to the class.

Since the organizer in Table 10.1 is set up for compare and contrast, you can use the EDI-EL Relationship Vocabulary Strategy in your sentence frames. In the example below, the word *distinction* is used in the sentence frame, and a Contextualized Definition is provided for the word *distinction*.

Students, what was one distinction, or difference, between Hamilton's and Jefferson's views on tariffs? Look over your graphic organizers and explain to your partner. Partner "A" goes first. You should say, "One distinction between Hamilton's and Jefferson's views on tariffs was _____."

Table 10.1 Compare Economic Ideas Graphic Organizer

	Hamilton	Jefferson	
Tariffs (taxes on goods coming in or out of a country)			CFU contrast ideas
War Bonds (government promise to pay back money borrowed to finance war)			CFU contrast ideas
Central Bank (bank that regulates money in a nation)			CFU contrast ideas
	CFU summarize	CFU summarize	

SUMMARY: SKILL DEVELOPMENT AND GUIDED PRACTICE

This chapter has described how to incorporate EL strategies while teaching Skill Development and Guided Practice to English Learners—teaching content while promoting language acquisition. EDI-EL lessons have always been text based, but we wrapped up this chapter by describing the EDI Literacy Approach for teaching declarative knowledge, in which students read about what they are being taught, implementing the Common Core shift of students learning from domain-specific text.

- **Provide Skill Development steps**. Steps should be strategic, showing students how to do it. Students should read the steps.
- **Rule of Two**. Use matched pairs of problems for all variations in the Independent Work. Teacher works first problem. Students work second one.
- **Internal Rule of Two.** If a given problem involves repetitive steps, have the students execute a repetitive step after you have modeled one first. You don't need to work the entire problem yourself.
- **Teach thinking processes**. Model the thinking used to solve problems. Ask CFU questions about the thinking processes you used and that the students used. Use sentence frames so ELs respond in complete sentences, practicing the new vocabulary from the lesson.
- **Focus on Vocabulary Development.** Continually define new words and then contextualize them to reinforce their meanings. Use one of the EDI-EL vocabulary strategies.

- **Focus on Language Objectives.** Incorporate Listening, Speaking, Reading, and Writing opportunities throughout the lesson. Teach student how to pronounce and read new words. Use tracked reading to improve reading fluency.
- **Content Access Strategies.** Continually use strategies that help ELs understand the English used in a lesson, such as slow, clear speech and Context Clues. When necessary, use Simplified or Elaborated Text to improve ELs' comprehension so they learn from what they are reading.
- **For Declarative Knowledge, use the EDI Literacy Approach.** Provide an overview during Concept Development. Go into greater detail during Skill Development and Guided Practice, reading and extracting information from a textbook (or suitable reading material) to complete a graphic organizer showing relationships among ideas.

How to Teach Skill Development and Guided Practice for Procedural Knowledge to English Learners

Using Matched Problems, written Skill Steps, and Rule of Two

1. Skill Development: Teacher works a problem first.
    A. **Teacher and students read a step.** Pre-pronounce and pre-read, if necessary. Define any new words. Use visual text.
    B. **Teacher executes a step**, modeling the thinking required. Pre-read text, if necessary. Define any new words. Speak slowly and clearly.
    C. **Teacher asks a Checking for Understanding question** about the thinking required to execute the step.
        - **Pair-share. Students explain** to each other how the teacher executed the step and the thinking required. Provide sentence frames using new vocabulary. Have students pair-share using complete sentences. Cue both partners to explain.
        - Call on non-volunteers. Provide corrective feedback on content and language. Re-teach, if necessary.

2. Guided Practice: Students work a matching problem step by step (usually on whiteboards).
    A. **Teacher pre-pronounces, pre-reads, and defines** any new words ELs are going to encounter.
    B. **Students execute steps** one at a time under teacher's direction.

C. **Students answer Checking for Understanding questions**, describing their intermediate answers and final answer and explaining how they determined their answer.

- Students pair-share using complete sentences. Provide sentence frames using new vocabulary. Cue both partners to explain.
- Call on non-volunteers. Provide corrective feedback on content and language. Re-teach, if necessary.

How to Teach Skill Development and Guided Practice for Declarative Knowledge to English Learners

Literacy Approach

1. **Provide an overview of the new information during Concept Development**.

2. **During Skill Development and Guided Practice, go into greater detail using text**.
   - Read from text to extract pertinent information to place in a graphic organizer that shows relationships between ideas.
   - Pre-read text, if necessary. Define any new words. Speak slowly and clearly.

3. **Rule of two**.
   - Steps mainly address the directions for completing the organizer.
   - Model extracting information from text and placing it in the organizer.
   - Have students extract information and place it in the organizer.

4. **Checking for Understanding**
   - Ask questions about where the information goes in the organizer and why.
   - Ask summarizing and compare and contrast questions about the information in the completed or partially completed organizer.
   - Provide sentence frames using new vocabulary. Have students pair-share using complete sentences. Have students point to information in text. Cue both partners to explain.
   - Call on non-volunteers. Provide corrective feedback on content and language. Re-teach, if necessary.

By this point in an EDI lesson, you have taught all the new content—Concepts and Skills. Now, all that is left before Closure is lesson Importance, when you teach students why the lesson is important to learn. You are going to convince them that the lesson is important and relevant.

11 How to Teach Lesson Importance to English Learners

In EDI lessons, Importance is the part of the lesson in which you explicitly teach your students why the lesson is worthwhile for them to learn. You convince your students that the lesson is important by providing compelling reasons along with examples that illustrate each reason. Generally, about five minutes is allocated to Importance.

> **Importance**
>
> Analyzing the economic policies of the New Deal is important because these policies still affect us today.
>
> *Social Security*
> *Workers' Compensation Insurance*

EDI lessons use three types of Importance reasons: (1) personal reasons—why the lesson is personally important to the students, (2) academic reasons—why the lesson is important at school (it's on the test; you need to know this for next year), and (3) real-life Reasons—why the lesson is important in real life or important to society. You don't need all three for every lesson; however, it's best to have a wide variety of reasons because some reasons will be more relevant to specific students than others.

The Importance reasons should use the Academic and Content Vocabulary from the lesson. Generally, the Learning Objective is embedded in the Importance reason. After each reason, you provide an example to illustrate what the reason means. You complete Importance with Checking for Understanding questions asking why the lesson is important to learn.

Learning Objective

Tell time to the nearest minute.

Importance

1. **Telling time** is important so you know when to do something.
   Watch your favorite TV show.
2. **Telling time** will be on the test Friday.
   What time is shown on the clock?
3. **Telling time** is important so everyone arrives at the same time.
   School starts at 8:05.

CFU

Does anyone else have another reason why it is important to tell time?

Which reason is the most important to you?

Avoid using an example as a reason. Provide Importance reasons followed by examples. In the reason below, students might think that density only applies to a ring.

Calculating density will enable you to determine whether a ring is made of gold.

Here is the generalizable reason followed by an example:

Calculating density will enable you to identify unknown materials.
   Is the ring made of gold?

The most effective Importance reasons and explanations are those that incorporate the specific attributes of the lesson's Concept definitions, allowing Importance to reinforce Concepts.

The generic reasons below don't reinforce concepts.

Determining the meaning of figurative language is important:

- You will be a better reader.
- You will be a better writer.
- It's on the state test.

Here are some Importance reasons derived from Concept definitions.

Concept Development

Figurative language is words or phrases that have meanings different from the literal meanings of the words.

Importance

Interpreting figurative language is important so you don't use literal meanings for figurative language.

I heard it straight from the horse's mouth.

Literal meaning: *I heard a horse say it.*

Figurative meaning: *I heard information directly from someone who knows.*

Concept Development

A **compound word** is two words joined together to make a new word.

Example compound words: bookshelf, notebook

Importance

You can **predict the meaning of compound words** by looking at the two words.

Birdhouse: A house for birds.

Concept Development

Perimeter is the length of the <u>distance around a polygon</u>.[1]

1 polygon—a flat figure with straight sides, such as a triangle, rectangle, or square

Importance

Calculating perimeters will enable you to build and design things.

What is the length of fence needed <u>to go around</u> a rectangular yard 2 meters by 5 meters?

LESSON IMPORTANCE IS IMPORTANT

Explicitly teaching students the importance—the relevance—of the lesson increases student motivation for learning. Students sometimes ask, "Why do I need to learn this?" During Importance you tell them why. Humans have a built in "What's in it for me?" attitude and will work harder when they think it is to their personal benefit. (For example, teenagers are motivated to read and study the motor vehicle laws because they want to pass the driver's license test.) Showing students the relevance of each lesson motivates them to learn.

From John: I always try to be very convincing during Importance. During middle school and high school lessons, I connect the lesson to real life, especially to jobs and careers, and success in life. One language arts lesson I taught recently included three reasons why the lesson was important. I then added my own fourth reason, passionately describing how what we were learning today could help them in jobs that required creativity. I had the students write which reason of the four reasons was most important to them on their whiteboards. When the boards went up, three-fourths of the students had my reason, which wasn't in the original lesson. When I called on individual students, they described how important creativity was for a job they might get.

However, one student violently disagreed. She wrote all four reasons on her whiteboard and said, "You are all wrong! Every one of the reasons is important." She went on to describe in detail how each reason was important. Importance can add interest and motivation to any lesson.

CREATING STUDENT MOTIVATION

Teachers often say they wish their students were more motivated to learn. Explicit Direct Instruction includes three specific practices that motivate students.

1. **Calling on non-volunteers**. This motivates students to pay attention because you might call upon them at any time.

2. **Importance**. Teach students why each lesson is important for them to learn.

3. **"I can do it**." The best motivator for students is being able to do the work. This is self-motivation at its best. Humans love to work on puzzles. However, puzzles are not fun if they are too easy or too hard.

When students learn something new and they can do it by the end of the lesson, they are self-motivated. Even doing the homework is interesting because they can do it. The "I can do it" moment is the goal of every EDI lesson.

WHEN DO YOU TEACH IMPORTANCE?

Importance can be taught at any time during the lesson, as soon as the students understand what they are being taught. This usually means that you can't start a lesson with Importance because students don't know the new content yet. Generally, you need to have at least completed Concept Development before going to Importance. At DataWORKS, we had been teaching Importance after Concept Development. We are now placing Importance after Guided Practice. At this point, students have a better grasp of the lesson, plus the lesson flows better with Concept Development going directly to Skill Development without being interrupted by Importance.

Now let's go over the three steps for teaching EDI Importance to English Learners.

How to Teach EDI Importance to English Learners

Using written Importance reasons with examples.

1. **Have students read** each reason chorally.

   A. Pre-read, if necessary

   B. Define vocabulary, if necessary

2. **Explain what each Importance reason means** using examples that illustrate the reasons.

   A. Define vocabulary, if necessary

   B. Speak clearly

3. **Check for Understanding:** Ask students why the lesson is important to learn.

   A. Ask volunteers for additional reasons

   B. Pair-share most important reason

   C. Call on non-volunteers for most important reason

EDI-EL Lesson Importance

1. Have students read each reason chorally.

   A. Pre-read, if necessary

   B. Define vocabulary, if necessary

(EDI-EL Vocabulary Development and Language Objectives: Listening, Speaking, Reading) To maximize reading opportunities for ELs, all EDI lesson components, including Importance, are text-based. But don't read the Importance reasons by yourself. Provide written reasons and have your students read the reasons with you. If students don't have matching handouts, then just have them read the reasons off the board or the screen.

By the time you reach Importance, you have already taught ELs to pronounce and read the Academic and Content words in the lesson. You can usually just cue students to read the Importance reason chorally without a pre-read.

However, for emergent readers (K–2), pre-read while students track and then have them read chorally (EDI-EL Tracked Choral Reading Strategy). If there are any new words, pre-pronounce them. Then define the words explicitly, or provide a contextualized definition.

For kindergarten and first-grade students, use simple Importance reasons and text with short sentences.

Importance

1. Knowing sight words helps you read.

   I see you. I see the man.

2. Knowing sight words helps you write.

   I go to school.

Avoid using pronouns in the reasons. ELs might lose track of what the pronouns refer to. Also, when using pronouns, English Learners are repeating pronouns instead of the new vocabulary you want them to learn and use.

Learning Objective

Distinguish between main idea and supporting details.

(Continued)

(Continued)

Importance

Distinguishing between main idea and supporting details is important.

1. It will help you find the most important information in text you read.

2. It will help you organize your own writing.

3. It is tested.

The pronouns in the three reasons above are not reinforcing the vocabulary in the lesson. Below, the new vocabulary is used in the three reasons.

Learning Objective

Distinguish between main idea and supporting details.

Importance

1. Distinguishing between main idea and supporting details will help you find the most important information in text you read.

2. Distinguishing between main idea and supporting details will help you organize your own writing.

3. Distinguishing between main idea and supporting details will help you do well on tests.

Although they appear to be wordy, the revised Importance reasons above provide additional opportunities for ELs to use the new vocabulary (EDI-EL Replace Pronouns With Nouns Strategy).

2. Explain what each Importance reason means using examples that illustrate the reasons.

A. Define vocabulary, if necessary

B. Speak clearly

After the choral reading of an Importance reason, you stop and explain what it means. It is best to include written examples. If you don't have written examples, then provide an oral example of what the Importance reason means. While explaining, use EDI-EL Content Access Strategies such as Speaking Clearly and Slowly, Defining Idioms, and providing Contextualized Definitions, if required.

3. Check for Understanding: Ask why the lesson is important.

A. Ask volunteers for additional reasons

B. Pair-share most important reason

C. Call on non-volunteers for most important reason

After presenting and explaining the reasons why the lesson is important to read, you are ready for Checking for Understanding questions. There are two Checking for Understanding questions for Importance that work for most EDI lessons.

CFU

1. Does anyone have another reason why this lesson is important? (volunteers)

This first question provides an opportunity for students to add their own ideas. Ask for volunteers because students are providing additional reasons from their background knowledge, not from what you have taught them. Students don't always come up with their own reasons, but you provide the opportunity. A pair-share can help students to start thinking. Sometimes, if you think of another reason yourself, you can add it to the list of reasons.

CFU

2. Which reason is the most important to you and why? (whiteboards, pair-share, non-volunteers)

Now you ask why the lesson is important. However, this specific question—asking for the most important reason—changes the Importance CFU from a recall question (name one reason) into a higher-order evaluation question. Students must evaluate the reasons and pick the best one. Always pair-share this question to engage all students in discussing why they selected their reason. Cue for a complete sentence using a sentence frame. Call on non-volunteers to answer.

At DataWORKS, we number the Importance reasons so we can use whiteboards to Check for Understanding. Students write the number of the reason they think is most important. Then we have students pair-share, defending the reason they selected. We use a sentence frame, such as *It is important to _____ because_____.*

Students must paraphrase the actual reason, not just state the number, and then explain why they selected it. *(Listening, Speaking, sentence frame, higher-order question).*

Let's watch a teacher present Importance. Mr. Adams is projecting his reasons directly on the whiteboard at the front of the class.

Importance

1. Calculating discounts and markups is important so you know how much to pay.

   Today only, jeans 25% off.

Mr. Adams points to the screen.

Students, you might be wondering why you need to learn to calculate discounts and markups. Let's read Reason 1 together. Go. "Calculating discounts and markups is important so you know how much to pay."

Now, he elaborates on Reason 1.

Students, when you read ads or go to the store, you can calculate the selling price. Look at the example. Let's read it. "Today only, jeans 25% off." From today's lesson, you know off *is one of the words used for discounts. The selling price will be 25% less than the original price.*

Mr. Adams didn't need to pre-read. His students have already read the new vocabulary several times during the lesson. The choral reading engaged his English Learners in Speaking and Reading and ensured that he was not talking too much by himself. He elaborated, explaining the reason and the example. He used extensive vocabulary including *calculate, selling price, off,* and *original price.*

Mr. Adams repeats the process for Reason 2 and the bulleted examples.

Importance

2. You might work at a store or own your own business and need to calculate discounts and markups.
   How much should we discount these items to sell them?
   Do we have enough markup to make a profit?

Mr. Adams continues, cueing his students to read the third reason and the sample test question.

> ### Importance
>
> 3. Discounts and markup are on the state test and the benchmark test this month.
>
>   *A calculator that is regularly priced at $30 is on sale at a 10% discount. What is the selling price of the calculator?*

Students, look at this sample question. You might be given a similar one. Look right here where it says "10% discount." I want all of you to underline "discount" on your handout. Also, underline the words "selling price." These words from today's lesson will be in test questions. When you see these words, you will know how to solve the problem.

Mr. Adams finished his reasons with a sample test question. However, he did not ask his students to solve the question. He asked his students to underline the vocabulary words from the lesson that are in the question. It is important that ELs recognize these words in test questions, so they know what type of question is being asked. Mr. Adams can have his students answer the question during Lesson Closure.

Mr. Adams turns to the class and inquires,

Students, does anyone else have another reason why it is important to calculate markups and discounts? Raise your hand if you do.

He waits for a few seconds. One student raises her hand. He calls on her. She explains that you need to know discounts and markups to become a teacher. He responds that this is a good reason and writes, "4. To become a teacher," on the board.

Students, write the number of the reason you think is the most important on your whiteboard, and then be ready to tell me why you selected the reason you did. You don't need to write the reason, just the number. Explain to your partner which reason you selected and why. Use a complete sentence. You should say something like this: "It is important to calculate discounts and markup because . . ." Explain the reason to your partner. Don't just read the number.

After waiting for the pair-share, he calls for whiteboards. *Chin-it.* The boards go up. He calls two non-volunteers and reminds one student to use a complete sentence.

While completing Importance, Mr. Adams provided an opportunity for volunteers to share their own reason. He provided a sentence frame. He used a pair-share so all ELs say their complete sentence and express their thoughts.

SUMMARY: LESSON IMPORTANCE

How to Teach EDI Importance to English Learners

Using written Importance reasons with examples

1. **Have students read each reason chorally**.

   A. Pre-read, if necessary

   B. Define vocabulary, if necessary

2. **Explain what each Importance reason means** using examples that illustrate the reasons.

   A. Define vocabulary, if necessary

   B. Speak clearly

3. **Check for Understanding:** Ask students why the lesson is important to learn.

   A. Ask volunteers for additional reasons

   B. Pair-share most important reason

   C. Call on non-volunteers for most important reason

Importance provides relevancy and increases students' motivation to learn. To teach Importance,

- Provide personal, real-life, and academic reasons why the lesson is important for students to learn.
- Provide reasons based on Concept definition attributes so the reasons reinforce Conceptual understanding.
- Include examples that illustrate each Importance reason.
- Incorporate lesson vocabulary into the Importance reasons and examples.
- Focus on Language. English Learners read the Importance reasons. They pair-share the reasons. They answer questions in complete sentences.

The EDI lesson is almost done now. Next comes Closure, to wrap up the lesson and to make sure students are ready for Independent Work, during which they practice what they were just taught. Turn the page.

12

How to Close a Lesson and Provide Independent Practice and Periodic Review for English Learners

C losure is a final, formal Checking for Understanding. When you reach Closure, you stop teaching and ask questions to verify that students have learned what you just taught.

Students, I have one last question. I want you to work Problem 14 on your whiteboard all by yourself. No pair-shares.

Including Closure in a lesson is important because it enables you to verify that students are ready to successfully complete the Independent Practice on their own. If students are not successful by Closure, don't assign problems yet. In EDI, you don't assign problems until students have *already* shown you that they know how to do them.

> In EDI, you don't assign problems until students have *already* shown you that they know how to do them.

Another use of Closure is to identify individual students who might need additional help. We have found that with EDI, you can't prejudge which students will be successful and which will need additional help. Present a well-crafted lesson to all students. Use Checking for Understanding and Closure to determine which specific students need help.

If you don't have time to complete a lesson, Closure should only cover the part of the lesson you actually taught. Then assign only those Independent Practice problems that match the ones you covered in class during the lesson.

From Silvia: Sometimes, we see Closure presented after students have already completed Independent Practice. Also, we have seen the new learning in a lesson being summarized by the teacher instead of by the students. In EDI, Closure completes the Content Presentation portion of an EDI lesson and verifies that students are prepared for Independent Practice.

LESSON CLOSURE FOR ENGLISH LEARNERS

How to Teach EDI Lesson Closure for English Learners

1. Ask Closure Checking for Understanding questions.

    A. Concept-related questions

    B. Execute skills

    C. Importance questions

    D. Vocabulary questions

    E. Summary questions: *What did you learn?*

    F. Super pair-share

2. Apply Content Access Strategies to Closure text.

3. Support Comprehension of Closure text.

    A. Support Closure text reading, if necessary

    B. Define Closure text vocabulary, if necessary

4. Identify Students for additional help, if necessary.

(EDI-EL Language Objectives: Reading) To support reading for English Learners, have the class read the Closure questions chorally. For emergent readers, pre-read with students tracking before the choral reading.

(Vocabulary Development) Avoid introducing any new vocabulary in Closure questions. The questions should incorporate the new vocabulary already taught during the lesson. For example,

In your own words, what is figurative language?

Interpret the figurative language in Paragraph 4.

Why is interpreting figurative language important?

The questions you ask during Closure address the lesson's Concepts, Skills, Importance, and Vocabulary. You can also include general Closure questions such as *What did you learn today?* Let's go over the types of Closure questions.

EDI-EL Lesson Closure

1. Ask Closure Checking for Understanding questions.

   A. Concept-related questions

In your own words, what is _____?

For Closure questions addressing Concept Definitions, allow students to pair-share and review the handouts or notes. Generally, students have not totally internalized (memorized) Concept definitions during one lesson. Directing them to look over their materials actually forces them to review the information one more time. Pair-sharing and explaining in their own words also provides additional repetitions, which helps students remember the new information.

Refer to your handout and explain to your partner in your own words.

What is figurative language?

In literature, what is hyperbole?

What is multiplication?

What is a quadrilateral?

What are the three solutions to a system of linear equations?

What was the New Deal?

What is separation of powers in the U.S. Constitution?

Besides asking for Concept definitions directly, you can ask questions related to Concepts.

Why is this sentence figurative language? I heard it from the horse's mouth.

Draw a right triangle and label the legs and hypotenuse.

B. Execute Skills for Closure

Skill-Based Closure questions ask students to work a problem or answer questions. Don't use pair-shares during Skill-Based Closure questions when students solve problems. You want to see whether students can successfully solve problems by themselves.

Provide a problem for students to work for Closure. Often, you can use a released state test question, if you have one that matches the lesson. Or, the final problems of Guided Practice can be used for Closure. Just have students work them on whiteboards with no pair-share.

If you did not have time to cover all the problem types during the lesson, then the Closure questions should only cover the problem types actually taught.

Solve Problem 18 on your whiteboards.

Identify the setting in the first paragraph on page 6. Write the setting on your whiteboard.

Students, I want you to show me you can solve a problem all by yourself. Write your answer on your whiteboard. Write it and hide it. Turn your whiteboard over when you have your answer. Don't show your partner or copy other students' whiteboards.

> **From Silvia:** Important! In EDI, the skill-based Closure question is the only time you don't use a pair-share. Use pair-shares for all other questions.

Skill-Based Closure questions for *declarative knowledge* can ask students for additional information or details. For these questions, allow students to refer to notes or handouts because they won't have memorized all the declarative information. Allow students to interact with the information one additional time.

Describe one of the specific reforms of the Progressive Reformers.

Describe one economic policy of the New Deal that dealt with providing a social safety net. What effect does that policy have on us today?

Refer to your notes and then explain to your partners.

C. Importance Closure questions

If you taught Importance early in the lesson, you can reinforce Importance by asking students one more time during Closure why the lesson is important to learn. If you taught Importance toward the end of the lesson, you can skip asking specific Importance questions again.

Use pair-shares for Importance Closure questions. You are not trying to measure whether students have memorized the Importance reasons. You want them to review, discuss, and think about it one more time.

Look at your handout and explain to your partner

Why is it important to identify characters in a story?

Why is writing a thesis statement important?

Why are Checks and Balances in the Constitution important?

Why is it important to be able to write a counterargument?

D. Vocabulary Closure questions

During Closure, you can also ask questions about any Academic Vocabulary words you taught. Let students refer to handouts and pair-share so they interact with the definitions again.

Students what does distinguish *mean?*

Students, what does interpret *mean?*

Refer to your handout and tell your partner in a complete sentence.

E. Summary Closure questions: What did you learn?

Besides the formal Concept, Skill, and Importance Closure questions, you can ask some more summary Closure questions.

What did you learn today about _____, and why is it important?

What will you tell your family tonight that you learned about ___ during this lesson?

How can you use what you learned today about _____ in the future?

How did we solve problems for _____ today?

F. Super Pair-Share Closure

For the Super Pair-Share Closure, have students stand up and face their partners and describe to each other everything they learned. Then call on non-volunteers to report out. After calling on non-volunteers, you can call on some volunteers, too.

Students, stand up and face your partners. Tell your partner everything you learned today. Then I am going to call on some of you to tell the class what you learned.

From John: I always watch the clock while I teach. I know I can't teach faster than the students' absorption rate—in other words, I can't just talk faster to complete a lesson—but I can pace myself to include a Closure for every lesson. Often, I just use the Super Pair-share. Having the students stand up energizes them and provides a strong ending for any lesson.

EDI-EL Lesson Closure

2. Apply Content Access Strategies to Closure text.

Closure readings and passages should be easy enough to read so English Learners can successfully apply their new knowledge of the Concepts and Skills taught in the lesson and not be slowed by difficult reading.

Closure is an excellent opportunity to select or modify readings using EDI-EL Content Access Strategies such as Easy-To-Read Text, Simplified Text (e.g., shorter sentences with fewer dependent clauses) and Elaborated Text.

EDI-EL Lesson Closure

3. Support Comprehension of Closure text.

A. Pre-read Closure text, if necessary

B. Define Closure text vocabulary, if necessary.

(EDI-EL Vocabulary Development and Language Objectives: Reading) We already discussed how Closure should use easy-to-read passages. However, if the Closure questions do require ELs to read difficult text, then pre-read the text so they can answer the questions. If there are new words

in the text, define them. Closure should measure English Learners' knowledge of the new content and not be a general reading comprehension or vocabulary test.

> Closure should measure English Learners' knowledge of the new content and not be a general reading comprehension or vocabulary test.

Closure With Pictures. If ELs in kindergarten or first grade are asked to circle pictures for answers, then tell them the names associated with the pictures. They may not know the specific name being used in the lesson. For example, if a drawing of a flower is used in a lesson for students to identify an initial *r* sound, then they need to be told that it's a *rose.*

(EDI-EL Listening and Speaking) To prevent any confusion, point to each picture and say the name. Have the students repeat the names with you so they know what name and sounds are associated with each picture.

Cornell Notes Closure. If your students are using Cornell Notes, direct students to write a summary of the lesson in their notes as part of Closure. Then call on non-volunteers to read their summaries for the whole class.

Incomplete Lesson. Remember, if you don't complete a lesson, Closure only addresses the parts of the lesson that you did cover. For example, if the lesson is on similes, metaphors, and personification, and you only covered similes and metaphors, then only ask questions related to similes and metaphors during Closure.

EDI-EL Lesson Closure

4. Identify Students for additional help, if necessary.

Closure can be a final check to identify indiv help. Pull them over to work with you while the the Independent Practice. If numerous students ra during Independent Practice, that's an indicator th tional instruction. Re-teach the class. You can then work the first few homework problems as additional Guided Practice until the students are ready to work by themselves.

Below are sample Learning Objectives and their corresponding Closures. You can see how the Concept, Skill, Importance, and general Closure questions relate to the Learning Objective.

[handwritten note: Apply to math by creating before instruct. Mid-way post instruction groups]

Learning Objective

Identify fractions as parts of a whole and parts of a group.

Closure

1. In your own words, what are fractions? *(Concept)*
2. Why is it important to be able to identify fractions? *(Importance)*
3. (whiteboards) What is the correct fraction for the **shaded** part. *(Skill, fraction as part of a whole)*

   a. 2/3
   b. 5/2
   c. 2/5

4. Circle the correct fraction for the **shaded** part. *(Skill, fraction as part of a group)*

   a. 1/2
   b. 1/3
   c. 2/3

5. What did you learn today about fractions? *(Summary Closure question)*

Learning Objective

Solve word problems using compound interest.

Closure

1. In your own words, what is compound interest? *(Concept)*
2. Why is it important to know how to solve word problems using compound interest? *(Importance)*
3. Victor deposits $1,000 in a saving account. How much money will he have after 2 years if the account pays 4% compounded annually. *(Skill, whiteboards, no pair-share)*

   a. Write the formula to use on your whiteboard.
   b. Solve the formula.

4. What did you learn today about compound interest, and why is it important? *(Summary Closure question)*
5. How can you use what you learned today about compound interest? *(Summary Closure question)*

INDEPENDENT PRACTICE

After Closure, students are ready for Independent Practice. You provide problems or questions for them to work by themselves that exactly match what you just taught them. In EDI, students can successfully complete Independent Practice as a direct result of the lesson you taught them, not their background knowledge. Remember, with EDI, you don't assign Independent Practice until the students have proven during Guided Practice and Closure that they know how to do the work.

The purpose of Independent Practice is to provide additional repetitions of the content to promote *retention* (so students remember it) and *automaticity* (so they can do it quickly and accurately). This means that the purpose of Independent Practice is to *practice* the content, not to *learn* the content. Students learn the content from you during the teaching of the EDI lesson.

From Silvia: "Automaticity" means learning a skill to the level of a habit so you don't need to think about it while you do it. When adults subtract with regrouping (borrowing), they don't think about the algorithm of borrowing because they have done it enough times. In fact, they can do it without thinking about it. The first few times students subtract with regrouping, they spend a lot of mental energy thinking about the process. As they practice, their brain internalizes the process to where they can do it with little mental effort. Guided Practice, Independent Practice, and Periodic Review all contribute repetitions necessary for the brain to develop automaticity.

Independent Practice can take place in the classroom or at home. Classroom Independent Practice takes place when students work problems by themselves in the classroom. If they have questions, they can raise their hands, and you are available to assist.

During classroom Independent Practice, you can also pull out students you identified during the lesson as needing extra help and work with them. This is called an In-Class Intervention.

To keep the whole class engaged, you can use Structured Independent Practice. Tell students to work the first two or three problems and then write just the answers on their whiteboards. You have them raise their boards, and you check that everyone has done the problems. Repeat the process. This can be very effective in keeping all students on task. Some teachers use an egg timer and have students show what they have done every few minutes.

Homework is Independent Practice that students do at home. During homework, English Learners must be able to work problems by themselves. There is no teacher to assist. Although parents are willing to help their children, we have discovered that some parents are not able to *teach* their students standards-based, grade-level content at home. EDI lessons are designed and taught so students will be able to work problems at home without needing assistance.

PERIODIC REVIEW

Periodic Review (also called Distributed Practice) refers to multiple practice sessions spread out over time to promote retention in long-term memory. Practice sessions are initially scheduled close together and then less frequently. The rule of thumb for Distributed Practice is to review content the day after instruction, a week after instruction, two to three weeks after instruction, and again before high-stakes tests.

Periodic Review is important. Without this practice, students will forget about 80% of what they learned within 18 to 24 hours. This is the reason students can work problems successfully during class and then not be able to do them on a quiz or state test. The information was in their working memory (conscious memory) during the lesson but is not in their long-term memory. Their brains have not retained the information. No amount of encouragement or cheerleading will help because the information is not in long-term memory to be retrieved. A common mistake seen in schools is teaching a lesson and never reviewing it until shortly before an important exam.

Refer to Appendix A for a description of higher-order Constructed Response Questions that can be used during Closure or Periodic Review to advance English Learners' knowledge of new Concepts and Skills.

INDEPENDENT PRACTICE AND PERIODIC REVIEW FOR ENGLISH LEARNERS

Independent Practice and Periodic Review for English Learners

1. Provide problem types that match Skill and Guided Practice problems.

2. Apply Content Access Strategies to Independent Practice text.

3. Support Comprehension of Independent Practice text.

   A. Provide reading support, if necessary.

   B. Provide vocabulary support, if necessary.

4. Include Periodic Review.

1. Provide problem types that match Skill and Guided Practice problems.

Independent Practice and homework problems should be grouped (or identified) by problem type so you can assign problems that match what you taught. This is especially important if you did not cover the entire lesson. Assign only what was taught.

2. Apply Content Access Strategies to Independent Practice text.

Just like Closure passages, Independent Practice passages should be easy enough to read so English Learners can successfully work by themselves. Select or modify readings using EDI-EL Content Access Strategies such as Easy-To-Read Text, Simplified Text and Elaborated Text.

From John: I once saw problems labeled "for the brighter students." Silvia and I always thought why not let *all the students* be the "brighter students"? Teach everyone how to solve each problem type, then everyone is a brighter student.

3. Support Comprehension of Independent Practice text.

   A. Provide reading support, if necessary.
   B. Provide vocabulary support, if necessary.

(EDI-EL Vocabulary Development and Language Objectives: Speaking, Reading) The principles we discussed for Closure apply to Independent Practice. Look over the Independent Practice before assigning it. If the Independent Practice requires ELs to read text, including word problems in math, you may need to pre-read. If Independent Practice uses new vocabulary, define these words. Independent Practice should have ELs practicing new Skills just taught. It is not a reading comprehension or vocabulary assessment. Students are practicing what they were just taught. If emergent readers are to circle pictures for answers, you may need to tell them, and have them repeat, the names associated with the pictures.

4. Include Periodic Review.

Periodic Review is important to help students retain new information. When planning lessons, think about when to include additional practice.

Periodic Review can be provided as warm-up problems or "problem of the day." Sometimes Activating Prior Knowledge reviews a previously taught skill.

One warning—for Periodic Review, you usually need to work a problem first to remind students how to do it. Periodic Review is not an assessment to see whether students remember. It's additional repetitions so they *will* remember. When you don't work a problem first, the students who don't remember will stare at the walls and don't benefit from practicing. Use the Rule of Two. You do a problem first and then the students do one.

Pair-shares are important during Periodic Review. Have students explain to each other how they solved the problems. These pair-shares provide additional repetitions as students discuss their work.

SUMMARY: CLOSURE AND INDEPENDENT PRACTICE

Closure is a final Checking for Understanding to ensure students are ready for Independent Practice. Closure also provides another repetition of the material as students look at notes and pair-share to answer some questions. Closure problem-solving questions are the only EDI questions done without pair-shares, helping you identify individual students for additional support.

During Independent Practice, students work by themselves, either in the classroom or at home. Independent Practice problems always match the problem types taught during the lesson. Students identified as needing extra help can work with the teacher, while other students work independently in the classroom.

Periodic Review, working additional problems over time, is important so students remember what you taught them. Work a problem first to remind students how to do it.

We've now covered all the EDI lesson components, the EDI delivery strategies, and the EDI English Learner strategies. In the next chapter, we'll look at the feedback John received from a principal after teaching Explicit Direct Instruction lessons in language arts and math to English Learners. Then we'll wrap it up with a listing of all the EDI-EL practices used in this book.

How to Teach EDI Lesson Closure for English Learners

I. Ask Closure Checking for Understanding questions.

   A. Concept-related questions

   B. Execute skills

   C. Importance questions

   D. Vocabulary questions

   E. Summary questions: *What did you learn?*

   F. Super pair-share

2. Apply Content Access Strategies to Closure text.

3. Support Comprehension of Closure text.

   A. Support Closure text reading, if necessary

   B. Define Closure text vocabulary, if necessary.

4. Identify Students for additional help, if necessary.

Independent Practice and Periodic Review for English Learners

1. Provide problem types that match Skill and Guided Practice problems.

2. Apply Content Access Strategies to Independent Practice text.

3. Support Comprehension of Independent Practice text.

   A. Provide reading support, if necessary.

   B. Provide vocabulary support, if necessary.

4. Include Periodic Review.

13

Well-Crafted, Powerfully Taught Lessons

Implementing Explicit Direct Instruction for English Learners

T his book has described important ideas and strategies for teaching English Learners who are learning content while simultaneously learning English. We discussed how English Learners learn best through well-crafted lessons, just as native English speakers do. Their brains function in the same way.

We described how to provide well-crafted lessons, how to modify English so it is more understandable, and how to support English language acquisition through embedded vocabulary development and Language Objectives of Listening, Speaking, Reading, and Writing in every lesson.

English Learner Needs

Learn content

Learn English

> **Teachers meet English Learner needs by**
>
> Providing well-crafted lessons
>
> Modifying English so ELs understand the lesson
>
> Supporting English language acquisition every day

Teaching English Learners

- English Learners need to learn grade-level content while simultaneously learning English.
- English Learners learn best through well-crafted lessons, just as native English speakers do (because their brains function the same way).

In Explicit Direct Instruction for English Learners, teachers use

- Components to design a lesson
- Strategies to deliver a lesson
- Continuous non-volunteer Checking for Understanding
- English Language Acquisition Strategies, Vocabulary Development, and Language Objectives
- Content Access Strategies to make English easier to understand
- Continuous student engagement every one to two minutes

The research-based EDI-EL strategies work in the classroom in all content areas, from kindergarten through 12th grade.

Your next step is implementation. You have made a great first step, reading this book. On the DataWORKS website (www.dataworks-ed.com), you will find sample EDI lessons, TAPPLE posters, videos of EDI in real classrooms, and other instructional materials.

PRACTICE EDI FOR ENGLISH LEARNERS TO AUTOMATICITY

All that's left now is for you to practice the strategies to automaticity. Automaticity means you can do them without consciously thinking about how to do them. You just do them.

Automaticity is important because human brains have a limited working memory capacity. Adults can only hold about five to nine items in working memory at the same time. To get around this, our brains automate repetitive tasks so we don't need to use up precious working memory thinking about them. For example, you can tie your shoes or even drive a car with little mental effort because you have practiced to automaticity, to a habit. Now it's as if your subconscious does the thinking for you. Much of what we do becomes habit. Then we can think about something else, such as the specific content we are teaching in a lesson.

Practice is important in developing automaticity in EDI for English Learners. When you reach automaticity, your cup of sticks with student names is nearby, and you always reach in for a random name of a student to answer a question. You consistently remember to teach English Learners how to pronounce words and provide word meanings. You work a problem, modeling your thinking, and then you have students work a matching problem. You ask questions about how the problem was solved. You provide sentence frames. ELs pair-share and answer questions in complete sentences using new vocabulary.

Teaching is fun. ELs are engaged. ELs are learning.

From Silvia: If you are like me, lessons fly by so fast during engaging EDI lessons that you wonder where the time went. But you are not doing all the work yourself. You teach, then the students do the heavy lifting—explaining, pair-sharing, reading, answering questions.

From John: It's as easy as 1, 2, 3:

1. Teacher explains to students.

2. Students explain to each other.

3. Learning verified with higher-order questions.

The next part of this chapter describes feedback from a principal after watching EDI lessons. It's an insightful analysis of strategies teachers want to use after watching Explicit Direct Instruction for English Learners in action with their students. The lessons met the EDI-EL vision: *All students, including English Learners, successfully taught, at school, grade-level work, every day.*

Following the feedback, an outline of all the EDI-EL practices described in this book completes this chapter. You can use it as a quick reference.

FEEDBACK ON EDI LESSONS

From John: Silvia and I have taught EDI lessons from K to 12th grade in all content areas. This next section describes the feedback from two EDI demo lessons I taught.

I visited a school to teach EDI-EL demo lessons in both language arts and math. The principal and teachers watched as I taught their students, which included a high percentage of English Learners. The lessons were grade-level lessons and were very successful with all students. I used released questions from the annual state test for Closure questions and had 100% correct answers in both lessons.

When I go to schools to teach EDI demonstration lessons, I start with a prebrief meeting to go over the design of the lesson and to describe the EL strategies I'm going to use. Then we walk to a classroom of students and I teach. Afterwards, we debrief to describe the lessons and the student results during the lesson. Usually, teachers then teach the same lesson they just observed. On this particular day, however, I taught two lessons, one in ELA and one in math.

At the end of the day, the observation teams and I met for a final time to summarize what we learned over the course of the day. The principal took notes of the discussion to be shared with all teachers, not just those who were with me for the lessons.

Below are generalizations that went out in an e-mail from the principal following our final debriefing session. I have added my comments in parentheses.

Good Afternoon Teachers,

Thank you for participating in yesterday's exceptional professional development activity. A special thank you to John Hollingsworth for sharing his knowledge and insight with us and the guest teachers from our neighboring schools who also observed.

I have included some generalizations and schoolwide expectations of what we learned from today's English language arts and math EDI Lesson Demonstrations:

- All students participated

  (All students, included ELs, actively participated throughout the lesson, including answering questions, choral readings, whiteboards, pair-shares, and gestures.)

- Train students to answer in complete sentences

- Use sentence frames, if needed

  (I provided sentence frames to promote English Learners' use of complete sentences using the new Academic and Content Vocabulary contained in the lesson. Hearing the ELs talk with the new vocabulary was impressive, and you could hear ELs improve during the lesson. In fact, one teacher reported that students sounded like "academic scholars." As students are cued to use complete sentences, they start using them on their own. The principal wants complete sentence and sentence frames to be used throughout the school.)

- Pre-pronounce Academic words

  (I pronounced new words and pre-read text. This allowed all students, including beginning ELs, to successfully pronounce and read the material used in the lesson.)

- Practice choral reading every day to increase general fluency
- Include Academic Reading every day in every lesson

  (The teachers were amazed how much ELs read, even during the math lesson. I had students reading throughout the lesson—Learning Objective, Concept definitions, Skill steps, Importance, and so forth. For difficult text, I always pre-read. For easy text, we read chorally.)

- Use whiteboards to show proficiency combined with an oral description or explanation

  (Besides checking answers, I promoted oral language when using whiteboards. I had students describe their answer, explain how they got their answer, or tell why it was the correct answer. Students had to orally justify whiteboard answers, not just show me the answer. All ELs expressed their ideas during pair-shares before raising their boards.)

- Use engagement strategies

  - Pair-share
  - Point to words
  - Point to your partner's paper
  - Write the word
  - Look at screen/board/paper
  - Circle words
  - Gestures

(I used whole-class strategies that create student engagement. The principal noted several of them above. I sometimes repeated a practice until all students joined in. Having English Learners pair-share while pointing to and explaining pertinent information on their partners' paper is my favorite engagement strategy. For ELs, it combines Listening, Speaking, Reading, and higher-order thinking into one activity.)

- Train all students in Engagement Norms

    (DataWORKS has created Student Engagement Norms. These norms formalize many of the EDI English Learner practices such as pair-share, answering in complete sentences, and tracked reading. I trained students in the norms at the beginning of the lessons and referred to the poster during the lessons. After seeing my demo lessons, the principal wanted all teachers to use the norms in all classes. Below is the poster we use. It is available for downloading on the DataWORKS website, www.dataworks-ed.com.)

Source: © 2009 DataWORKS Educational Research.

- Use attention signals—call and response technique

    (Attention signals are part of the DataWORKS Student Engagement Norms. I said, "Eyes front," and students responded, "Backs straight." Because of the extensive use of pair-shares with English Learners, attention signals are important to quickly regroup the class's attention to the teacher.)

- Check for Understanding (CFU) using higher-order questions constantly
- Use higher-order questions that begin with How or Why—process questions

  (I constantly asked higher-order questions. Remember, ELs have the capability to think and process information at high levels even if they can't completely express their thoughts orally in English. Process questions are an easy way of generating higher-order questions. I had ELs justify their answers. I asked how and why questions: How did I get the answer? How did you get the answer? Why is that the answer?)

- Re-teach if two students in a row cannot answer CFU questions

  (I re-taught a couple of times when students couldn't answer my CFU questions. This can happen in any lesson. By continually asking CFU questions and re-teaching occasionally, I had all the English Learners with me every step for the entire lesson.)

- Never let them off the hook

  (I consistently called on non-volunteers. I used "I'll come back to you" a few times to differentiate for individual students. The teachers commented how this also transformed a couple of students who thought they could tune out during the lesson.)

- Classroom arrangements must have students facing teacher

  (I rearranged some desks during the lessons. Students need to be next to each other to pair-share, and they need to be able to see the text-based lesson presentation at the front of the class. Sometimes, I see classrooms with students in groups facing each other rather than the front of the classroom. This makes it difficult to focus students on the lesson.)

- Don't use new vocabulary to Activate Prior Knowledge—Use the idea

  (During the debrief, we discussed how in EDI, Activating Prior Knowledge does not ask ELs what they already know about new Content Vocabulary words. Instead, Activating Prior Knowledge activates what students already know about the ideas represented by new Content Vocabulary, rather than the new word itself. Alternatively, Activating Prior Knowledge can quickly teach a subskill that will be used during Skill Development and Guided Practice.)

- Concepts vs. Skills. Focus on Concepts first

  (During the debriefing, teachers noted the difference between Concept Development [presentation of definitions and examples of the Concepts] and Skill Development [executing a skill such as "solve" or "distinguish between"]. They also recognized the importance of having solid Concept Development for English Learners in math lessons before manipulating numbers during Skill Development and Guided Practice. This matches the Common Core Standards' focus on developing students' conceptual knowledge in mathematics.)

- Remember "Rule of Two"—matched pairs with homework that also matches

(Of course, "Rule of Two" refers to the use of matched problems in Skill Development and Guided Practice. Plus, the homework problems must match, too. My EDI lessons were set up with matching problems and matching Independent Practice.)

SUMMARY: EXPLICIT DIRECT INSTRUCTION (EDI) FOR ENGLISH LEARNERS

Explicit Direct Instruction Vision

- Ensuring student success at the *lesson* level
- All students, *including English Learners,* successfully taught, at school, grade-level work, every day
- GIFT—Great Initial First Teaching
- Well-crafted, powerfully taught lessons in which students learn more the first time they are taught
- School reform that addresses the success of initial classroom instruction

English Learner Needs

- **Grade-level Content and English.** English Learners need to learn grade-level content while simultaneously learning English.
- **Explicit Direct Instruction.** To maximize learning, English Learners need well-crafted, well-taught lessons. ELs' brains learn in the same manner as native English speakers'.
- **Content Access.** English Learners need to understand the English used during the lesson. You do this by purposefully using Content Access Strategies that make the English you use—both orally and from text—easier to understand.
- **English Language Acquisition.** English Learners need to advance their knowledge of English every single day. You accomplish this by embedding Vocabulary Development (two to seven new words) and Language Objectives (Listening, Speaking, Reading, and Writing) into every lesson, every day, for the whole year.

EDI English Learner Strategies

Support Vocabulary Development in Every EDI Lesson

Vocabulary Development

1. Contextualized definitions

2. Develop concept

3. Attach a label

4. Multiple-meaning words

5. Homophones

6. Synonyms

7. Definitions

8. Word morphology

9. Relationship vocabulary

Support Oral Language Development in Every EDI Lesson

Language Objectives

Listening and Speaking

1. Clear enunciation

2. Physical pronunciation

3. Connect to known sounds

4. Minimal pairs

5. Word chunking for pronunciation

6. Backwards syllabication

7. Inflectional endings emphasis

8. Inflectional endings buildup

9. Pair-share

Reading

1. Tracked reading
   a. Air tracking

2. Read whole word

3. Use phonics rules

4. Syllabication

5. Initial sounds word reading

Writing

1. Write new words on whiteboards

2. Write vocabulary-based answers on whiteboards

3. Elaboration writing

Make English Easier to Understand

Content Access

Comprehensible Delivery

1. Speaking clearly

   a. Speaking slowly

   b. Using formal register when speaking

   c. Inserting pauses between words

   d. Extending vowels

   e. Stressing consonants

   f. Emphasizing each syllable

2. Making sentences easier to understand

   a. Breaking long sentences into several shorter sentences

   b. Shortening sentences by removing unnecessary information

   c. Simplifying sentences by rearranging and removing dependent clauses

3. Controlling vocabulary

   a. Deleting and replacing unnecessary words

4. Connecting to cognates

5. Defining idioms

6. Replacing pronouns with nouns

   a. Replacing pronouns with nouns to increase clarity

   b. Replacing pronouns with nouns to reinforce use of new vocabulary

   c. Clarifying pronoun reference explicitly

7. Clarifying passive voice

    a. Strategically selecting or creating active voice materials

    b. Explaining passive voice when necessary

Context Clues

1. Contextualized definitions

2. Facial expressions

3. Gestures

4. Visuals

    a. Written text

    b. Pictures with definition

5. Realia

6. Analogies, similes, and metaphors

7. Graphic organizers

Supplementary Materials & Adaptations of Existing Materials

1. Selecting text and passages that are easier to read

2. Simplified text

    a. Reducing quantity of difficult words

    b. Reducing sentence length

    c. Simplifying sentences

3. Elaborated text

    a. Making implicit information explicit

    b. Using clear text structure

    c. Adding context clues

EXPLICIT DIRECT INSTRUCTION (EDI): THE WELL-CRAFTED LESSON

Learning Objectives Focus the Lesson for Both Teachers and Students

- **Learning Objectives:** These come directly from grade-level state standards and must match Independent Practice. First, teach students how to pronounce and read the Learning Objective.

Then, over the course of the entire lesson, you teach them how to execute the Learning Objective.

- Deconstruct the Standards: Break a content standard into multiple, teachable Learning Objectives.

Move Prior Knowledge From Long-Term Memory to Working Memory So It's Available to Use

- **Activate Prior Knowledge:** This explicitly reveals a connection between what students already know and what they are about to learn.
- Use a Subskill Review to go over subskills used in the new lesson.
- Use a Universal Experience to connect relevant life experiences to new learning.

Provide Conceptual Knowledge

- **Concept Development:** This requires written, bulletproof definitions (that ELs read) followed by examples (and non-examples) that illustrate the attributes contained in the written definition.
- **Critical Attributes:** Use written, bulletproof concept definitions that contain critical attributes that explicitly define the concept. While teaching, refer to these attributes in the definitions and examples. Explain how non-examples are missing critical attributes.
- **Work the Page:** Using a visual presentation, physically point back and forth between written concept definitions, examples, and non-examples while explaining what the definition means.

Show Students How to Do It

- **Skill Development:** Teacher works problems, explicitly modeling thought processes to show all students, including ELs, exactly how to work the problem.

Students Practice Under Your Guidance

- **Guided Practice:** Now students work a matching problem, usually on whiteboards. Checking for Understanding questions should ask students to describe how the problem was solved, not just the answer itself.
- **Rule of Two:** Use matched Skill Development and Guided Practice problems. Teacher models solving the first one. Students do the second one. Ask CFU questions about thinking processes used to solve the problem.

- **Internal Rule of Two:** If a specific problem has repetitive steps, have the students do some of the repetitive steps after you have modeled how to do one first.

Generate Student Motivation

- **Importance:** Convince students that the lesson is important to learn. Provide personal, academic, and real-life examples.
- Non-volunteers: Calling on non-volunteers generates motivation.
- I can do it! The best motivator of all is students being able to do the work. At the conclusion of well-crafted, powerfully taught lessons, students say, "I can do it!"

Verify Student Learning Before Assigning Independent Practice

- **Closure:** Close a lesson by asking final Checking for Understanding questions to make sure students have learned—*before* assigning Independent Practice.
- **Intervention:** Identify students who may need additional help.

Students Practice to Remember

- **Independent Practice and Periodic Review:** These provide repetition to transfer information into students' long-term memory so it can be retrieved later. Students always work problems that match what was taught.
  - ○ Independent Practice (in class)
  - ○ Homework (out of class)
  - ○ Periodic Review (practice spread out over time)

EXPLICIT DIRECT INSTRUCTION (EDI): THE POWERFULLY TAUGHT LESSON

Verify Students Are Learning While You Are Teaching

Checking for Understanding—TAPPLE

Use pair-shares and non-volunteer Checking for Understanding continuously throughout every lesson to verify that all students, including ELs, are learning what you are teaching. Have students pair-share and answer in complete sentences using the new vocabulary taught in the lesson. Provide corrective feedback to English Learners for content errors and for language errors.

TAPPLE

Teach first

Ask a specific question

Pause, Pair-share, students **P**oint to answers

Pick a non-volunteer

Listen to the response

Effective Feedback

Corrective Feedback

- Cues and prompts
- "I will come back to you."
- De-escalate to a multiple-choice question
- Have students read the answer
- Language error correction (Correct all language errors)
  - ○ Explicit language error correction
  - ○ Implicit language error correction
  - ○ Elicit a correction

Higher-Order Questions

Ask questions that cannot be answered by reading back a sentence from the text. Students must use their own words, explain examples, justify and interpret answers, answer how and why questions, and so forth.

Public Voice

Students answer questions in a loud voice that all students can hear.

Stand and Deliver

Students stand up and deliver responses in a loud voice so all students see them and hear the response.

Help Students Learn and Remember

Rhythm of Teaching for English Learners

There is a rhythm to teaching English Learners—pronouncing words, defining words, pre-reading, choral reading, explaining, pair-shares, Checking for Understanding.

Teaching Strategies

- Explaining: Teach by telling
- Modeling: Teach by talking aloud, revealing inner thinking processes
- Demonstrating: Teach using physical objects

Cognitive Strategies

Strategies that help students remember information such as repetition, memory aids, mnemonics, gestures, and graphic organizers (to show relationships between information).

Cross-Reference the Brain

Used to help remember new words. You say the word, and the students call out the synonym. You say the synonym and students call out the word.

Automaticity

- Students learn academic processes to automaticity so they can execute them quickly and accurately.
- Teachers use instructional EL practices—such as pair-shares and calling on non-volunteers—automatically without having to think about them.

Point

- Teachers point to information on the board or screen as they explain to students what it means.
- Students point to information on paper as they explain during pair-shares.

Create Student Engagement

Engagement: In EDI, teachers create engagement by having students do something every one to two minutes—whiteboards, pair-shares, tracked and choral reading, answering Checking for Understanding questions, and so forth.

Appendix A

Sample Explicit Direct Instruction Lessons for English Learners

Note: All images in the lesson plans, except the DataWORKS logo, are from iStock.com.

Included in this Appendix are sample EDI-EL lessons with clearly labeled components. Lessons start with a Learning Objective and Activate Prior Knowledge. Concept Development includes written definitions, along with examples and non-examples (if applicable). Skill Development and Guided Practice include steps and Rule of Two matched problems—the first one for the teacher to model and the second one for the students to work. The lessons include Importance and Closure. They conclude with Independent Practice and Periodic Review.

The lessons contain vocabulary definitions. However, many important English Learner Strategies are added orally as you teach. For example, you use slow speech and insert contextualized definitions. You pre-read and have students read chorally with you. You direct students to pair-share using complete sentences.

COMMON CORE TESTING

The assessments being developed for the Common Core State Standards contain various types of questions. Selected Response questions are multiple-choice questions where students select one or more correct answers. Constructed Response questions require students to think and reason to create their own responses. Performance Tasks require students to gather information and prepare a final writing or presentation in response to a prompt.

CONSTRUCTED RESPONSE QUESTIONS

Explicit Direct Instruction lessons already include many higher-order Constructed Response questions. For example, Concept Development questions ask students to explain examples and non-examples.

The sample EDI lessons often include additional problems labeled as "Constructed Response" that deepen English Learners' understanding of new Concepts and Skills. The table below shows the types of higher-order Constructed Response questions we use.

Types of Constructed Response Questions

1. Agree or disagree, why	Stephen added $3 + 2$ and got the answer 4. Do you agree with his answer? Why or why not? Jane said that *pretty* is a noun. John said that *parrot* is a noun. Which person do you agree with? Why?
2. Error Analysis	$$\begin{array}{r} 103 \\ -\ 29 \\ \hline 84 \end{array}$$ Ms. Smith said Joe's answer was incorrect. What is wrong with Joe's answer? How can he fix it? Where did he make a mistake?
3. Give an example	Write a sentence with a subordinating conjunction. Refer to your list of subordinating conjunctions. Write a word problem that can be solved using the perimeter formula.
4. Justify a correct answer	$$\begin{array}{r} 103 \\ -\ 29 \\ \hline 74 \end{array}$$ Mr. Jones said that Matthew's answer is correct. Why is Matthew correct? Explain.
5. Recognize the need for a skill in real-life scenarios	Sarah wants to find the distance around her school. Can she use area to solve this problem? Why or why not? 1. How much carpet is needed to cover the living room floor? 2. How much baseboard is needed to go around the living room? Which question can be solved using area? Why?

6. Ask procedural questions	Given $3x - 4 = 12$, what would be the first step of solving this equation? Describe how you solve for x?
7. Decontextualize real-life problems	Applying skills from a lesson to real-life problems that do not have clear steps for solving. A school has 105 computers and 8 classrooms. Each classroom must have 14 computers. How many more computers do they need to buy?
8. Larger scope of similar problems	ELA: Read longer paragraphs, write more sentences, etc. MATH: Longer word problems, larger numbers, more complex figures, inclusion of unneeded information.

9. Analysis of all multiple-choice responses	Which sentence contains an abstract noun?
	   A. Two third graders have a friendship.
	   B. Two third graders played with a basketball.
	   C. Two third graders ate hot dogs.
	Explain the correct answers.
	Explain the incorrect answers.

10. Backward or Reverse logic	Ask a reverse question.
	   A. (forward) Show shaded figure as fraction.
	   B. (reverse) Show fraction as shaded figure.

Additional sample lessons are available on our website www.dataworks-ed.com.

Name _____

We will identify the compare-and-contrast pattern
in informational text$_1$.

CFU

What are we going to do?
What is *informational text*?
"Informational text means _____."

Activate Prior Knowledge

What is the same with Snoopy and Lucky?
What is different with Snoopy and Lucky?

Snoopy	Lucky

Make Connection

Students, you already know
how to find things that are the
same and different. Now, we
will find things that are the
same and different in text.

Vocabulary

$_1$ (informational text) writing that
gives facts

DataWORKS
Educational Research
READY TO TEACH^{SM} EDI® Lessons
©2012 All rights reserved.

CCSS 4th Grade Reading Informational Text 4.5
Describe the overall structure (e.g., chronology, comparison, cause and effect, problem
and solution) of events, ideas, concepts, or information in a text or part of a text.

Concept Development

The **compare-and-contrast pattern** is writing that tells how <u>two</u> or <u>more</u> <u>things</u> are **similar** or **different**.
- *_Compare_ means to tell how things are similar, the same, or alike.*
- *_Contrast_ means to tell how things are different.*
- *Sometimes compare-and-contrast patterns use **clue** words:*

Clue Words for Compare (*similar, alike*)	Clue Words for Contrast (*different*)
like, likewise, also, too, both, same, similar	unlike, different from, but, whereas, on the other hand[2]

Compare-and-contrast pattern:

> 1. Frogs and toads **both** have big mouths and sticky tongues. 2. However, frogs and toads have **different** legs. 3. Frogs have long back legs for jumping. 4. Toads have short back legs to hop from one place to another.
>
> 36 words

Not an example of compare-and-contrast pattern:

> 1. Frogs have big mouths and sticky tongues to catch food. 2. A frog's eyes are on the top of its head so it can see while mostly under water. 3. Frogs have long back legs for jumping.
>
> 35 words

CFU

Which example below is a comparing sentence? How do you know?
Which example below is a contrasting sentence? How do you know?
"Sentence ____ is an example of _____ because _____."

A Frogs and toads also lay eggs to have babies.
B Unlike frogs that have slimy skin, toads have dry skin.

What is the difference between the example and non-example? Explain your answer.
In your own words, what is a compare-and-contrast pattern?
"A compare-and-contrast pattern is _____."

Vocabulary

[2] (on the other hand) (idiom) means to look at something in a different way

The **compare-and-contrast pattern** is writing that tells how <u>two</u> or <u>more things</u> are **similar** or **different**.

Clue Words for Compare *(similar, alike)*	Clue Words for Contrast *(different)*
like, likewise, also, too, both, same, similar	unlike, different from, but, whereas, on the other hand

Identify the compare-and-contrast pattern in informational text.

❶ Read the passage carefully.
   ⓐ Identify₃ the two things being compared, if any. (circle)
   ⓑ Identify the compare-and-contrast clue words, if any. (underline)
❷ Identify if the informational text is written in the compare-and-contrast pattern. (circle Yes or No)
❸ Describe₄ the text structure₅. *"The text is/is not compare-and-contrast pattern because _____."*

---

1. Spiders and insects both have an exoskeleton[1]. 2. Insects have three body segments[2], whereas spiders have only two body segments. 3. Insects have six legs. 4. Spiders, on the other hand, have eight legs. 5. Both spiders and insects have joints[3] in their legs so they can bend them.

45 words

[1] hard outer body
[2] parts divided into sections
[3] places where two bones meets

Compare-and-contrast text?   Yes   No

---

1. Apples and bananas are both fruit. 2. Bananas are long and yellow, whereas apples are round and can be red, green, or yellow. 3. Also, apples and bananas grow on trees. 4. Apples have larger brown seeds, but bananas have smaller black seeds.

40 words

Compare-and-contrast text?   Yes   No

CFU

ⓐ How did I/you identify what two things were being compared?
ⓑ How did I/you identify the compare-and-contrast clue words?
❷ How did I/you identify the compare-and-contrast pattern?
❸ How did I/you describe the text structure?

Vocabulary

[3] find
[4] tell about
[5] (text structure) pattern of writing

CCSS 4th Grade Reading Informational Text 4.5
Describe the compare and contrast pattern in informational text.

The **compare-and-contrast pattern** is writing that tells how <u>two</u> or <u>more things</u> are **similar** or **different**.

Clue Words for Compare *(similar, alike)*	Clue Words for Contrast *(different)*
like, likewise, also, too, both, same, similar	unlike, different from, but, whereas, on the other hand

Identify the compare-and-contrast pattern in informational text.

1 Read the passage carefully.

  a Identify the two things being compared, if any. (circle)

  b Identify the compare-and-contrast clue words, if any. (underline)

2 Identify if the informational text is written in the compare-and-contrast pattern. (circle Yes or No)

3 Describe the text structure. *"The text is/is not compare-and-contrast pattern because _____."*

---

1. Birds are animals that have feathers. 2. They mainly live in trees and bushes. 3. Birds lay eggs in the nests that they build and raise their young until they are old enough to fly. 4. Birds eat seeds, worms, and small insects. 5. There are hundreds of different types of birds, each with their own song.

53 words

Compare-and-contrast text?   Yes   No

---

1. The first movie theater, or "picture house," was built in 1896 and admission was only three cents. 2. By 1905, the first Nickelodeon movie theatre was built, and admission was five cents. 3. You could watch a 10-minute film called *The Great Train Robbery* there. 4. The first full-length movie wasn't shown until 1913.

52 words

Compare-and-contrast text?   Yes   No

CFU

1a How did I/you identify what two things were being compared?

1b How did I/you identify the compare-and-contrast clue words?

2 How did I/you identify the compare-and-contrast pattern?

3 How did I/you describe the text structure?

CCSS 4th Grade Reading Informational Text 4.5
Describe the compare and contrast pattern in informational text.

The **compare-and-contrast pattern** is writing that tells how <u>two</u> or <u>more things</u> are **similar** or **different**.

1 *Identifying the compare-and-contrast pattern in informational text will help you better understand text that tells how things are the same or different.*

> Tornadoes and hurricanes are both very violent storms. Tornadoes are storms that form on land, different from hurricanes that form over water.

2 *Identifying the compare-and-contrast pattern in informational text will help you do well on tests.*

> **Sample Test Question:**
>
> **Read the essay Suzy wrote about desert animals for science class.**
>
> 72. How did Suzy organize the information about desert predators?
>
>   A She used a series of steps in a process.
>   B She stated a cause and then gave effects.
>   C She wrote how things are alike and different.
>   D She made a statement and then gave reasons why it's true.
>
> Support your answer using information from Suzy's essay:
> _____
> _____
> _____

Does anyone else have another reason why is it important to identify the compare-and-contrast pattern in informational text? (Pair-Share)

Which reason is most important to you? Why?
You may give me one of my reasons or one of your own.
It is important to me to identify compare-and-contrast pattern because _____."

CCSS 4th Grade Reading Informational Text 4.5
Describe the compare and contrast pattern in informational text.

The **compare-and-contrast pattern** is writing that tells how <u>two</u> or <u>more things</u> are **similar** or **different**.

Clue Words for Compare (*similar, alike*)	Clue Words for Contrast (*different*)
like, likewise, also, too, both, same, similar	unlike, different from, but, whereas, on the other hand

Skill Closure

Identify the compare-and-contrast pattern in informational text.

1. Read the passage carefully.
   a. Identify the two things being compared, if any. (circle)
   b. Identify the compare-and-contrast clue words, if any. (underline)
2. Identify if the informational text is written in the compare-and-contrast pattern. (circle Yes or No)
3. Describe the text structure. *"The text is/is not compare-and-contrast pattern because _____."*

> 1. Dogs and cats are animals. 2. They both have four legs and a tail. 3. Dogs bark, but cats meow. 4. Dogs and cats also need food and water to live. 5. Dogs need people to provide them with food and shelter, whereas cats can hunt and live on their own.
>
> 47 words

Compare-and-contrast text?   Yes   No

> 1. A lake is a big body of water. 2. Most lakes have fresh water in them. 3. People like to go to the lake to fish, swim, or ride in a boat. 4. The water for lakes comes from the melting snow that travels down through the rivers.   45 words

Compare-and-contrast text?   Yes   No

Constructed Response Closure

Why is the passage below NOT a compare-and-contrast pattern? Explain your answer.

> 1. A blacksmith is a person who makes and repairs things made of metal. 2. A blacksmith makes and fixes metal by heating the metal over a hot flame. 3. A blacksmith makes and fixes things like horseshoes and tools.   36 words

Summary Closure

What did you learn today about identifying the compare-and-contrast pattern in informational text? (Pair-Share)

_____

_____

_____

_____

Name

The **compare-and-contrast pattern** is writing that tells how <u>two</u> or <u>more things</u> are **similar** or **different**.

Clue Words for Compare (*similar, alike*)	Clue Words for Contrast (*different*)
like, likewise, also, too, both, same, similar	unlike, different from, but, whereas, on the other hand

Identify the compare-and-contrast pattern in informational text.

❶ Read the passage carefully.
  ⓐ Identify the two things being compared, if any. (circle)
  ⓑ Identify the compare-and-contrast clue words, if any. (underline)
❷ Identify if the informational text is written in the compare-and-contrast pattern. (circle Yes or No)
❸ Describe the text structure. *"The text is / is not compare-and-contrast pattern because _____."*

---

1. Basketball and soccer are both sports. 2. Like soccer, basketball is played with a round ball. 3. Soccer is played by kicking the ball with feet, whereas basketball is played with hands. 4. Soccer is played with 11 players, different from basketball that is played with five players.

45 words

Compare-and-contrast text?   Yes   No

Describe the text structure.

_____

_____

---

1. Ocean Beach is near San Diego, California. 2. The water is salty, and the sands are beautiful colors of brown. 3. It stretches out to the horizon[1]. 4. People like to go surfing and swimming there. 5. The town is small and quiet.

[1] where the land or sea seems to meet the sky

39 words

Compare-and-contrast text?   Yes   No

Describe the text structure.

_____

_____

Learning Objective

We will solve two-step equations.

CFU

What are we going to learn?

Activate Prior Knowledge

An **equation** states₁ two expressions are equal.
Inverse operations are operations that <u>undo</u> each other.

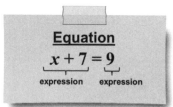

Equation

$x + 7 = 9$

expression   expression

Inverse Operations

+ and −

• and ÷

Solve the one-step equations.

1. $x + 7 = 9$

2. $x + 3 = 7$

Make Connection

Students, you already know how to solve one-step equations. Now we will solve two-step equations.

3. $4x = 16$

4. $2x = 4$

Vocabulary

¹ (states) says or tells

DataWORKS
Educational Research
READY TO TEACH℠ EDI® Lessons
©2012 All rights reserved.

7th Grade Expressions and Equations 7.4.a
Solve word problems leading to equations of the form $px + q = r$
and $p(x + q) = r$, where p, q, and r are specific rational numbers.

Concept Development

A **two-step** equation contains₂ two operations.

$$2x + 3 = 7 \qquad \frac{x}{4} - 5 = 1$$

addition · subtraction · multiplication · division

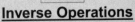

Inverse Operations

+ and −

• and ÷

A **two-step equation** requires₃ two inverse operations to solve for the variable.
- To keep an equation **balanced, inverse operations** must be done on <u>both sides</u> of the equation.

Solving Two-Step Equations

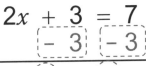

① Inverse Operation

② Inverse Operation

$$2x + 3 = 7$$
$$-3 \quad -3$$
$$\frac{2x}{2} = \frac{4}{2}$$
$$x = 2$$

Balance ①

Balance ②

The **solution** is the value of the variable that makes the equation <u>true</u>.

Checking a Solution

$$2x + 3 = 7$$

Solution

$x = 2$

$$2x + 3 = 7$$
$$2(2) + 3 \stackrel{?}{=} 7$$
$$7 = 7$$
True

NOT a Solution

$x = 4$

$$2x + 3 = 7$$
$$2(4) + 3 \stackrel{?}{=} 7$$
$$11 \neq 7$$
False

CFU

Which of the following is an example of a two-step equation? How do you know?

"___ is an example of a *two-step equation* because _____."

A $5x = 6$ B $5x - 4 = 6$ C $x - 4 = 6$

Which two inverse operations would be used to solve the two-step equation $5x - 4 = 6$? How do you know?

"The two *inverse operations* that would be used to solve are _____ and _____ because _____."

How do you check if a solution is correct or incorrect?

"To check if a *solution* is correct or incorrect, you _____."

Vocabulary

² (contains) has within it
³ (requires) needs [synonym]

7th Grade Expressions and Equations 7.4.a
Solve two-step equations.

A **two-step equation** contains two operations.
A **two-step equation** requires two inverse operations to solve.
  • *To keep an equation **balanced**, inverse operations* must be done
  on both sides of the equation.

Inverse Operations
+ and −
• and ÷

The **solution** is the value of the **variable** that makes the equation true.

Solve two-step equations.

① Read the problem and identify (underline) important information.
  ⓐ Connect the problem to the given two-step equation.
② Isolate₄ the term with the variable.
③ Solve for the variable.
④ Check and interpret the solution.
  Hint: Answer the question.

1. What is the unknown value of x in the two-step equation?

$$\frac{x}{2} - 3 = -2$$

2. What is the unknown value of x in the two-step equation?

$$\frac{x}{5} - 6 = -3$$

3. A gym membership charges a flat fee₅ to sign up, as well as a monthly rate. Jessica paid $50 to sign up and $25 each month. If Jessica has paid $175 to the gym, how long has she been a member?

$$25m + 50 = 175$$

4. A book club membership charges a flat fee to sign up, as well as an annual rate₆. Maurice paid $15 to sign up and $7 each year. If Maurice has paid $36 to the book club, how long has he been a member?

$$7y + 15 = 36$$

ⓐ How did I/you connect the problem to the given two-step equation.
② How did I/you isolate the term with the variable?
③ How did I/you solve for the variable?
④ How did I/you check the solution?

Vocabulary

4 (isolate) separate to be alone
5 (flat fee) one-time payment
6 (annual rate) payment once a year

DataWORKS
Educational Research

7th Grade Expressions and Equations 7.4.a
Solve two-step equations.

A **two-step equation** contains <u>two operations</u>.
A **two-step equation** requires <u>two inverse operations</u> to solve.
  • *To keep an equation* **balanced**, *inverse operations* *must be done*
  on <u>both sides</u> *of the equation.*

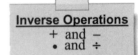

Inverse Operations
+ and −
• and ÷

The **solution** is the value of the **variable** that makes the equation <u>true</u>.

Solve two-step equations.

1. ❶ Read the problem and identify(underline) important information.
   ⓐ Connect the problem to the given two-step equation.
2. ❷ Isolate the term with the variable.
3. ❸ Solve for the variable.
4. ❹ Check and interpret the solution.
   Hint: Answer the question.

5. The length of a rectangular computer monitor is 20 cm. The perimeter of the monitor is 72 cm. What is the width of the computer monitor?

$$2w + 2l = P$$
$$2w + 2(20) = 72$$
$$2w + 40 = 72$$

6. The length of a rectangular cell phone screen is 2 in. The perimeter of the cell phone screen is 10 in. What is the width of the cell phone screen?

$$2w + 2l = P$$
$$2w + 2(2) = 10$$
$$2w + 4 = 10$$

7. A middle school hosted a fall festival to raise money for both grades in the school. The seventh grade class used their half of the money to buy a $750 chemistry set. After buying the chemistry set, the 7th graders had $350 left over. How much money did the school earn at the fall festival?

$$\frac{m}{2} - 750 = 350$$

8. Maria's grandmother gave Maria money to share with her two sisters. The three girls split the money evenly and Maria used her share to buy a computer that cost $550. After buying the computer, she had $25 leftover. How much money did Maria's grandmother give Maria and her sisters altogether?

$$\frac{m}{3} - 550 = 25$$

CFU

ⓐ How did I/you connect the problem to the given two-step equation.
❷ How did I/you isolate the term with the variable?
❸ How did I/you solve for the variable?
❹ How did I/you check the solution?

Importance

A **two-step equation** contains two operations.
A **two-step equation** requires two inverse operations to solve.

• *To keep an equation **balanced**, **inverse operations** must be done on both sides of the equation.*

The **solution** is the value of the **variable** that makes the equation true.

1 *Solving two-step equations will help you solve problems in other classes.*

> If the temperature in Russia is 20° Celsius then what is the temperature in Fahrenheit.
>
> $$F = 1.8C + 32$$
> $$F = 1.8(20) + 32$$
> $$F = 36 + 32 = 68$$
>
> The temperature in Fahrenheit is **68°**.

2 *Solving two-step equations will help you do well on tests.*

Sample Test Question:

42. What is the value of x if $-3x + 2 = -7$.

   A $x = -6$
   B $x = -3$
   C $x = 3$
   D $x = 6$

Check your solution in the space below:

Sample Test Question:

43. Joan needs $60 for a class trip. She has $32. She can earn $4 an hour mowing lawns. If the equation shows this relationship, how many hours must Joan work to have the money she needs?

$$4h + 32 = 60$$

   A   7 hours
   B   17 hours
   C   23 hours
   D   28 hours

CFU

Does anyone else have another reason why it is important to solve two-step equations? (pair-share)

Which reason is most important to you? Why?
You may give one of my reasons or one of your own.
"It is important to me to solve two-step equations because _____."

A **two-step equation** contains <u>two operations</u>.
A **two-step equation** requires <u>two inverse operations</u> to solve.
   • *To keep an equation* **balanced**, *inverse operations* *must be done on* <u>both sides</u> *of the equation*.
The **solution** is the value of the **variable** that makes the equation <u>true</u>.

Skill Closure

Solve two-step equations.

1. Read the problem and identify(underline) important information.
   a. Connect the problem to the given two-step equation.
2. Isolate₄ the term with the variable.
3. Solve for the variable.
4. Check and interpret the solution.
   Hint: Answer the question.

Inverse Operations
$+$ and $-$
$\bullet$ and $\div$

1. The length of the basketball backboard is 2 m. The perimeter of the backboard is 6 m. What is the width of the basketball backboard?

$$2w + 2l = P$$
$$2w + 2(2) = 6$$
$$2w + 4 = 6$$

Constructed Response Closure

Write an example of a two-step equation. How do you know that it is an example of a two-step equation?

_____

_____

_____

Summary Closure

What did you learn today about solving two-step equations?

_____

_____

_____

_____

Name

A **two-step equation** contains two operations.
A **two-step equation** requires two inverse operations to solve.
- *To keep an equation **balanced**, **inverse operations** must be done on both sides of the equation.*

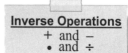

Inverse Operations
+ and −
• and ÷

The **solution** is the value of the **variable** that makes the equation true.

Solve two-step equations.

❶ Read the problem and identify(underline) important information.
  ⓐ Connect the problem to the given two-step equation.
❷ Isolate the term with the variable.
❸ Solve for the variable.
❹ Check and interpret the solution.
  Hint: Answer the question.

---

1. What is the unknown value of x in the two-step equation?

$$\frac{x}{4} + 8 = 5$$

2. What is the unknown value of x in the two-step equation?

$$-3x - 12 = -3$$

---

3. A cell phone service charges a flat fee for activation[1], as well as a monthly rate. Petra paid $145 to sign up and $50 each month. If Petra has paid $395, how long has she had her cell phone service?

$$50m + 145 = 395$$

---

4. The length of a football field is 360 ft. The perimeter of the football field is 1040 ft. What is the width of the football field?

$$2w + 2l = P$$
$$2w + 2(360) = 1040$$
$$2w + 720 = 1040$$

5. Bill and his four friends earned money doing chores for their neighbors. Bill spent $15 of his share on a new book and had $20 left. How much money did Bill and his friends earn doing chores?

$$\frac{m}{5} - 15 = 20$$

Vocabulary

[1] start

7th Grade Expressions and Equations 7.4.a
Solve two-step equations.

Appendix B

How to Manage the Classroom for Pair-Shares

Pair-shares are most effective after you have strategically set up the partners and created a pair-share-friendly classroom. Here are some specific strategies we have used in the classroom that contribute to effective and successful pair-sharing.

ARRANGE DESKS FOR PAIR-SHARES

Desks need to be suitably arranged so students have physical access to their pair-share partner. Move the desks, if necessary. Most teachers are sliding rows of desks close together. Arrange desks so all students can see the teacher and the board.

PAIR-SHARE WITH GROUPS OF TWO STUDENTS

Pair-share with groups of two. When students work in larger groups, one student usually ends up doing much of the work while the others watch. Use one group of three if you have an odd number of students. Have instructional aides and paraprofessionals pair-share with the students they are helping so the students are prepared to successfully answer questions.

USE STRATEGIC PAIRING

Group individual students into strategic pairs that will maximize learning for students. For example, ELs should be paired with fluent English speakers. Non-English speakers should be paired with a student who can serve as an interpreter. Special-needs students should be grouped with a student who is able to be supportive. When students are absent, immediately move students around so everyone has a partner.

ROTATE THE PAIRS

It's a good idea to form new pair-sharing partners periodically. This allows students to interact with a broader range of partners.

Classroom discipline problems can often be reduced by changing partners or moving students from the back of the classroom to a seat in the front. Also, it's not a good idea to isolate one student by himself because then he does not benefit from the pair-share interaction. Keep all students in partners. If you have an odd number of students, then there will be one group of three students.

We have found that when pair-shares are used extensively, students will request to move when they don't have a partner.

LABEL STUDENTS IN THE PAIRS

When we first started using pair-shares extensively, we noticed that some students were dominating the pair-shares and others were rarely speaking. To include all students, assign labels to the students. Most teachers are using "A" partners and "B" partners so they can cue students. The easiest method is to label alternating rows as "A" and "B." Some teachers use other names for the partners. We have seen peanut butter and jelly for partners. We have heard boats and oars.

During the lesson you mix up the pair shares with cues such as:

A, read today's learning Objective to B.

B, explain to A the definition of a quadrilateral.

A first and then B, explain how to solve this density problem.

Peanut butter tell jelly how to find the topic sentence in a paragraph.

When you call on students to respond, you can ask questions involving the pair-share itself: *What did your partner say about . . .?"*

TRAIN STUDENTS TO PAIR-SHARE

Invest time in training your students to talk to each other. During DataWORKS demo lessons we often discover that students are reluctant to talk to each other. They are used to listening to the teacher. It takes a while before they fully understand that they are supposed to talk in class during the pair-shares. Once the students are trained and practice pair-sharing, they get better and better.

From John: I visited a school where the teacher had trained kindergartners to pair-share. What happened was amazing. The students sat on the carpet cross-legged facing the teacher attentively listening to her. Suddenly, she gave the command "Sharing Position." All the students spun 90 degrees on their bottoms to face each other in pairs. She directed them in what to tell their partner. As the students finished, she gave the command "Listening Position." Every student spun back to face the teacher. It was very effective.

In a fourth-grade class, I taught an EDI demo lesson on multiple-meaning words. I paired off the students and used extensive pair-shares throughout the lesson. Later in the day, I saw one of my students with a different teacher. Shortly into the lesson, he raised his hand and in a straightforward, matter of fact way, said to the teacher, "Isn't this where you should tell us to explain to our partners what this means?"

Wow! The student was doing instructional coaching for me. I have seen several examples such as this. As students are trained in the practices, they get better and better and little time is spent in directing student behavior.

PROVIDE AN ATTENTION SIGNAL

Classes run more efficiently when you use a consistent signal to call for students' attention when ending pair-shares. There are two types: (1) a teacher-only signal and (2) call-and-response. Both work. Call-and-response attention signals require students to actively do something as they stop talking and turn to face you.

Teacher: *One, two, three. Eyes on me.*

Students: *One, two. Eyes on you.*

Teacher: *Eyes front.*

Students: *Back straight.*

You can use school-relateds signals.

Teacher: *Lincoln*

Students: *Panthers*

To prepare students to complete their pair-share conversations, you can include warning signals such as, *15 seconds . . . 10 seconds . . . three, two, one, eyes FRONT.* As you start using the warning signals, you often don't even need the attention signal.

Appendix C

Why Pair-Shares Are Important for English Learners

Pair-shares are extremely important for English Learners, and here are 16 reasons why. Each one alone justifies the power of pair-shares.

1. **English Learners orally answer *every* question.** Pair-shares go beyond having students think of an answer. Now, all of them are actually saying the answer aloud. Think about it. Every EL orally answers every question all day long. As you cue for complete sentences, all students are using new Academic and Content Vocabulary and language structures.

2. **Wait time is built in.** When ELs pair-share, you have already provided wait time for students to prepare answers to Checking for Understanding questions. You don't need to mentally count off eight seconds of silence.

3. **Listening and Speaking is included.** Pair-shares are the primary method of incorporating Listening and Speaking Language Objectives into every lesson. And when you use sentence frames, every EL is practicing saying and hearing new Academic and Content Vocabulary.

4. **Student engagement improves.** During pair-shares, all students are engaged. Pair-shares are one of the few whole-class engagement practices. (Other whole-class strategies include whiteboards, gestures, and choral reading.)

5. **Students remember more.** Pair-sharing is also a cognitive strategy. The additional interaction with the material (reading it, hearing it, seeing it, and saying it) facilitates holding the information in

students' working memory longer and, ultimately, in transferring the information into their permanent, long-term memory. It takes mental effort to hold information in working memory. Unless interacted with or repeated, information in working memory fades and is lost in 10 to 30 seconds. Only the information that is transferred into permanent, long-term memory can be recalled for a quiz or state test. You directly support student brains in remembering information when you have students pair-share.

From John: I recently taught a demo EDI science lesson at a high school, and then three teachers taught the same lesson. After school, the science teachers, the principal, the Assistant Superintendent, and I met to discuss the strategies we had practiced. As we sat in a circle of student desks, the principal opened up the discussion, "I talked to the students in the classes you taught today. They said that they especially liked the pair-shares. They told me that saying the words and describing the Postulates of the Kinetic Molecular Theory to each other helped them learn and remember."

6. **Increases student-talk to teacher-talk ratio.** Consistent use of pair-shares is how you add student talk to a lesson. And the student talk involves Academic and Content Vocabulary, not playground conversational language.

7. **English Learners practice composing sentences.** During pair-shares, students, including ELs, are practicing putting together English sentences they are going to use to respond.

8. **Provides language translation time.** When a non-English speaker is strategically paired with a student who is able to translate, then the pair-share provides the mechanism for information to be transferred to the non-English speaker. The CFU question cues the translator with the specific information to translate and talk about.

From John: I personally experienced the importance of using pair-shares for translations during an EDI math demonstration lesson I recently taught. Four teachers were observing in the back of the room. I called on a non-volunteer who turned out to be an EL student giving her first answer in English. In a clear voice, this is exactly what she said, "Prime factorization is finding all the prime factors you multiply together to get a composite number." The teachers' mouths dropped open. The teachers rose in unison and gave a standing ovation from the back of the room. When the lesson was over, one of the teachers told me, "John, that's the first response she has ever made, and you should have seen the look on the partner who had been translating during the pair-shares. She had the most encouraging, 'you can do it' look in her eyes."

9. **Short attention span is addressed.** Teachers have reported how pair-shares help students with short attention spans. This is because the frequent talking with a partner breaks up the length of time students must sit quietly listening to the teacher.

10. **Provides first re-teach.** Pair-shares provide the first re-teaching opportunity during a lesson, and the students do it for you. During pair-shares, you ask students to explain their answers to each other and to correct any errors. When using whiteboard responses, you direct students to look for errors if they have different answers.

11. **Improves classroom management.** Having students pair-share improves classroom management as all students actively participate in a directed whole-class activity.

12. **Instruction is more interactive, engaging, and interesting for the students.** Pair-share is the number one way of providing student interaction. And lessons are more interesting for students when they do something rather than sit passively through the lesson.

13. **Provides academic socialization.** During pair-shares, English Learners carry on purposeful and focused discussions with each other using academic English rather than conversational English. This helps prepare them for the type of discussions they will need in the future in the workplace.

14. **Guides Instructional Aides.** Just as pair-shares provide opportunity for translations, pair-shares provide a structured time for paraprofessionals to explicitly help students. Aides can join in on the pair-shares, help students clarify and prepare their answers, and, if necessary, provide a quick re-teach. The pair-share time allows the aides time to act without talking over the teacher.

From John: I was teaching a language arts lesson during a DataWORKS summer school program. In the back of the room, a special needs student sat with a full-time aide. They were doodling on their whiteboards. I walked back to talk with the aide. I said that each time I asked a question she should use the pair-share time to prepare her student to correctly answer. She put down their whiteboards and began explaining and pair-sharing with her student.

I was calling on random non-volunteers and, sure enough, in a few minutes, the special needs student's name came up. I walked over to her, repeated the question, and waited for her response. She looked right up at me, tilted her head, and gave me the correct answer. I replied, "Good answer!" I turned and said, "Class, let's give her a round of applause." I looked back at her and could see a big, proud smile on her face. I don't know what happened when she went home that night, but this is what I picture: "Mommy, the teacher called on me at school today. I had the right answer."

15. **Reduces affective filter.** English Learners are less nervous about answering questions because they have practiced their answer with their partner before being called upon to answer in front of the whole class.

16. **Students do part of the work of teaching.** Instead of the teacher doing all the work, students do the some of the work during pair-shares.

From Silvia: I have observed many classes where insufficient wait time is provided for ELs. When an English Learner doesn't respond immediately, the teacher either gives the answer herself or calls on another student. Pair-shares allow ELs to be better prepared to answer. Also, be ready to provide additional wait time for individual students to respond even after a pair-share. Remember: Always provide sufficient wait time.

Pair-shares are so powerful that students attest to how much it helps them in their classes. Below are survey responses from English Learners who attended a DataWORKS StepUP Academy summer school program where we accelerate ELs using EDI lessons to pre-teach next year's standards during the summer.

Write a sentence telling how you felt when the teacher asked you to talk to your neighbor or partner. (5th grade)

1. When my partner tells me the answer, it gives me details and it gets more interesting.

2. I was better prepared to answer questions.

3. It helps me because we put all of our ideas together.

4. Yes, it helps me because I could correct the answer with new answer.

5. It helps me on reading the sentence.

6. It helped me because we worked together so we could learn more.

7. Yes, it helps me to talk to my partner because I could think about my answer before giving the answer to the teacher.

8. Partner talk helped me remember what I learned.

9. It helped me not be nervous.

10. Sometimes my neighbor let me know if I had the right answer or not.

11. I knew some more stuff that I did not know, and I learned more stuff.

Appendix D

How to Address Subskill Gaps

At DataWORKS, we use a three-pronged approach to subskill gaps so we can teach grade-level lessons to all students, including English Learners: (1) Improve subskills within the context of an EDI lesson, (2) Differentiate to work around subskills, (3) Improve subskills directly. Many of the strategies address reading fluency and arithmetic.

(1) Improve subskills within the context of an EDI lesson.

Pre-read difficult text in lessons. One of the delivery techniques in EDI is the teacher pre-reading difficult text in a lesson. This is followed with a choral reading by all the students. Struggling readers can read almost any text if it is read first by the teacher.

Incorporate Oral Reading Fluency practice into every lesson every day, all year long. With EDI, reading fluency practice is incorporated into every lesson with pre-reads and choral readings of the Learning Objective, the Concept Definitions, and other academic English embedded in the lesson. Reading these parts of the lesson improves student reading every hour, every day.

Review a subskill during Activate Prior Knowledge. One method of reducing subskill errors is to review and teach a (below grade-level) subskill during the Activate Prior Knowledge portion of an EDI lesson. Select a specific subskill students will be using during Skill Development and Guided Practice. Limit the subskill review to about five minutes to maximize the time available for the new grade-level content.

Identify, point out, and correct subskill errors during the lesson. When students make errors related to the *new* content you are teaching, you stop and re-teach because the purpose of the lesson is to teach students the *new* content. However, when students make subskill errors, you cannot stop and re-teach a subskill to mastery inside of another lesson. The approach we are successfully using is to identify, point out, and correct the subskill error, and then move on, staying focused on teaching the new content.

Subskill errors in math are easy to detect when you use whiteboards because you can see them. Here is an example:

From John: The other day I was teaching a lesson on evaluating algebraic expressions when I saw some subskill errors. Here is how I handled them.

I was using PowerPoint. I pointed to the screen and said, "Students, I want you to evaluate the expression $x^2 + 5x$ when $x = 6$. Use your whiteboards. When you're done, show your whiteboard to your partner and explain to your partner how you solved it. Partner A go first, then partner B. I waited as they worked the problem. I gave my first signal, "Be ready to chin-it in a minute." "Chin-it" was my signal to hold up whiteboards. I waited a little longer and called, "Three, two, one, CHIN-IT."

I scanned around the room looking carefully at the whiteboards. A few students had miscalculated 6^2 as $6 \times 2 = 12$ instead of $6 \times 6 = 36$. I saw the errors and turned to the board and wrote $6^2 = 6 \times 6 = 36$. I pointed to it and said, "Students, this is the notation for 6 squared—six times six which equals 36. I want you to check your whiteboard and your neighbor's whiteboard. Correct them, if necessary, and be ready to hold them up again."

During debriefing after my lesson, the teachers who watched me commented on how quickly I corrected the exponent errors without stopping to teach exponents. At the end, all the students had the correct answers on their whiteboards.

I discussed this with the teachers. I told them that I should have been more preemptive during the problem I solved first. I should have more clearly modeled my thinking when I evaluated for $x = 3$. I should have clearly verbalized that 3^2 is 3 times 3 which is 9. This would have preempted the error in the problem the students were going to work next.

Model math subskills. As you work problems during Skill Development, model subskills by clearly verbalizing your thoughts out loud as you work the problem. For example, *I move the decimal over two places to the left to convert 7 percent to point zero seven. Now I multiply .07, the decimal equivalent of 7%, times 125. Seven times 5 is 35 . . . five carry three . . .*

From Silvia: Modeling subskills is what John realized he should have done during the lesson he just described on evaluating algebraic expressions.

(2) Use differentiation to work around subskill errors.

We have just described addressing subskill errors during a lesson. We will stop for a moment here and describe some additional strategies we use to work around subskill gaps. Then we'll describe methods we use to improve student subskills directly.

When teaching English Learners with subskill gaps, you can often *differentiate around the gaps.* This means you provide some mechanism or support to allow students to bypass or work around their subskill gaps while you continue to teach them grade-level concepts and skills. This allows you to continue to provide all your students with equal opportunity to access grade-level content. (We'll talk about directly improving subskills in a moment.)

Here are some examples of preemptive differentiation techniques you can use that will allow students to participate in grade level-lessons even if they have subskill gaps.

Reduce reading levels. Locate passages written at a lower reading level covering the same content. Lower only the reading difficulty, not the concepts and skills being taught. For example, the Objective, *Analyze how the author's use of figurative language affects tone,* can be taught using easy-to-read materials. Remember, the grade level of a lesson is determined by the concepts and skills being taught, not the reading level of the instructional materials used to teach the content.

> **From Silvia:** The Common Core State Standards are calling for increased complexity of text as students advance in grade. However, they also call for teachers to provide scaffolding and support so it's possible for students reading below grade level to be successful. The EDI vocabulary development, teacher pre-reading, and student choral reading provide support so students reading below level can be successful.

Give students calculators and then teach grade-level mathematics. For example, students can calculate compound interest quickly using calculators to solve the following: Future Value = $P (1 + r)^Y$. This would be a long arithmetic problem to work by hand. A teacher may be able to work only a few problems by hand, changing the focus of the lesson away from compound interest to arithmetic. With calculators, many more problems and problem types can be solved. You focus more on conceptual knowledge and less on arithmetic.

Provide math facts tables for students to use. Typically, they are taped to the desks for the students to refer to. Show students how to use the tables and occasionally model looking up a math fact during a lesson. At DataWORKS, we often include math facts on the back of student whiteboards.

Use simple numbers. For example, have students calculate sales tax of 5% on a $10 item instead of 7.25% sales tax on a $9.98 item. The problem is the same. Only the arithmetic is simplified, not the concept being taught.

(3) Improve student subskills directly.

Besides differentiating around subskill gaps, schools and districts can provide additional systems and support to improve student subskills directly. There are various programs that schools use for remediation. Here are a few practices that we have used successfully at DataWORKS.

Provide math facts clinics. Provide clinics to **memorize** math facts. Many math facts lessons we see are conceptual lessons rather than memorization lessons. They refer to multiplication as being repeated addition such as 4 + 4 + 4 = 12. Other lessons refer to arrays, such as 4 rows of 3 objects have the same number of objects as 3 rows of 4 objects. Yet, if someone asks these students what is 3 times 4, they can't answer.

The multiplication facts clinics that DataWORKS successfully uses focus on *memorization* of facts. We use multi-modality repetition by saying, hearing, reading, and writing facts over and over and over. The repetition transfers math facts *into* students' long-term memory. By the way, quizzing students on math facts with flash cards or timed tests is practice in *recalling* the facts—retrieving the facts from long-term memory. DataWORKS focuses on repetition to place the facts into memory. Many students can't tell you the answer to 7 x 9 because the answer, 63, is not in their long-term memory to be retrieved. You can refer to our website (www.dataworks-ed.com) for the worksheets we use to help students memorize multiplication facts.

Provide Reading Fluency practice. The best method we have used to improve reading fluency is repeated oral readings of the same passage 3 to 18 times. These are *not* cold reads, round-robin reading, or silent reading. The session starts with the teacher pre-reading one or two sentences at a time orally while students track with their fingers looking at each word as it is read. Then all the students read together chorally. Periodically, the teacher stops and directs each student to read the selection again to their partners.

We have effectively used this approach for a half hour of reading fluency practice every day during our summer school StepUP Academies. Often during reading fluency practice, we have students pre-read the expository text passages they will encounter later during EDI lessons.

We have students read expository passages because expository text tends to have a better range of academic English than narrative stories. We often use science and social science text for reading fluency. Although we are not teaching the content, students learn from the reading as a side benefit.

Incorporate Oral Reading Fluency practice into every lesson every day, all year long. With EDI, students practice reading in every lesson, every hour, all year long. It's built in. You pre-read and then students chorally read the Learning Objective, the Concept definitions, and other academic English embedded in the lesson. Teachers comment on how much students read during EDI lessons, even in math.

Appendix E

English Phonemes

Below are some examples of English phonemes. English uses a large number of phonemes which have multiple spelling patterns for the same sound. Information on phonemes is included in the *Common Core State Standards ELA Appendix A,* starting on page 17.

Being aware of the large number of spelling patterns can be useful when showing ELs how to read specific words incorporated in EDI lessons. As they learn spelling patterns, they can use this information to read other words.

English has 18 consonant sounds with multiple spelling patterns.

> ### 12 SPELLING PATTERNS
> ### FOR CONSONANT *K* SOUND
>
> c, ck, ch, cc, qu, q, cq, cu, que, kk, kh, ke
>
> **c**at, **k**ey, ta**ck**, **ch**ord, a**cc**ount, li**qu**or, Ira**q**,
>
> a**cq**uaint, bis**c**uit, mos**que**, tre**kk**er, **kh**an, ma**ke**

English has 7 digraphs which are pairs of letters that represent a single speech sound.

> ### 12 SPELLING PATTERNS FOR DIGRAPH *Sh* SOUND
>
> ti, ci, ssi, si, ss, ch, s, sci, ce, sch, sc, tion
>
> **sh**in, na**ti**on, spe**ci**al, mi**ssi**on, expan**si**on, ti**ss**ue, ma**ch**ine, o**ce**an, **sch**ist, cre**sc**endo

English has 5 short vowel sounds.

13 SPELLINGS FOR SHORT VOWEL e SOUND

e, ea, a, ai, ie, eo, u, ae, ay, ei, ue, eb, eg

met, weather, many, said, friend, jeopardy, bury, aesthetic, says, heifer, guess, debt, phlegm

English has 6 long vowel sounds which say the name of the letter.

22 SPELLINGS FOR LONG VOWEL e SOUND

e, y, ee, ea, e_e, i_e, ie, ei, ei_e, ey, ae, ay, oe, eo, is, eip, ie_e, i, ea_e, it, eigh, ois

be, city, bee, beach, cede, machine, field, deceit, deceive, key, Caesar, quay, amoeba, people, debris, receipt, believe, ski, leave, esprit, Raleigh, chamois

English has three r-controlled sounds which occur when an "r" changes the way the preceding vowel is pronounced. R-controlled vowels are neither long nor short. When vowels are followed by "r," the sound is blended with "r" and a special sound or phoneme is made.

EXAMPLE: 3 SPELLINGS FOR R-CONTROLLED ar SOUND

ar, er, ear, a_e, aa

car, sergeant, heart, are, bazaar

English has 7 diphthongs, vowel sounds in which the first vowel gradually moves toward a second vowel so that both vowels form one syllable.

EXAMPLE: 5 SPELLINGS FOR DIPHTHONG oi SOUND

oi, oy, aw, uoy oy_e

foil, toy, lawyer, buoy, gargoyle

Appendix F

Teach English Learners on Grade Level

At DataWORKS, we developed **Curriculum Calibration**, a process where we collect student assignments from schools and compare the assignments to standards. We determine the percentage of assignments given to students that are on grade level for language arts, math, science, and social science for each grade level. Our goal—for a school to be considered standards-based—is for 90% of student assignments to be on grade level.

Over the years, we have analyzed more than 2 million assignments. We have found large numbers of students, including English Learners, who were not taught *grade-level* content. Schools that perpetually present below-grade-level content to students are, in fact, remedial schools. Students taught below grade level have a hard time answering questions on annual state tests that assess student knowledge of grade-level content. Below are five reasons to teach English Learners on grade level every day.

Why is teaching on grade level so very, very important for English Learners?

1. Teaching all students (including English Learners) on grade level provides equal opportunity to learn.

2. Students (including ELs) cannot learn grade-level content they are not taught.

---

3. Students (including ELs) perform no higher than the assignments they are given. Students taught below grade level perform below grade level.

4. Students (including ELs) test higher—even if their grades go down—when they are taught on grade level. It's better to get C's on grade-level work than A's and B's on below-grade-level assignments.

5. State tests assess ELs with grade-level questions.

Appendix G

Guidelines for Designing Standards-Based Pacing Guides

A t DataWORKS, we have helped several districts develop Pacing Guides that describe when to teach specific lessons. Here are some of the guidelines we use for pacing to ensure students are taught the grade-level content they need to know to do well on state testing.

Guidelines for Creating Pacing Guides

1. Make sure you are pacing the state standards and not pages-per-week in a textbook.

2. Focus on grade-level lessons. This usually means you need to analyze your instructional materials carefully. We have found that some instructional materials are not always on grade level. And some standards might be missing.

3. Teach grade-level lessons from the first day of school. Standards-based schools teach on grade level every day. (At least 90% of all lessons are on grade level.) Remedial schools teach lessons that are below grade level.

4. Remediation (filling in below-grade level gaps) must be in addition to—not in place of—grade-level instruction. Students in remedial programs fall one year further behind each year they are in a remedial program where they receive no access to grade-level content.

5. Include Periodic Review (distributed practice) so students are exposed to the same standard multiple times over the year. This promotes retention in long-term memory.

6. Include catch-up days. At DataWORKS, we only pace four days per week. The fifth day is a catch-up day.

7. Pace the completion of tested standards so there is time for additional periodic review before state testing.

Appendix H

How to Design an EDI Learning Objective for English Learners

We have developed a six-step methodology you can use for writing Learning Objectives.

How to Design a Learning Objective for English Learners

1. Select a standard.

2. Underline the part of the standard you are going to teach.

3. Reword to make it grammatically correct, if necessary.

4. Verify that the Independent Practice matches the Learning Objective. (Refer to released test questions, if available.)

5. Write Checking for Understanding questions for the Learning Objective.

6. Identify where to incorporate English Learner strategies: Language Objectives, Content Access Strategies, Vocabulary Development.

1. Select a standard.

This sounds easy. You open your standards and select a standard from your grade level to teach, and then create a lesson using materials from your textbook. Most likely, you work in reverse. You have a district pacing guide or curriculum guide that lists textbook pages to teach. Either way, it's important to ensure that you are teaching *grade-level* lessons every day, not just any lesson.

Standards-based education—teaching from Learning Objectives taken directly from state standards—represents a shift in thinking about what to teach. In the standards era that we are in now, schools teach concepts and skills contained in a standard using appropriate instructional materials that match a standards-based Objective. Standards-based lessons focus on standards rather than completing worksheets or pages in a book.

> 2. Underline the part of the standard you are going to teach.
>
> 3. Reword to make it grammatically correct, if necessary.

At DataWORKS, we have had various methods of writing Learning Objectives over the years. Here is the simplest method of writing a Learning Objective there is. It's easy to do, and it's always on grade level. Many standards contain multiple Learning Objectives, so just underline the part of the standard you are going to teach right now. Reword it, if necessary.

Common Core State Standard for Kindergartners:

> With prompting and support, identify characters, settings, and major events in a story.

Learning Objective ▶

Identify characters in a story.

It's that simple! You don't need to have extra phrases such as "The student will be able to . . ." Just start the Objective with the skill, the verb.

If you want, you can add "Today, we will . . ." For example, *Today, we will identify characters in a story.* The reason to use "we" is so you can do choral readings of the Objective with the students. If the Learning Objective is written in second person, the students will all be looking directly at you when they chorally read, *You will identify the characters in a story.* In short, start all Learning Objectives with the skill (verb) or "Today, we will . . ."

It is important that the words for the Learning Objective come from the standards. This ensures that the Objective matches a standard and that it is on grade level. Also, if you analyze sample released test questions, you will see that the words from the standards show up in the test questions and answers. When you substitute other words, you are removing the specific rigorous Academic and Content Vocabulary words your students need to be taught and will be tested on. Students don't need to understand every word in the Learning Objective during the initial reading. You will teach the meaning of the words over the course of the lesson.

From John: Some schools I am working with are using first-person Learning Objectives. It sounds a little funny when the teacher reads it, but it works when students say, "Today, I will solve multi-step linear inequalities." Also, the Checking for Understanding question becomes very directed: "Jason, what are you going to do today?"

4. Verify that the Independent Practice matches. (Refer to released test questions, if available.)

After you have written an Objective, verify that the Independent Practice matches. The Independent Practice can be either practice problems from the textbook or problems that you provide. Either way, the problems must match the Learning Objective.

It's important that you verify the Independent Practice while you prepare the Learning Objective. Often the entire lesson is written, and then you discover that the homework problems don't match.

From Silvia: We often see students struggle because they are being asked to do Independent Practice that they were not taught how to do. One area to watch is the skill. For example, students are taught to identify cause-and-effect patterns in informational text, yet at the end of the lesson they are asked to write a cause-and-effect essay. Writing is a different skill than identifying. Always make sure the Independent Practice matches the Learning Objective.

REFER TO RELEASED QUESTIONS WHEN PREPARING LESSONS

While you are verifying that the Independent Practice matches the Learning Objective, also check that the Independent Practice matches how the state tests the standard.

Most state departments of education (and the Common Core test developers) provide released questions for annual state tests. Educators don't always agree with how the standards are tested. However—and this is important—the released questions reveal what the test writers think the standards mean and shows the rigor of the vocabulary used. So, while you are verifying that the Independent Practice matches the Learning Objective, also verify that the lesson matches how the standards are tested.

From John: Some people say that this is "teaching to the test." No one actually knows how to "teach to the test," or we would have 100% proficient students everywhere. What we are saying is to teach the standards that are being tested. And teach the standards in the manner in which they are being assessed. You are not teaching students how to answer one specific released question but how to answer the types of questions that the test writers use to assess students' knowledge of the standards.

COMMON CORE RELEASED QUESTIONS

Two consortia are preparing test questions for the Common Core Standards: Smarter Balanced Assessment Consortium (www.smarterbalanced.org) and Partnership for Assessment of Readiness for College and Careers (www .parcconline.org). Although Common Core testing has not started yet, sample questions are available.

5. Write Checking for Understanding questions for the Learning Objective.

Checking for Understanding questions for the Learning Objective are easy to write. There are a few variations, but basically they all ask the same thing.

What are we going to do today?

What is our Objective for today?

What are we going to _____ today?

In the blank space above, insert the skill that matches your Objective.

What are we going to analyze today?

What are we going to describe today?

What are we going to calculate today?

Note that the Learning Objective CFU question does not ask the students what the concept is. That's not been taught yet. For example, if your objective is *Describe plate tectonics,* the CFU question is *What are we going to do today?* or *What are we going to describe?* The question cannot be *What is plate tectonics?* You haven't taught it yet. The CFU question, *In your own words, what is plate tectonics?* will come during Concept Development, *after* you have taught what plate tectonics is.

> **6. Identify where to incorporate English Learner strategies: Language Objectives, Content Access Strategies, Vocabulary Development.**

Analyze the text in the Learning Objective and identify words that could be hard for ELs to pronounce. Identify Academic words that need to be defined. You teach pronunciation and some definitions as you present the Learning Objective to your students. Note that you only define Academic Vocabulary words. The Content Vocabulary contained in the Learning Objective is formally taught during Concept Development.

Here are two examples of teachers writing Learning Objectives.

Mrs. Robertson is sitting in her room after school preparing for tomorrow's math lesson. The textbook chapter is covering circumference of circles and area of plane figures. She reads the standard printed on the first page of the chapter.

> Develop and use formulas to determine the circumference of circles and the area of triangles, parallelograms, trapezoids, and circles and develop strategies to find the area of more complex shapes.

She looks over the chapter. There are pages on circumference and area. She underlines the part of the standard she will teach tomorrow:

> Develop and <u>use formulas to determine the circumference of circles</u> and the area of triangles, parallelograms, trapezoids, and circles and develop strategies to find the area of more complex shapes.

She writes her Learning Objective: *Today, we will use formulas to determine the circumference of circles.* She writes a CFU question: *What are we going to do today?* She looks over the practice problems in the student workbook and selects the specific problems that address circumference. She looks at some sample test questions and sees that the circumference questions are word problems. She checks the textbook to locate word problems.

To support English Learners, she will pre-pronounce *circumference* before reading the Objective and have the students say it several times. As a reminder, she writes "L S R" (Listening, Speaking, and Reading) above the word *circumference* in her notes. She adds the definition of *formula* (a mathematics rule written in symbols) to the student handout. During Concept Development, she will present the two formulas for calculating circumference: $C = \pi d$ and $C = 2\pi r$. She adds the definition of *determine* (to find out or to figure out) to the handout.

Mr. Wu teaches chemistry. His standard is as follows:

Students know that the kinetic molecular theory describes the motion of atoms and molecules and explains the properties of gases.

The part about "describing the motion of atoms and molecules" will be taught as part of the lesson and doesn't need to be included in the Objective. He underlines some key words in the standard. He skips the nonspecific verb, *know.* Reading further, he underlines *describe* as the skill.

Students know that the <u>kinetic molecular theory describes</u> the motion of atoms and molecules and explains the properties of gases.

Learning Objective: Describe the kinetic molecular theory.

He looks at his Objective. This would work fine. However, he decides to add two more words: "of gases."

Learning Objective: Describe the kinetic molecular theory of gases.

This clarifies the focus of the lesson: it's about gases. Mr. Wu opens the textbook to locate the appropriate pages that describe the postulates of the kinetic molecular theory. He identifies matching problems at the end of the chapter for Independent Practice.

To support English Learners, he will pre-pronounce *kinetic* and *molecular* and *theory* before he presents the Learning Objective. The first two words could be confusing. They both appear to have a silent *e: kine*-tic and *mole*-cular. They are actually pronounced as ki-net-ic and mo-lec-u-lar. He writes a note to himself: *preempt silent* e *error; include Listening, Speaking, Reading.*

Annotated References

In this section, we have grouped our references into 10 specific categories and annotated them. This will make it easier for readers to research specific areas. A total alphabetical reference list follows. The 10 annotated categories here include the following:

Teaching in a Meaningful Way

Scaffolding Language

Vocabulary Instruction for English Learners

Planned Interactions in Class

Setting High Expectations

Activating Prior Knowledge

Reading Comprehension

Vocabulary Research

Using Direct Instruction

Using Visuals

Teaching in a Meaningful Way

Teach content, literacy, and language in an integrated and meaningful way:

- Teach language through meaningful content and themes, targeting both content and language objectives in every lesson.
- Integrate all four language skills (reading, writing, listening, and speaking) in every lesson.
- Develop English oral language proficiency in the context of literacy instruction.
- Include frequent opportunities to practice reading with a variety of rich materials, in meaningful contexts.

August, D., & Shanahan, T. (Eds.). (2008). *Developing reading and writing in second-language learners.* Report of the National Literacy Panel on Language-Minority Children and Youth. The Center for Applied Linguistics and the International Reading Association. Florence, KY: Routledge.

Cloud, N., Genesee, F., & Hamayan, E. (2009). *Literacy instruction for English language learners: A teacher's guide to research-based practices.* Portsmouth, NH: Heinemann.

Echevarria, J., Vogt, M., & Short, D. J. (2004). *Making content comprehensible for English learners: The SIOP model* (2nd ed.). Needham Heights, MA: Allyn & Bacon.

Goldenberg, C. (2008). Teaching English language learners: What the research does—and does not—say. *American Educator, 32*(2), 8–22, 42–44.

Goldenberg, C., & Coleman, R. (2010). *Promoting academic achievement among English learners.* Thousand Oaks, CA: Corwin.

Institute of Education Sciences (IES). (2007). *Effective literacy and English language instruction for English language learners in the elementary grades.* Washington, DC: IES, National Center for Education Evaluation and Regional Assistance.

Short, D. J., & Fitzsimmons, S. (2007). *Double the work: Challenges and solutions to acquiring language and academic literacy for adolescent English language learners.* New York: Carnegie Corporation.

Scaffolding Language

Scaffold language based on students' English proficiency to make sure it is comprehensible, using the following:

- visuals and realia (objects from real life)
- hands-on materials
- graphic organizers
- gestures
- modified speech
- adapted text (i.e., simple sentence structure, elaboration)
- leveled readers
- repetition/re-reading
- narrow reading (reading several texts about the same topic)

Build on what students already know and help them develop background knowledge they need.

- Validate and build on home and community language, literacy, and culture.
- Use texts with familiar content and topics before moving on to unfamiliar ones.
- Help students develop needed background knowledge on unfamiliar topics and cultures.

Vocabulary Instruction for English Learners

- Provide multiple opportunities for students to encounter and produce the targeted words in different contexts and through different tasks, such as reading and peer-to-peer interaction.
- Have students develop their own definitions of the words.
- Revisit and review words with students.
- Teach word analysis and vocabulary learning strategies for inferring meaning of unknown words.
- Pre-teach key vocabulary before reading or learning tasks.
- Make word meanings accessible by drawing on students' prior knowledge, providing student-friendly definitions and contextual information through meaningful text, visuals, gestures, and examples.
- Use students' first language (e.g., cognates—train/tren, and L1 text) to support vocabulary development.

August, D., Carlo, M., Dressler, C., & Snow, C. (2005). The critical role of vocabulary development for English language learners. *Learning Disabilities Research & Practice, 20*(1), 50–57.

Calderon, M. (2008, April). ESL strategies for teaching vocabulary and reading. Teachers of English to Speakers of Other Languages (TESOL), New York, NY. Keynote Address.

Carlo, M. S., August, D., McLaughlin, B., Snow, C. E., Dressler, C., Lippman, D., Lively, T., et al. (2003). Closing the gap: Addressing the vocabulary needs of English language learners in bilingual and mainstream classrooms. *Reading Research Quarterly, 39*(2), 188–315.

Planned Interactions in Class

Provide ample opportunities for carefully designed interaction with teacher and peers.

- Instructional conversations
- Cooperative learning (common goal, assigned roles, group and individual accountability)
- Modified guided reading
- Pair reading
- Retelling and summarizing in pairs
- Think-pair-share
- Role plays, reader's theater

August, D., & Shanahan, T. (Eds.). (2008). *Developing reading and writing in second-language learners.* Report of the National Literacy Panel on Language-Minority Children and Youth. The Center for Applied Linguistics and the International Reading Association. Florence, KY: Routledge.

August, D., Carlo, M., Dressler, C., & Snow, C. (2005). The critical role of vocabulary development for English language learners. *Learning Disabilities Research & Practice, 20*(1), 50–57.

Calderon, M. (2008, April). ESL strategies for teaching vocabulary and reading. Teachers of English to Speakers of Other Languages (TESOL), New York, NY. Keynote Address.

Carlo, M. S., August, D., McLaughlin, B., Snow, C. E., Dressler, C., Lippman, D., Lively, T., et al. (2003). Closing the gap: Addressing the vocabulary needs of English language learners in bilingual and mainstream classrooms. *Reading Research Quarterly, 39*(2), 188–315.

Cloud, N., Genesee, F., & Hamayan, E. (2009). *Literacy instruction for English language learners: A teacher's guide to research-based practices.* Portsmouth, NH: Heinemann.

Drucker, M. J. (2003). What reading teachers should know about ESL learners. *The Reading Teacher,* 22–29.

Echevarria, J., & Hasbrouck, J. (2009). *Response to intervention and English learners.* Washington, DC: Center for Research on the Educational Achievement and Teaching of English Language Learners. Retrieved from http://www.cal.org/create/resources/pubs/CREATEBrief_ResponsetoIntervention.pdf

Echevarria, J., Vogt, M., & Short, D. J. (2004). *Making content comprehensible for English learners: The SIOP model* (2nd ed.). Needham Heights, MA: Allyn & Bacon.

Goldenberg, C. (2008). Teaching English language learners: What the research does—and does not—say. *American Educator, 32*(2), 8–22, 42–44.

Institute of Education Sciences (IES). (2007). *Effective literacy and English language instruction for English language learners in the elementary grades.* Washington, DC: IES, National Center for Education Evaluation and Regional Assistance.

Orosco, M. J., & Klingner, J. (2010). One school's implementation of RTI with English language learners: Referring into RTI. *Journal of Learning Disabilities, 43*(3), 269–288.

Short, D. J., & Fitzsimmons, S. (2007). *Double the work: Challenges and solutions to acquiring language and academic literacy for adolescent English language learners.* New York: Carnegie Corporation.

Tharp, R. G. (1997). *From at-risk to excellence: Research, theory, and principles for practice* (Research Report 1). Santa Cruz, CA: Center for Research on Education, Diversity & Excellence. Retrieved from http://www.cal.org/resources/Digest/crede001.html

Trumbull, E., & Pacheco, M. (2005). *Leading with diversity: Cultural competencies for teacher preparation and professional development.* Providence, RI: The Education Alliance at Brown University and Pacific Resources for Education and Learning.

Setting High Expectations

Present ELs with challenging curricular content. Curricula should be organized around "big questions," involve authentic reading and writing experiences, and provide textual choices as well as meaningful content for students.

Set high expectations for ELs. ELs will perform much better if placed according to academic achievement rather than language proficiency; placement in challenging classes with quality instruction will enable them to learn more.

Callahan, R. (2005). Tracking and high school English learners: Limiting opportunities to learn. *American Educational Research Journal, 42*(2), 305–328.

Activate Prior Knowledge

A number of researchers argue that when teachers make an effort to learn about students' existing "funds of knowledge," and when they encourage students to relate that knowledge to the subjects studied in class, students tend to become more engaged in the lesson and their reading comprehension improves (Gonzalez et al., 1993; Moje et al., 2004).

Gonzalez, N., Moll, L. C., Floyd-Tenery, M., Rivera, A., Rendon, P., Gonzalez, R., & Amanti, C. (1993). *Teacher research on funds of knowledge: Learning from households* (Educational Practice Report 6). Washington, DC: National Center for Research on Cultural Diversity and Second Language Learning.

Moje, E. B., Ciechanowski, K. M., Kramer, K., Ellis, L., Carrillo, R., & Collazo, T. (2004). Working toward third space in content area literacy: An examination of everyday funds of knowledge and discourse. *Reading Research Quarterly, 39*(1), 38–69.

Reading Comprehension

Besides learning the basics of reading, ELs need to receive explicit instruction about reading comprehension strategies (Bernhardt, 2005; Denti & Guerin, 2004; Garcia & Godina, 2004).

Bernhardt, E. (2005). Progress and procrastination in second language reading. *Annual Review of Applied Linguistics, 25,*133–150.

Denti, L., & Guerin, G. (2004). Confronting the problem of poor literacy: Recognition and action. *Reading & Writing Quarterly, 20,* 133–22.

Garcia, G. E., & Godina, H. (2004). Addressing the literacy needs of adolescent English language learners. In T. Jetton & J. Dole (Eds.). *Adolescent literacy: Research and practice* (pp. 304–320). New York: Guildford Press.

Rand Reading Study Group. (2001). *Reading for understanding: Toward a R&D program in reading comprehension.* Prepared for the Office of Educational Research and Improvement (OERI), U.S. Department of Education. Santa Monica, CA: RAND.

Vocabulary Research

Knowledge of words, word parts, and word relationships is critical if students are to understand topics in a content area and develop strong reading comprehension and test-taking skills (Graves, 1986, 2006).

For ELs, teachers may also need to distinguish between content-specific words (e.g., hypotenuse, equilateral), process words (e.g., scan, draft, clarify), and words related to English structure (e.g., prefix, *photo-*; suffix, *-ly*; Echevarria, Vogt, & Short, 2004; Graves, 2006).

Brown, C. L. (2007). Supporting English language learners in content reading. *Reading Improvement, 44,* 32–39.

Carlo, M. S., August, D., McLaughlin, B., Snow, C. E., Dressler, C., Lippman, D., Lively, T., et al. (2003). Closing the gap: Addressing the vocabulary needs of English language learners in bilingual and mainstream classrooms. *Reading Research Quarterly, 39*(2), 188–315.

Carlo, M. S., August, D., & Snow, C. (2005). *Sustained vocabulary-learning strategy instruction for English-language learners.* In E. H. Hiebert & M. Kamil (Eds.), *Teaching and learning vocabulary: Bringing research to practice.* (pp. 137–154). Mahwah, NJ: Lawrence Erlbaum.

Coxhead, A. (1998). *An academic word list.* English Language Institute Occasional Publication 18. Wellington, NZ: Victoria University of Wellington.

Coxhead, A., & Nation, P. (2001).The specialized vocabulary of English for academic purposes. In J. Flowerdew & M. Peacock (Eds.), *Research perspectives on English for academic purposes* (pp. 252–267). Cambridge: Cambridge University Press.

Echevarria, J., Vogt, M., & Short, D. J. (2004). *Making content comprehensible for English learners: The SIOP model* (2nd ed.). Needham Heights, MA: Allyn & Bacon.

Francis, D. F., et al. (2006). *Practical guidelines for the education of English language learners: Research-based recommendations for serving adolescent newcomers, Vol. 2.* (Under cooperative agreement grant S283B050034 for U.S. Department of Education). Portsmouth, NH: RMC Research Corporation, Center on Instruction (COI).

Gersten, R., et al. (2007). *Effective literacy and English language instruction for English learners in the elementary grades: A practice guide* (NCEE 2007–4011). Washington, DC: U.S. Department of Education. Retrieved from http://ies.ed.gov/ncee/

Graves, M. F. (1986). Vocabulary learning and instruction. In E. Z. Rothkopf (Ed.), *Review of Research in Education, 13*, 49–89.

Graves, M. F. (2006). Teaching Word-Learning Strategies. In *The Vocabulary Book: Learning & Instruction* (pp. 91–118). New York: Teachers College Press.

Institute of Education Sciences (IES). (2007). *Effective literacy and English language instruction for English language learners in the elementary grades.* Washington, DC: IES, National Center for Education Evaluation and Regional Assistance.

Kieffer, M. J., & Lesaux, N. K. (2007). Breaking down words to build meaning: Morphology, vocabulary, and reading comprehension in the urban classroom. *The Reading Teacher, 61*(2), 134–144.

Lively, T., August, D., Carlo, M., & Snow, C. (2003). *Vocabulary improvement program for English language learners and their classmates.* Baltimore, MD: Brookes.

Nagy, W. E., Anderson, R. C., & Herman, P. A. (1987, Summer). Learning word meanings from context during normal reading. *American Educational Research Journal, 24*(2), 237–270.

Scarcella, R. (2003a). *Academic English: A conceptual framework.* The University of California Linguistic Minority Research Institute. Technical Report. Oakland, CA: University of California.

Scarcella, R. (2003b). *Accelerating academic English: A focus on the English learner.* Oakland, CA: University of California.

Stahl, S. A., & Nagy, W. E. (2006). *Teaching word meanings.* Mahwah, NJ: Lawrence Erlbaum.

Zwiers, J. (2005). The third language of academic English. *Educational Leadership, 62*, 60–63.

Zwiers, J. (2008). *Building academic language: Essential practices for content classrooms, Grades 5–12.* San Francisco: John Wiley & Sons.

Using Direct Instruction for English Learners

A 2004 review of effective reading programs found that most of the programs that are effective with "language learners were adaptations of programs also found to be successful with English-dominant students" (Slavin & Cheung, 2004, p. 55). The reviewers noted that Direct Instruction has "been extensively evaluated with a wide variety of students" (p. 55).

A 2003 review of experimental studies of reading programs for English language learners found Direct Instruction to be among the programs with the strongest evidence of effectiveness (Slavin & Cheung, 2003).

Slavin, R. E., & Cheung, A. (2003). *Effective programs for English language learners: A best-evidence synthesis.* Baltimore, MD: Johns Hopkins University, CRESPAR.

Slavin, R., & A. Cheung, A. (2004). How do English language learners learn to read? *What Research Says About Reading, 61*(6), 55.

Using Visuals

Intervention studies and several observational studies have noted that the effective use of visuals during instruction can lead to increased learning. Rousseau et al. (1993) used visuals for teaching vocabulary (i.e., words written on the board and pictures), and Saunders et al. (1998) incorporated the systematic use of visuals for teaching, reading, and language arts. Visuals also play a large role in the Cognitive Academic Language Learning Approach (CALLA), shown to be related to growth in language development.

Rousseau, M. K., Tam, B. K. Y., & Ramnarain, R. (1993). Increasing reading proficiency of language-minority students with speech and language impairments. *Education and Treatments of Children, 16,* 254–271.

Saunders, W., O'Brien, G., Lennon, D., & McLean, J. (1998). Making the transition to English literacy successful: Effective strategies for studying literature with transition students. In R. Gersten & R. Jimenez (Eds.), *Promoting learning for culturally and linguistically diverse students: Classroom applications from contemporary research* (pp. 99–132). Belmont, CA: Wadsworth.

Bibliography

Adams, G. L., & Engelmann, S. (1996). Research in direct instruction: 25 years beyond DISTAR. Seattle, WA: Educational Achievement Systems.

American Federation of Teachers. (2004). *Building from the best, learning from what works: Five promising remedial reading intervention programs.* Washington, DC: American Federation of Teachers. Retrieved from http://www.aft.org/pubs-reports/downloads/teachers/remedial.pdf

Anderson, J. R., Corbett, A. T., Koedinger, K., & Pelletier, R. (1995). Cognitive tutors: Lessons learned. *Journal of the Learning Sciences, 4*(2), 167–207.

August, D., Carlo, M., Dressler, C., & Snow, C. (2005). The critical role of vocabulary development for English language learners. *Learning Disabilities Research & Practice, 20*(1), 50–57.

August, D., & Hakuta, K. (Eds.). (1997). *Improving schooling for language minority children: A research agenda.* Washington, DC: National Academy Press.

August, D., & Shanahan, T. (Eds.). (2008). *Developing reading and writing in second-language learners.* Report of the National Literacy Panel on Language-Minority Children and Youth. The Center for Applied Linguistics and the International Reading Association. Florence, KY: Routledge.

Baker, S., Gersten, R., & Lee, D. (2002). A synthesis of empirical research on teaching mathematics to low-achieving students. *The Elementary School Journal, 103*(1), 51–73.

Bandura, A. (1977). *Social learning theory.* New York: General Learning Press.

Baumann, J. F., Jones, L. A., & Seifert-Kessell, N. (1993). Using think alouds to enhance children's comprehension monitoring abilities. *The Reading Teacher, 47*(3), 184–193.

Bellon, J., Bellon, E., & Blank, M. (1992). *Teaching from a research knowledge base: A development and renewal process.* New York: Macmillan.

Bernhardt, E. (2005). Progress and procrastination in second language reading. *Annual Review of Applied Linguistics, 25,*133–150.

Black, M. J., & Yacoob, Y. (1997). Recognizing facial expressions in image sequences using local parameterized models of image motion. *International Journal of Computer Vision, 25*(1), 23–48.

Borman, G., Hewes, G. M., Overman, L. T., & Brown, S. (2003). Comprehensive school reform and student achievement: A meta-analysis. *Review of Educational Research, 73*(2), 125–230.

Brewster, C., & Fager, J. (2000, October). *Increasing student engagement and motivation: From time-on-task to homework.* Retrieved from http://www.nwrel.org/request/oct00/textonly.html

Brown, C. L. (2007). Supporting English language learners in content reading. *Reading Improvement, 44*, 32–39.

Calderon, M. (2008, April). ESL strategies for teaching vocabulary and reading. Teachers of English to Speakers of Other Languages (TESOL), New York, NY. Keynote Address.

California State Board of Education. (1997). *English language arts content standards for California public schools.* Sacramento: California Department of Education Press.

Callahan, R. (2005). Tracking and high school English learners: Limiting opportunities to learn. *American Educational Research Journal, 42*(2), 305–328.

Carlo, M. S., August, D., McLaughlin, B., Snow, C. E., Dressler, C., Lippman, D., Lively, T., et al. (2003). Closing the gap: Addressing the vocabulary needs of English language learners in bilingual and mainstream classrooms. *Reading Research Quarterly, 39*(2), 188–315.

Carlo, M. S., August, D., & Snow, C. (2005). *Sustained vocabulary-learning strategy instruction for English-language learners.* In E. H. Hiebert & M. Kamil (Eds.), *Teaching and learning vocabulary: Bringing research to practice.* (pp. 137–154). Mahwah, NJ: Lawrence Erlbaum.

Celce-Murcia, M., Brinton, D., & Goodwin, J. (1996). *Teaching pronunciation: Reference for teachers of English to speakers of other languages.* Cambridge: Cambridge University Press.

Chall, J. S. (2000). *The academic achievement challenge: What really works in the classroom?* New York: Guilford Press.

Chamot, A. U., & O'Malley, J. M. (1994). *Instructional approaches and teaching procedures.* In K. S. Urbschat & R. Pritchard (Eds.), *Kids come in all languages: Reading instruction for ESL students.* Newark, DE: International Reading Association.

Cloud, N., Genesee, F., & Hamayan, E. (2009). *Literacy instruction for English language learners: A teacher's guide to research-based practices.* Portsmouth, NH: Heinemann.

Coxhead, A. (1998). *An academic word list.* English Language Institute Occasional Publication 18. Wellington, NZ: Victoria University of Wellington.

Coxhead, A., & Nation, P. (2001).The specialized vocabulary of English for academic purposes. In J. Flowerdew & M. Peacock (Eds.), *Research perspectives on English for academic purposes* (pp. 252–267). Cambridge: Cambridge University Press.

Davey, B. (1983). Think-aloud: Modeling the cognitive processes of reading comprehension. *Journal of Reading, 27*(1), 44–47.

DeCapua, A. (2008). *Grammar for teachers: A guide to American English for native and non-native speakers.* New York: Springer Science + Business Media.

Denti, L., & Guerin, G. (2004). Confronting the problem of poor literacy: Recognition and action. *Reading & Writing Quarterly, 20*, 113–122.

Drucker, M. J. (2003). What reading teachers should know about ESL learners. *The Reading Teacher,* 22–29.

Dutro, S., & Moran, C. (2003). *Rethinking English language instruction: An architectural approach.* In G. Garcia (Ed.), *English learners reaching the highest level of literacy* (pp. 227–258). Newark, DE: International Reading Association.

Echevarria, J., & Hasbrouck, J. (2009). *Response to intervention and English learners.* Washington, DC: Center for Research on the Educational Achievement and

Teaching of English Language Learners. Retrieved from http://www.cal.org/ create/resources/pubs/CREATEBrief_ResponsetoIntervention.pdf

Echevarria, J., Vogt, M., & Short, D. J. (2004). *Making content comprehensible for English learners: The SIOP model* (2nd ed.). Needham Heights, MA: Allyn & Bacon.

Echevarria, J., Vogt, M. E., & Short, D. (2008). *Making content comprehensible for English learners: The SIOP model* (3rd ed.). Boston: Allyn & Bacon.

Ekman, P., & Friesen, W. V. (1969). The repertoire of nonverbal behavior: Categories, origins, usage, and coding. *Semiotica, 1,* 49–98.

Elley, W. B. (1991). Acquiring literacy in a second language: The effect of book-based programs. *Language Learning, 41,* 375–411.

Erman, B., & Warren, B. (2000). The idiom principle and the open choice principle. *Text, 20,* 29–62.

Evertson, C. M., Emmer, E. T., & Brophy, J. E. (1980). Predictors of effective teaching in junior high mathematics classrooms. *Journal of Research in Mathematics Education, 11*(3), 167–178.

Evertson, C. M., et al. (1980). Relationships between classroom behaviors and student outcomes in junior high mathematics and English class. *American Educational Research Journal, 17*(1), 43–60.

Francis, D. F., et al. (2006). *Practical guidelines for the education of English language learners: Research-based recommendations for serving adolescent newcomers, Vol. 2.* (Under cooperative agreement grant S283B050034 for U.S. Department of Education). Portsmouth, NH: RMC Research Corporation, Center on Instruction (COI).

Gagne, R. (1974). *Essentials of learning for instruction* (2nd ed.). Hinsdale, IL: The Dryden Press.

Garcia, G. E., & Godina, H. (2004). Addressing the literacy needs of adolescent English language learners. In T. Jetton & J. Dole (Eds.). *Adolescent literacy: Research and practice* (pp. 304–320). New York: Guildford Press.

Gersten, R., et al. (2007). *Effective literacy and English language instruction for English learners in the elementary grades: A practice guide* (NCEE 2007–4011). Washington, DC: U.S. Department of Education. Retrieved from http://ies.ed.gov/ncee/

Glasersfeld, E. von. (1991). *Radical constructivism in mathematics education.* Dordrecht, The Netherlands: Kluwer Academic.

Goldenberg, C. (2008). Teaching English language learners: What the research does—and does not—say. *American Educator, 32*(2), 8–22, 42–44.

Goldenberg, C., & Coleman, R. (2010). *Promoting academic achievement among English learners.* Thousand Oaks, CA: Corwin.

Goldenberg, C., Rueda, R., & August, D. (2006). *Sociocultural influences on the literacy attainment of language-minority children and youth.* In D. August & T. Shanahan (Eds.), *Developing literacy in second-language learners: Report of the National Literacy Panel on Language-Minority Children and Youth* (pp. 269–347). Mahwah, NJ: Lawrence Erlbaum.

Goldstein, E. B. (2008). *Cognitive psychology: Connecting mind, research, and everyday experience* (2nd ed.). Belmont, CA: Thomson Wadsworth.

Gonzalez, N., Moll, L. C., Floyd-Tenery, M., Rivera, A., Rendon, P., Gonzalez, R., & Amanti, C. (1993). *Teacher research on funds of knowledge: Learning from households* (Educational Practice Report 6). Washington, DC: National Center for Research on Cultural Diversity and Second Language Learning.

Good, T. L., & Grouws, D. A. (1979). The Missouri Mathematics Effectiveness Project: An experimental study in fourth-grade classrooms. *Journal of Educational Psychology, 71*(3), 355–362.

Graham, S. (2005). *Strategy instruction and the teaching of writing: A meta-analysis.* In C. A. MacArthur, S. Graham, & J. Fitzpatrick (Eds.), *Handbook of writing research.* (pp. 187–207). New York: Guilford Press.

Graves, M. F. (1986). Vocabulary learning and instruction. In E. Z. Rothkopf (Ed.), *Review of Research in Education, 13,* 49–89.

Graves, M. F. (2006). Teaching Word-Learning Strategies. In *The Vocabulary Book: Learning & Instruction* (pp. 91–118). New York: Teachers College Press.

Griffiths, R. (1990). Speech rate and NNS comprehension: A preliminary study in time-benefit analysis. *Language Learning, 40*(3), 311–336.

Hake, R. (1992). Socratic pedagogy in the introductory physics laboratory. *The Physics Teacher, 30*(9), 546–552.

Hennings, D. G. (1993). On knowing and reading history. *Journal of Reading, 36*(5), 362–370.

Hiebert, J., & Carpenter, T. (1992). Learning and teaching with understanding. In D. A. Grouws (Ed.), *Handbook of research on mathematics teaching and learning* (pp. 65–97). New York: MacMillan.

Hunter, R. (2004). *Madeline Hunter's mastery teaching: Increasing instructional effectiveness in elementary and secondary schools.* Thousand Oaks, CA: Corwin.

Institute of Education Sciences (IES). (2007). *Effective literacy and English language instruction for English language learners in the elementary grades.* Washington, DC: IES, National Center for Education Evaluation and Regional Assistance.

Ivey, G. (2002). Building comprehension when they're still learning to read words. In C. C. Block & M. Pressley (Eds.), *Comprehension instruction: Research-based best practices* (pp. 234–246). New York: Guilford Press.

Ivey, G., & Broaddus, K. (2001). 'Just Plain Reading': A survey of what makes students want to read in middle school classrooms. *Reading Research Quarterly, 36*(4), 350–371.

Juel, C. (1994). *Learning to read and write in one elementary school.* New York: Springer-Verlag.

Katona, G. (1940). *Organizing and memorizing.* New York: Columbia University Press.

Kieffer, M. J., & Lesaux, N. K. (2007). Breaking down words to build meaning: Morphology, vocabulary, and reading comprehension in the urban classroom. *The Reading Teacher, 61*(2), 134–144.

Klahr, D., & McCoy Carver, S. (1988). Cognitive objectives in a LOGO debugging curriculum: Instruction, learning, and transfer. *Cognitive Psychology, 20*(3), 362–404.

Kramer, V. R., Schell, L. M., & Rubison, R. M. (1983). Auditory discrimination training in English of Spanish-speaking children. *Reading Improvement, 20,* 162–168.

Krashen, S. (2004). *The power of reading.* Westport, CT: Libraries Unlimited.

Lakoff, G., & Johnson, M. (2008). *Metaphors we live by.* Chicago: University of Chicago Press.

Laufer, B. (2000). Avoidance of idioms in a second language: The effect of L1-L2 degree of similarity. *Studia Linguistica, 54,* 186–196.

Lively, T., August, D., Carlo, M., & Snow, C. (2003). *Vocabulary improvement program for English language learners and their classmates.* Baltimore, MD: Brookes.

Lumsden, L. (2000). *Student motivation to learn.* ERIC Document Reproduction Service No. ED370200.

Marzano, R. J. (1998). *A theory-based meta-analysis of research on instruction.* Aurora, CO: Mid-Continent Research for Education and Learning.

Marzano, R. J., Pickering, D. J., & Pollock, J. E. (2001). *Research-based strategies for increasing student achievement.* Alexandria, VA: Association for Supervision & Curriculum Development.

Mathes, P. G., et al. (2003). A comparison of teacher-directed versus peer-assisted instruction to struggling first-grade readers. *The Elementary School Journal, 103*(5), 459–480.

Mayer, R. E. (1974). Acquisition processes and resilience under varying testing conditions for structurally different problem solving procedures. *Journal of Educational Psychology, 66*(5), 644–656.

Mayer, R. E., Stiehl, C. C., & Greeno, J. G. (1975) Acquisition of understanding and skill in relation to subjects' preparation and meaningfulness of instruction. *Journal of Educational Psychology, 67,* 331–350.

Mehrabian, A. (1971). *Silent messages.* Belmont, CA: Wadsworth.

Moje, E. B., Ciechanowski, K. M., Kramer, K., Ellis, L., Carrillo, R., & Collazo, T. (2004). Working toward third space in content area literacy: An examination of everyday funds of knowledge and discourse. *Reading Research Quarterly, 39*(1), 38–69.

Murray, B. (1999). Tuning into the sounds in words. *The Reading Genie.* Retrieved from http://www.auburn.edu/academic/education/reading_genie/tuning.html

Nagy, W. E., Anderson, R. C., & Herman, P. A. (1987, Summer). Learning word meanings from context during normal reading. *American Educational Research Journal, 24*(2), 237–270.

National Governors Association Center for Best Practices, Council of Chief State School Officers. (2010). *Common core state standards.* Washington, DC: Author.

National Institute of Child Health and Human Development. (2000). *Report of the National Reading Panel. Teaching children to read: An evidence-based assessment of the scientific research literature on reading and its implication for reading instruction: Reports of the sub-groups* (NIH Publication No. 00–4754). Washington, DC: U.S. Government Printing Office.

National Research Council. (2000). *Inquiry and the national science education standards: A guide for teaching and learning.* Retrieved from http://en.wikipedia.org/wiki/English_as_a_foreign_or_second_language#Systems_of_simplified_English

Nokes, J. D., & Dole, J. A. (2004). Helping adolescent readers through explicit strategy instruction. In T. L. Jetton & J. A. Dole (Eds.), *Adolescent literacy research and practice* (pp. 162–182). New York: Guilford Press.

Oh, S. Y. (2001). Two types of input modification and EFL reading comprehension: Simplification versus elaboration. *TESOL Quarterly, 35*(1), 69–96.

Olshavsky, J. E. (1976–1977). Reading as problem-solving: An investigation of strategies. *Reading Research Quarterly, 12*(4), 654–674.

Orosco, M. J., & Klingner, J. (2010). One school's implementation of RTI with English language learners: Referring into RTI. *Journal of Learning Disabilities, 43*(3), 269–288.

Pearson, P. D., & Dole, J. A. (1987). Explicit comprehension in instruction: A review of research and new conceptualization of instruction. *Elementary School Journal, 88*(2), 151–165.

Pearson, P. D., & Gallagher, M. C. (1983). The instruction of reading comprehension. *Contemporary Educational Psychology, 8*(3), 317–344.

Policy Studies Associates. (1995). Raising the educational achievement of secondary school students: An idea book. *Summary of Promising Practices Vol 1.* Washington, DC: U.S. Department of Education.

Rand Reading Study Group. (2001). *Reading for understanding: Toward a R&D program in reading comprehension.* Prepared for the Office of Educational Research and Improvement (OERI), U.S. Department of Education. Santa Monica, CA: RAND.

Reese, L., & Goldenberg, C. (2006). Community contexts for literacy development of Latina/o children: Contrasting case studies. *Anthropology and Education Quarterly, 37,* 42–61.

Rittle-Johnson, B. (2006). Promoting transfer: Effects of self-explanation and direct instruction. *Child Development, 77*(1), 1–15.

Robertson, W. C. (2008). Teaching conceptual understanding to promote students' ability to do transfer problems. *Research Matters to the Science Teacher, 34–45.*

Rosenshine, B., & Meister, C. (1992, April). The use of scaffolds for teaching higher-learning cognitive strategies. *Educational Leadership, 49*(7), 26–33.

Rosenshine, B., & Stevens, R. (1986). Teaching functions. In M. C. Wittrock (Ed.), *Handbook of research on teaching* (3rd ed., pp. 376–391). New York: MacMillan.

Rousseau, M. K., Tam, B. K. Y., & Ramnarain, R. (1993). Increasing reading proficiency of language-minority students with speech and language impairments. *Education and Treatments of Children, 16,* 254–271.

Rowe, M. B. (1972). *Wait-time and rewards as instructional variables, their influence on language, logic, and fate control.* Chicago: National Association for Research in Science Teaching.

Rowe, M. B. (1986). Wait time: Slowing down may be a way of speeding up. *Journal of Teacher Education, 37*(1), 43–50.

Sanders, N. M. (1966). *Classroom questions: What kinds.* New York: Harper & Row.

Saunders, W., O'Brien, G., Lennon, D., & McLean, J. (1998). Making the transition to English literacy successful: Effective strategies for studying literature with transition students. In R. Gersten & R. Jimenez (Eds.), *Promoting learning for culturally and linguistically diverse students: Classroom applications from contemporary research* (pp. 99–132). Belmont, CA: Wadsworth.

Scarcella, R. (2003a). *Academic English: A conceptual framework.* The University of California Linguistic Minority Research Institute. Technical Report. Oakland, CA: University of California.

Scarcella, R. (2003b). *Accelerating academic English: A focus on the English learner.* Oakland, CA: University of California.

Shanahan, T. (2004). Overcoming the dominance of communication: Writing to think and learn. In T. L. Jetton & J. A. Dole (Eds.), *Adolescent literacy research and practice* (pp. 59–74). New York: Guilford Press.

Shanahan, T. (2005). *The National Reading Panel Report: Practical advice for teachers.* Naperville, IL: Learning Point.

Shanahan, T., & Beck, I. L. (2006). Effective literacy teaching for English-language learners. In D. August & T. Shanahan (Eds.), *Developing literacy in second-language learners* (pp. 415–488). Mahway, NJ: Lawrence Erlbaum.

Shaywitz, S. E., Fletcher, J. M., Holahan, J. M., Schneider, A. E., Marchione, K. E., & Stuebing, K. K. (1999). Persistence of dyslexia: The Connecticut Longitudinal Study at Adolescence. *Pediatrics, 104,* 1351–1359.

Short, D. J., & Fitzsimmons, S. (2007). *Double the work: Challenges and solutions to acquiring language and academic literacy for adolescent English language learners.* New York: Carnegie Corporation.

Skinner, E., & Belmont, M. (1991). *A longitudinal study of motivation in school: Reciprocal effects of teacher behavior and student engagement.* Unpublished manuscript, University of Rochester.

Slavin, R. E., & Cheung, A. (2003). *Effective programs for English language learners: A best-evidence synthesis.* Baltimore, MD: Johns Hopkins University, CRESPAR.

Slavin, R., & A. Cheung, A. (2004). How do English language learners learn to read? *What Research Says About Reading, 61*(6), 55.

Snow, C. E., Burns, M. S., & Griffin, P. (Eds.). (1998). *Preventing reading difficulties in young children.* Washington, DC: National Academies Press.

Sousa, D. (2003). *The leadership brain: How to lead today's schools more effectively.* Thousand Oaks, CA: Corwin.

Sousa, D. (2005). *How the brain learns* (3rd ed.). Thousand Oaks, CA: Corwin.

Spires, H. A., Gallini, J., & Riggsbee, J. (1992). Effects of schema-based and text structure-based cues on expository prose comprehension in fourth graders. *Journal of Experimental Education, 60*(4) 307–320.

Stahl, R. J. (1990). *Using "think-time" behaviors to promote students' information processing, learning, and on-task participation. An instructional module.* Tempe, AZ: Arizona State University.

Stahl, S. A., & Nagy, W. E. (2006). *Teaching word meanings.* Mahwah, NJ: Lawrence Erlbaum.

Stallings, J. A. (1974). *Follow-through classroom observation 1972–1973—Executive Summary.* Menlo Park, CA: SRI International.

Stallings, J., et al. (1978). *Early childhood education classroom evaluation.* Menlo Park, CA: SRI International.

Stallings, J., et al. (1980). *How to change the process of teaching basic reading skills in secondary schools.* Menlo Park, CA: SRI International.

Taylor, B., Harris, L., Pearson, P. D., & Garcia, G. E. (1995.) *Reading difficulties: Instruction and assessment* (2nd ed.). New York: Random House.

Tharp, R. G. (1997). *From at-risk to excellence: Research, theory, and principles for practice* (Research Report 1). Santa Cruz, CA: Center for Research on Education, Diversity & Excellence. Retrieved from http://www.cal.org/resources/Digest/crede001.html

Tobin, K. (1987, Spring). The role of wait time in higher cognitive-level learning. *Review of Educational Research, 57*(1), 69–95.

Trumbull, E., & Pacheco, M. (2005). *Leading with diversity: Cultural competencies for teacher preparation and professional development.* Providence, RI: The Education Alliance at Brown University and Pacific Resources for Education and Learning.

Vosniadou, S., et al. (2001). Designing learning environments to promote conceptual change in science. *Learning and Instruction, 11*(4–5), 381–419.

Walberg, H. J., Paschal, R. A., & Weinstein, T. (1985). Homework's powerful effects on learning. *Educational Leadership, 42*(7), 76–79.

Watkins, C., & Watkins, T. (2004). The components of direct instruction. In N. E. Marchand-Martella, T. A. Slocum, & R. C. Martella (Eds.), *Introduction to direct instruction* (pp. 28–65). Boston: Allyn & Bacon.

Whitehurst, G. (2000). What we know from educational research: A summary. Mathematics Summit Meeting, Washington, DC. Retrieved from http://www .ed.gov/rschstat/research/progs/mathscience/whitehurst.html

Wigdor, A. K. (1999, October). *Education research: Is what we don't know hurting our children?* Testimony before the House of Representatives Subcommittee on Basic Research, Committee on Science. Retrieved from http://www7.national academies.org/ocga/testimony/Education_Research.asp

Wolfe, P. (1998). How the brain learns. *Educational Leadership, 56*(3) 61–64.

Young, D. J. (1999). Linguistic simplification of SL reading material: Effective instructional practice? *Modern Language Journal, 83*(3), 350–366.

Zwiers, J. (2005). The third language of academic English. *Educational Leadership, 62*, 60–63.

Zwiers, J. (2008). *Building academic language: Essential practices for content classrooms, Grades 5–12*. San Francisco: John Wiley & Sons.

Index

CORWIN
A SAGE Company

The Corwin logo—a raven striding across an open book—represents the union of courage and learning. Corwin is committed to improving education for all learners by publishing books and other professional development resources for those serving the field of PreK–12 education. By providing practical, hands-on materials, Corwin continues to carry out the promise of its motto: **"Helping Educators Do Their Work Better."**

DataWORKS
Educational Research

DataWORKS Educational Research has a vision . . .

All students, including English Learners, successfully taught, at school, grade-level work, every day.

DataWORKS provides tools, materials, and training aimed at helping teachers be successful during whole-class instruction so more students learn more the first time they are taught.

- **Powerful lessons**—high student success obtained through effective lesson design and delivery.
- **Student engagement**—100% student participation in their own learning.
- **Language acquisition**—English Learners learn content and language during every lesson.
- **Instructional decisions**—teachers use non-volunteer Checking for Understanding to make real-time decisions so all students attain high levels of success.